PRAISE FOR *ORGANIZING FOR POWER*

"What an excellent look at the significance of class struggle and progressive social movements in the Boston metropolitan area! This is a book that goes beyond examining the institution of unions, but instead focuses on the multifarious efforts to refound a genuine labor movement. Though this book focuses on the Greater Boston area, the examples explored and the lessons learned have a value throughout the country. That the book focuses so clearly on one geographic site of struggle helps it to avoid a level of generality that frequently undermines other analyses."

—BILL FLETCHER JR., aut⸻ *Solidarity Divided* and *They're Ban⸻ ty Other Myths about Unions*

"These fresh⸻ cent labor struggles in the greater Bosto⸻ understudied region of the United States. ⸻ a sobering, yet hopeful portrait of organizing ⸻ increasingly precarious working people— including immigrants, women, and people of color—to challenge and transform the neoliberal order."

—RUTH MILKMAN, author of *Immigrant Labor and the New Precariat*

"As America has ineluctably transformed into a postindustrial economy, so has the character and nature of its working class. *Organizing For Power: Building a Twenty-First Century Labor Movement in Boston* is a comprehensive guide to understanding the formative changes in the American class structure and how organized labor can regain relevance to a chaotic spectrum of contemporary workers. Drawing on the shifting landscape of Boston, Chomsky and Striffler's book is essential reading for grasping the opportunities and challenges of trade unions in the United States today."

—IMMANUEL NESS, author of *Organizing Insurgency: Workers Movements in the Global South*

"*Organizing for Power* offers an uncommonly comprehensive yet granular view of a single city labor movement's attempt to cope with structural and demographic change in the early twenty-first century. Striffler and Chomsky have convened an impressive array of postindustrial Boston's labor brain trust—including academic activists, union leaders and alt-labor strategists—to sketch a path forward on both the organizational and political fronts."

"With political polarization and legislative paralysis forestalling progressive innovations at the federal level, unionists and community activists have rightly looked to cities like Seattle, Chicago, Los Angeles, and Boston to build power and construct social policies designed to give workers—of all ethnicities, sexual orientations, and legal statuses—a voice in twenty-first-century America. In this splendid collection, Aviva Chomsky and Steve Striffler have put in dialogue a wide-ranging set of activists and academics who offer important and insightful accounts of how the Hub City has become a terrain of struggle where the working-class has won important battles, even in an era bookended by Ronald Reagan and Donald Trump. Their stories bare careful reading—and emulation!"

ORGANIZING FOR POWER

BUILDING A TWENTY-FIRST CENTURY
LABOR MOVEMENT IN BOSTON

Edited by
Aviva Chomsky and Steve Striffler

Haymarket Books
Chicago, IL

Published in 2021 by
Haymarket Books
P.O. Box 180165
Chicago, IL 60618
773-583-7884
www.haymarketbooks.org
info@haymarketbooks.org

ISBN: 978-1-64259-277-1

Distributed to the trade in the US through Consortium Book Sales and Distribution (www.cbsd.com) and internationally through Ingram Publisher Services International (www.ingramcontent.com).

This book was published with the generous support of Lannan Foundation and Wallace Action Fund.

Special discounts are available for bulk purchases by organizations and institutions. Please email orders@haymarketbooks.org for more information.

Cover design by Rachel Cohen.

Printed in Canada.

Library of Congress Cataloging-in-Publication data is available.

10 9 8 7 6 5 4 3 2 1

CONTENTS

Race, Immigration, and Labor in Boston

Aviva Chomsky and Steve Striffler

> Boston's economy is booming, but many Boston residents continue
> to struggle to make ends meet. The unemployment rate has fallen
> to pre-recession levels, but the median income has remained
> unchanged for a generation. A quarter of full-time, full-year
> workers, and just under half of all labor force participants, earn
> less than $35,000.[1]

In July of 2017, twelve hundred nurses at the Tufts Medical Center
carried out a one-day strike—the largest nurses' strike in Massachusetts
history, and the first one in Boston in more than thirty years. By the end
of the year, the union signed a compromise contract that won enhanced
staffing to improve conditions for nurses who had been overloaded with
up to five patients at a time, along with raises and some management
concessions to sweeten the unwanted transition from a defined-benefit
pension to a defined-contribution retirement plan—a 401(k). In part
because the union had framed the action in terms of patient safety
and quality health care, the strike quickly got the support of local
labor unions, including apparently unlikely allies like the Building &
Construction Trades Council and the Teamsters. Boston mayor Marty
Walsh, a former union leader himself, and other community leaders also
backed the strikers. The strike captured the attention of the news media,
which provided the nurses with generally sympathetic coverage.[2]

Was the nurses' strike a sign of increased or resurgent militancy,
solidarity, and working-class power? Or is it to be understood as an
inspirational, but ultimately isolated, expression of worker discontent that
would do little to reverse the decades-long decline of union density and

working-class power in the city? Or a mix of both? Only time will tell, though in the intervening period since the summer of 2017, the United States has experienced a remarkable wave of strikes, with New England playing its part. The February 2018 West Virginia teachers' strike started it, quickly followed by statewide walkouts in Oklahoma and Arizona as well as teacher revolts throughout the country. By the fall, close to eight thousand Marriott workers were striking in eight cities, including Boston. And some thirty thousand Stop and Shop workers went out on strike throughout New England supermarkets in April 2019, only to be followed by fifty thousand GM workers nationwide that fall.

In all of these cases high levels of community and political support for the workers contributed to broad public approval of unions—driven in part by increased concerns about runaway inequality. All of this suggests that we are perhaps at a pivotal moment, with the labor movement poised between decades-long decline and potential revival. To be sure, labor unions are decimated and powerful interests continue the political-economic assault against working people. It is far too early to suggest that the strike wave has altered the balance of power in any significant way. Yet, as recent revolts suggest, more and more people are concluding that not only is the system rigged, but that a labor movement rooted in unions and community organizations may provide one of the few ways of blocking or even reversing this decades-long attack on working people.

In this respect, the nurses' strike is instructive of some of the obstacles labor faces, which of course are not unique to Boston. This was not a case where management quickly caved when confronted with a powerful union backed by community support. Prior to the one-day strike, the nurses had negotiated for well over a year in more than thirty long and bitter meetings. Their demands around pay, benefits, and working conditions were modest, and focused more on forcing the hospital to meet regional standards than achieving radical change. The nurses' backs were up against the wall, and achieving the kind of unity and courage needed to pull off a strike took years of hard work—but by no means assured success. Tufts' immediate response was to lock out the nurses and hire out-of-town scabs, threatening patient safety.[3] This arrogance ultimately proved to be Tufts' undoing, but it is nonetheless suggestive of how brazen and confident today's employers can be when dealing with labor. Had Tufts not been one of the crown jewels in Boston's vaunted "global healthcare innovation" economy, or had it handled the conflict with a bit more discretion, the nurses might not have received such overwhelming support and attention from labor, community groups, and the media.

It is also unlikely that the strike produced a sea change within the health care industry, let alone altered the balance of power more broadly between workers and capital. While Tufts ceded on the all-important staffing issue, nurses were forced to give up their defined-benefit pensions, albeit with the sweetener of additional employer contributions to the hospital's 403(b) retirement plan. Union bargaining committee chair Mary Cornacchia concluded, somewhat ambiguously, that "it is a win for us, a compromise, but both sides did do a lot of compromising to get to where we're at now."[4] Moreover, when the Massachusetts Nurses Association attempted to scale up in 2018, sponsoring a ballot measure to mandate safe staffing levels statewide, the state's Health and Hospital Association mobilized massively against it and the initiative was resoundingly defeated.

The nurses' strike, the hardline response by Tufts, and the mobilization and risks involved in the move to the electoral arena, offer a glimpse at how the working class, as well as forms of labor organizing both within and outside of unions, have changed in the Boston region during the past several decades. While in some ways the trajectory of Boston's labor movement mirrors nationwide trends, the area's particular pattern of collapse and recovery, progressive politics and provincialism, and racial division and immigration can deepen our understanding of the multiple structural challenges facing the twenty-first-century labor movement, and how unions and other working-class organizations are struggling to overcome them.

In this respect, the greater Boston region is an ideal place to study this larger conflict, in part because it presents a complex picture of the nature and strength of organized labor and what is sometimes referred to as "alt-labor"—new forms of worker and working-class organization. The city upholds a reputation for being liberal and union-friendly, and organized labor continues to wield significant political clout. The election of Boston Building Trades Council president Marty Walsh as mayor in 2013, and the blueness of Massachusetts as a whole, testify to the continued political influence of organized labor. And yet, despite labor's relative strength in Boston and Massachusetts, the labor-liberal alliance has never been particularly militant, and has often aimed more at delivering gains to a small sector of relatively privileged (and often white) workers than at empowering working people or addressing the gross inequalities that have long plagued the city. The union fortress has at times defended its walls and protected members' interests, but it has been less capable of going on the offensive or expanding coverage to include broader sectors of the working class.[5]

Taking the greater Boston region as its lens, our anthology explores the political-economic transformation of the United States and its labor movement since the late twentieth century. The neoliberal era—characterized by deregulation, deindustrialization, free trade, and public sector cutbacks—has weakened labor's traditional core and its political clout, even as immigration and the growth of the informal and service economies have created new potential sites for labor militancy. These changes have also challenged unions to rethink older strategies and explore new forms of solidarity with allies outside its historic comfort zone. The nurses framed their strike in terms of the larger public good—what has come to be known as "social justice unionism"—and their successful appeal to more traditional unions like the Teamsters and Building Trades is but one of many instances in which Boston labor is beginning to respond in innovative ways to the disintegration of the New Deal order that had shaped it. These transformations, including organized labor's struggle to navigate a changing landscape, have created new conditions and sites of militancy that have led working people who were historically excluded from the house of labor to devise alternative strategies, approaches, and organizations.

The chapters in this book explore these new spaces, approaches, and organizations, which have challenged how we think about the past, present, and future of the labor movement and the larger working class. How do unions look to redefine themselves, and help advance broader working-class interests outside the workplace, while also retaining and expanding workplace-based organizing and power? What types of alternative forms of labor and community organizing based both within and beyond the immediate workplace are emerging, and how do they help (or hinder) working people in advancing their interests? Finally, in what ways do these various forms of organizations interact with each other, and what does this mean for the future of the labor movement?

Themes and Overview

In the epilogue of James Green and Hugh Carter Donahue's seminal 1979 study entitled *Boston's Workers: A Labor History*, the authors summarized the challenges facing Boston workers in the post-World War II period.[6] They identified key issues that have remained relevant to the city's workers in the four decades since the book was published. One theme that was central to Green and Donahue's work, and to this volume, is the structural changes that have shaped Boston's labor market. Since *Boston's Workers* was published, the city's postwar decline was reversed by the so-called Massachusetts Miracle of the 1980s and beyond, which created vast wealth and distinguished Boston from other deindustrialized cities of the northeast. The high tech, financial, education, tourism, and medical industries have created a sharply divided local labor market in the context of national neoliberal retrenchment, particularly in the privatization of public education and other government cutbacks. Waves of new immigrants came into the racially divided city and entered both the top and the bottom tiers of the new economy.

The low-wage, precarious economy serving Boston's better-off is populated primarily by immigrant and other workers of color who live in an expensive region with a limited safety net. Massachusetts, and in particular the Boston area, are among the most expensive regions in the country.[7] The city itself ranked first in the nation in inequality in 2014, although researchers cautioned that its large student population could be depressing the lower levels of the income spectrum. Nevertheless, the city's Office of Workforce Development acknowledged that "too many Boston residents are having trouble accessing economic opportunity. One in five Bostonians lives in poverty—close to one in three children under eighteen—and a far greater share earn too little to afford the high cost of living in the city."[8] Not surprisingly, people of color suffer the highest unemployment rates and the highest poverty rates in the city.[9] Median household earnings are $79,802 for non-Hispanic whites, $38,454 for Blacks, and $30,883 for Hispanics.[10] While people of color comprise 53 percent of Boston's population, union leadership is still predominantly white, and unions have not been immune to the city's racial divide.

A second theme addressed by Green and Donahue as well as this volume is the role of organized labor in Boston. Massachusetts has historically enjoyed strong unions that have been important players within the city's political life while insuring relatively high wages and strong benefits for a significant portion of the working class. Yet Boston's unions have suffered from some of the same political, internal, and structural forces that have decimated unions nationwide. Union density has fallen to about 12 percent in Massachusetts, and unions are overwhelmingly concentrated in the public sector (with over 50 percent density, versus 6.4 percent in the private sector).[11] Like their counterparts around the country, unions in Boston struggle between seeking to protect the declining, but still considerable, power and benefits that organized labor has won for the unionized sector of the workforce, and attempting to recreate a social movement unionism in alliance with immigrant, ethnic, and other community organizations.[12] These represent different visions of unions' role in society, the constituency of unions, and what kind of working class the labor movement represents. This debate, in Boston as elsewhere, has produced both tension and innovation within the labor movement.

The final theme is the lives and organizations of Boston's precarious workers, both inside and outside traditional labor unions. A number of our case studies highlight different types of strategies and campaigns pursued by low-wage workers in Boston and beyond under adverse political and economic conditions. It is not surprising, given the region's combination of economic expansion and inequality, that workers have sought multiple and alternative ways of organizing and fighting for their rights. Black workers have combined struggles for access and autonomy both inside and outside of unions. On the margins of Boston's famed universities, food service workers and adjunct faculty are fighting for union representation. Raise Up Mass, a union-community coalition, has fought for state-level legislation to raise the minimum wage and provide benefits for workers regardless of union membership. Sex workers struggle against policing, while immigrant-based worker centers struggle against wage theft.

Organizing for Power paints a picture of labor in Boston that is both dynamic and grim. As the nurses' strike demonstrated, although the political and economic forces arrayed against workers and their organizations are powerful and well-organized, workers continue to struggle for dignity, improved wages, and decent lives. The diversity of Boston's working class is both its strength and its weakness. Divided by language, culture, race, and workplace, and facing both anti-union and anti-working-class policies at the national level, Boston workers nevertheless have the strength of their many histories to draw on, and the energy of their hopes and dreams.

This anthology emerges from an ongoing dialogue between politically engaged academics and area labor activists to reflect upon the challenges facing the labor movement today. Part I of the book, "Labor, Power, and Inequality in Boston," consists of three chapters that explore transformations in the city's recent history, with a particular focus on how economic shifts since the 1970s have not only increased inequality (impacting different groups in distinct ways), but have posed particular challenges for labor unions' ability to advance the interests of working people as a whole. Part II, "Boston's Workers and Unions Confront the Twenty-First Century," examines how labor organizations and working people have tried to survive and organize on this shifting terrain.

Boston's Labor History in National and Historical Context

The making of Boston's working class was deeply shaped by industrialization and the associated waves of immigration from England, French Canada, and Ireland in the early nineteenth century, and from southern and eastern Europe in the latter half of the century. After European immigration was curtailed in the 1920s, Boston, like other industrial cities in the north, received new migrants: African Americans from the US South, followed by Puerto Ricans in the 1960s, and other immigrants of color from Latin America and Asia in the later twentieth century. The city's economy was global from the start. Shipping, trade, and finance were pivotal industries and their ties to slavery and the plantation economies of the West Indies and the US South ran deep.

In Boston as elsewhere in the country, nineteenth-century immigrant and labor radicalism was mostly subsumed and contained by the rise of the American Federation of Labor (AFL) by the early twentieth century. The AFL had a long history of representing white, native-born craft workers and excluding immigrants, workers of color, and lower-paid, marginal workers. In much of the country, the Congress of Industrial Workers' (CIO) industrial unionism surged in the 1940s and 50s and challenged the exclusivity of the AFL while bringing Black and white workers together in unprecedented ways. In so doing, the CIO greatly expanded the reach of the labor movement among new sectors of low-wage workers and workers of color.

As Green and Donahue showed, however, Boston's trajectory was particularly unfriendly to the industrial unionism of the mid-century. The city's economy was based in small-scale, lighter industries like shoes and textiles, which began to experience industrial decline early in the century. Although most studies of deindustrialization in the United States rightly focus on the 1980s and 1990s, in Boston the process started much earlier. The mainstays of Boston's unionized industries, "meat packing, printing,

rail transport, textiles, docks, and light manufacturing" all went into
steep decline after World War II. Government-funded urban renewal
projects created some jobs, but "its long-term effects were to expand
the low-wage, nonunion service and clerical sectors."[13] Thus Boston's,
and New England's, industrial workers faced the challenges of capital
flight, plant closures, and industrial decline a half a century before
deindustrialization confronted what came to be known as the Rust Belt.[14]

Boston's trajectory of labor organizing was also out of step with that
of the country's industrial heartlands. As Green and Donahue explain,
"when a new industrial union movement, the CIO, arose to challenge AFL
business unionism in the mid-1930s, Boston's workers took a backseat to
the workers in the great, mass-production industrial centers . . . [The]
working class as a whole did not take the great step forward in Boston that
it took in other cities."[15] The city's unions retrenched into what Heiwon
Kwon and Benjamin Day call "political collective bargaining," a top-down
strategy exchanging loyalty to politicians for favors to their members.[16]
Postwar migrants and immigrants to Boston faced a far less hospitable
economy and labor movement than in many other northern cities.

New postwar immigrants entered low-wage sectors of the economy,
and upward mobility was curtailed due to limited opportunities for
gaining access to better, unionized employment. The first generation
saw migration as a door to opportunity, but, especially among migrants
of color, their children confronted joblessness, discrimination, and
segregation. The civil rights and liberation movements of the 1950s and
1960s reflected their frustrations, raised expectations, and made them
much less willing to accept poor working and living conditions.[17]

The 1970s: A Key Decade?

Labor historians have pointed to the 1970s as a transformational decade.[18]
Global economic restructuring and deindustrialization, a concerted
attack on unions, civil rights gains, the beginning of a new influx of
immigrant workers from Latin America, and the Wars on Crime and
Drugs coincided and inter-related to shift the contours of labor in the
United States. Women and people of color pushed for unionization
in the aftermath of gains associated with the civil rights and women's
movements. The business class went on the offensive and successfully
reduced the power of unions and working people. Private sector unions
lost ground in the workplace and in the political arena. Growth in

the public sector partially masked unions' decline in the private sector. Some white workers, encouraged by their employers and conservative politicians, turned their frustrations against the very groups who had just acquired basic rights and were pushing for economic justice—women and workers of color.[19]

In Boston, deindustrialization was well underway by the 1970s. By 1980, 54 percent of Boston's workers labored in office-related activities—the highest proportion in the country.[20] In 1972, Boston employed a third of the metropolitan region's workforce; by 1992, this was down to one fourth as the suburbs attracted both new businesses and relocations from the city. Even manufacturing grew in the larger metropolitan area, while declining by 44 percent in the city proper between 1972 and 1990. Boston also lost thirty thousand retail jobs between 1970 and 1990, while the retail industry exploded in the suburbs. The new suburban jobs were much less likely to be unionized.[21]

The city's population fell from 801,444 in 1950 to 562,994 in 1980.[22] Much of the population decline was due to white flight, as federal policies encouraged suburban development through highway construction and low-interest mortgage loans. Routes 128 and then 495 circled the city and laid the foundation for a booming new high-tech industrial corridor that drew its workers from the expanding suburbs. School desegregation—dubbed "forced busing" by its opponents—came late to Boston, and it was met with violent protest. Like elsewhere in the northeast, desegregation ended at municipal boundaries, becoming a further motivation for white flight.[23]

The 1970s saw the beginning of a new surge in immigration nationwide, primarily of people of color from Latin American and Asia. Black migrants to Boston in the 1950s and 60s had come from the US South. In the 1970s this pattern shifted and the Black population grew primarily with migrants from the Caribbean. These immigrants entered an already racially divided city and labor force, in the context of industrial decline.

The relationship of Boston's unions with its populations of color, including the new groups of immigrants of color, has been complex. Green and Donahue pointed out that the city's history of strong ethnic politics and the absence of heavy industry and CIO-style unions undermined the development of a multiracial working-class identity and politics. "Lacking the experience of integrated unionism created by the CIO in other cities," they write, "Boston unions have failed by and large to meet the city's racial crisis" of the 1970s they wrote at the end of that decade.[24] When Boston's Black and other workers of color mobilized in the 1960s and 70s, it was outside as much as inside of unions, and it was for access to jobs, housing, and schools as much as for greater rights in the workplace. Rising activism by workers of color coincided with ongoing job contraction, making it less likely that white males would open their unions to women and minority workers. As Green and Donahue explain, "in an economy of scarce jobs and scarce housing, in which economic security is harder to obtain, efforts to desegregate in any area—schools, jobs, neighborhoods—will be perceived as a threat by many white workers, even in cases where desegregation benefits everyone by increasing federal and state funding." Boston-area labor unions focused less on defending the interests of the working class as a whole than on protecting the "limited privileges enjoyed by their white members." Within a contracting economy, trade "unions, which earlier won immigrant workers steady jobs and better working conditions," had become "part of the problem rather than part of the solution as far as minority workers are concerned."[25]

Women and people of color carried on their struggles both inside and outside the workplace. Community organizations like 9to5, the United Community Construction Workers and the Third World Workers Association organized to press for the rights of women and workers of color for equal pay, treatment, and access to jobs. As Lane Windham noted, the women's organization 9to5 mobilized "the foremothers of what today is known as 'alt-labor,' the wave of workers' centers, associations, and campaigns that seek to build power for workers outside the collective bargaining paradigm in the early twenty-first century."[26] Several of this book's chapters explore the emerging relationships between traditional and "alt" labor movements.

Increasing Black mobilization was one factor leading Boston's employers to begin recruiting in Puerto Rico to fill low-wage positions. As a new generation of Puerto Rican migrants began to arrive in the mid-1960s, the city's Spanish-speaking population increased from one thousand in 1959 to seventeen thousand in 1969, and an estimated forty thousand by 1973.[27] As Michael Piore shows, Puerto Ricans were explicitly recruited to replace Black workers who were becoming less willing to accept conditions at the lowest-skill, lowest-wage jobs, especially in Boston's declining manufacturing sector.[28] Although they frequently entered into precarious sectors of the labor market like produce packaging, shoe manufacturing, and hospitals, close to half of the Puerto Rican workers in Piore's study held jobs in unionized workplaces. But the unions only reinforced the "bimodal job structure," providing strong representation to skilled, largely white workers, and providing Puerto Ricans with few services or benefits while ensuring that they subsidized a pension fund that few would ever draw upon.[29]

Race, Immigration, and Inequality in the Massachusetts Miracle

Boston's deindustrialization and its spatial and racial divides continued as the underside to the city's and the state's revival after 1980. Manufacturing jobs in the city fell from 70,000 in 1969 to 10,000 in 2013, and 7,000 in 2016.[30] In Massachusetts as a whole, manufacturing jobs plummeted from 500,000 in 1990 to 246,000 in 2018.[31] Healthcare and Social Assistance became the Commonwealth's largest employment category by 1995, and has only continued to grow since then, adding 40,000 workers between 2007 and 2011 and employing 16 percent of workers in the state.[32] The sector added 64,000 more jobs between 2012 and 2016, and by 2016 employed one of every six workers statewide.[33]

The 1980s brought the surge of growth in high technology and financial services known as the Massachusetts Miracle. After a downturn at the end of the 1980s, the state saw further economic expansion in the 1990s.[34] Barry Bluestone and Mary Huff Stevenson characterized Boston's trajectory during these two decades as a "triple revolution," made up of a demographic shift from white ethnic to multicultural, an industrial shift from "mill-based" to "mind-based," and a spatial shift from an economically-dominant central city to one that was part of a broader metropolitan region. The influx of high-tech industry temporarily turned the Boston area into the Silicon Valley of the east coast; it was followed by an upsurge in high-end services like health and education, finance, insurance, real estate, and business services.[35]

After 1980 Boston's population began to rise again, reaching 617,594 by 2010. As whites were leaving the city, people of color were arriving. Boston's population went from 18 percent "minority" in 1970 to 30 percent in 1980, 37 percent in 1990, 51 percent in 2000, and 53 percent in 2010.[36] In the process, Boston's Black population became poorer (as middle-income Blacks also left) and more concentrated in a few deteriorating neighborhoods as gentrification pushed African Americans out of mixed areas like the South End. New development in the city emphasized housing and amenities to attract young, single, overwhelmingly white professionals back to the city, further increasing social divisions and racial segregation.[37]

For the city's growing population of people of color, the Miracle brought growing poverty and inequality. Most of the new jobs were located outside the city in the Route 128 corridor, inaccessible to city residents without cars. Latin American immigration continued to grow substantially in the 1980s, making Latinos the largest minority group in Massachusetts.[38] Beyond Boston, Latino and other poor immigrants of color concentrated in smaller deindustrialized cities like Lawrence and Holyoke that shared with Boston's poor neighborhoods conditions of deteriorating housing and lack of access to suburban jobs. The Latino poverty rate, which had almost doubled during the 1970s, remained at around 37 percent during the 1980s, the highest rate in the country.[39] For white workers in Massachusetts, annual income grew 22 percent between 1979 and 1999, while for Black workers it fell by 1.7 percent, and for Hispanics by 9.7 percent.[40] As Edwin Meléndez noted, "the beneficial impact of the economic expansion on Latino poverty was offset by the type of jobs created, the concentration of Latinos in those cities that suffered the brunt of blue-collar job losses, the relatively low educational attainment of working-age Latinos, and the growing number of households with only one potential wage-earner."[41]

The city itself became ever-more segregated, by both race and class. Neighborhoods like Roxbury and Mattapan became both Blacker and poorer, and for those populations upward mobility was becoming increasingly unrealizable.[42] New immigrants continued to join older populations of color, and Boston's Black population grew with migrants from Cape Verde, Haiti, Jamaica, and other parts of the Caribbean and Africa. (Some, though not all, Cape Verdeans identify as Black, as do a very few migrants from the Spanish-speaking Caribbean.) The Latino population, initially primarily Puerto Rican, came to incorporate Cubans, Dominicans, Central Americans, Mexicans, and others. But unlike much of the rest of the country, where Mexicans comprise the largest number of Latinos, in Massachusetts over 40 percent of Latinos were Puerto Rican in 2014, and only 5 percent were Mexican.[43] It is also notable that the proportion of foreign-born residents is actually greater among Boston's Black population (32.8 percent) than among the Latino population (32.2 percent).[44]

Relations between established communities of color and newer immigrants sometimes replicated the same kind of competition that

Green and Donahue described in the 1970s, where migrants compete with locals over a still-shrinking pie. Some of the city's initiatives to embrace diversity, transcend the racial divisions of earlier generations, and welcome immigrants seemed to only entrench older racial fault lines, continuing to exclude native-born African Americans. Thus, by the turn of the century Boston was home to what many considered to be a healthy, even booming economy, but also extreme economic inequality shaped by race and immigration. The chapters in Part I of this book trace these structural processes into the twenty-first century.

Unlike other American cities that have expanded their borders over the twentieth century, Boston consists of a geographically small city where unions, despite their shrinking numbers, still play an outsized political role, ringed by multiple growing suburbs where unions have failed to make significant inroads. Contrasts characterize the city itself, its metropolitan area, and the state of Massachusetts. Frenetic growth and gentrification in Boston's downtown has only sharpened the marginalization of poor, still-segregated urban neighborhoods, while leafy, exclusive suburbs border struggling, deindustrialized secondary cities like Lawrence and Springfield, home to new immigrants from the Global South and with poverty rates of up to 90 percent.

Harris Gruman, Massachusetts Political Director of the SEIU, argues that labor revitalization requires transcending the borders of the city of Boston to confront the state as a whole. In terms of its economy, he writes,

Massachusetts is like a large metropolitan system, and one significantly smaller than New York City or Los Angeles. It has 6 million inhabitants, and I can drive to my union's farthest-flung offices in under two hours. If we have pockets of extreme poverty in the old factory towns of Springfield and Lawrence, they relate to the overall affluence around them more like the Bronx does to New York City than a vast region like upstate New York or California's Central Valley does to those states. The desire of many legislators to Balkanize reform in Massachusetts by city or region is much like the efforts to concentrate economic reforms and community benefits within a single neighborhood of a large city or an affluent suburb or college town, and often worsens overall economic inequality at the state level.[45]

Gruman's chapter in this volume details SEIU's commitment to deepening ties with movements for progressive social change, one of the hallmarks of Boston's new unionism.

The SEIU is not alone in this stance. Labor-community alliances are now in vogue and new forms of solidarity have been emerging. As David Pihl, Jasmine Kerrissey, and Tom Juravich correctly point out in their 2017 accounting of Massachusetts labor, the "labor movement remains a powerful force in the Commonwealth working for fair and more just workplaces" and "has continued to launch creative campaigns to protect and expand workers' rights and standards of living."[46] Yet it is hard to tell whether recent manifestations of worker militancy are coalescing into something larger, or whether they are isolated expressions of anger from a working class that is sporadically rebellious and fed up, but without a clear path to building the collective strength necessary to consistently shape state and corporate power in meaningful ways.

Boston's Workers and Unions Confront the Twenty-First Century

The Massachusetts Institute for a New Commonwealth (MassINC) termed the first ten years of the new century as a "lost decade" for Massachusetts. The Miracle faded, and the state lost one hundred and fifty thousand jobs. Top earners increased their incomes by up to 10 percent, while low-wage workers saw their income stagnate or decline by up to 20 percent.[47] Massachusetts is now one of the most unequal states in the country, with Boston leading the way.[48] Nor did the post-2008 recovery do much to reverse these trends. In terms of expanding employment, Massachusetts recovered from the recession faster than the rest of the country, but over 85 percent of the new jobs were in low-wage sectors like food service, home health care, and cleaning services, and paid less than $38,000 a year.[49] Even as job creation picked up in the second decade of the century, unemployment remained significant, and disproportionately high for Black and Hispanic workers.[50] Boston's small size and high rate of suburbanization—one of the highest in the country—contributed to "extraordinarily high unemployment rates for central city residents, particularly for minority communities."[51] Wages for those at the lower end of the labor market failed to recover after the recession had technically ended.

Closely related to the city and state's sharpening inequality, union density continued its decline during the new century. Although the state's constantly threatened public sector still enjoys relatively high rates of unionization, this alone has not been able to compensate for the ongoing decline in union density within the private sector (now at around 6 percent), especially in the context of cutbacks that have created further hardship for working people. Manufacturing employment in the state declined by over 17 percent from 2007 to 2017, including a nearly 30 percent decline in high-tech areas such as computer, semiconductor, and electronics production—the core industries that had driven the Massachusetts Miracle. Unionized printing and publishing industries also shed jobs.[52] Despite a number of successful organizing campaigns, the Massachusetts labor movement could not unionize enough workers in major growth sectors such as health care, hospitality, and other services to make up for the overall decline.

Nationally, unions took stock of their declining fortunes in the form of two structural changes at the turn of the century. In 1995, the "New Voices" slate took leadership of the AFL-CIO, vowing to revitalize the labor movement by committing to a mass organizing campaign, particularly within growing low-wage sectors of the economy. Then, a decade later, some of the unions most associated with the New Voices broke off from the AFL-CIO entirely, forming the Change to Win coalition, and espousing almost the same goals that New Voices had proclaimed. Led by the SEIU (Service Employees), and to a lesser extent UNITE HERE (Hotel and Restaurant Workers), the United Farmworkers, the Laborers, and others joined together, vowing once again to prioritize organizing the low-wage service sector. Several large-scale nationwide campaigns seemed to show the promise of this new commitment, as home health-care workers, janitors, nurses, and hospitality workers were organized in large numbers.

It is interesting to note that the unions leading the New Voices and Change to Win almost all came out of an AFL union tradition, but with new energy and commitment to transcending the AFL's racial and gender exclusivity and to embracing immigrant and other workers of color. The AFL's roots were in pre-heavy industry, pre-NLRA, unregulated sectors that bear significant resemblance to unorganized and growing sectors of today's economy. AFL unions tended to be occupationally based rather than plant-based, decentralized, and focused on controlling local labor markets rather than relying on NLRB-sponsored elections. They have thus been well positioned to pursue new tactics like corporate campaigns and community mobilization.[53] In this respect, the historic weakness of the CIO in Boston that Green and Donahue lamented could become a strength as older AFL organizing strategies become newly relevant.

Critics, however, pointed out that even this massive commitment to organizing has failed to stem the tide of declining numbers.[54]

Boston unions have been slower to embrace some of these changes due to their tradition of Kwon and Day's "political collective bargaining"—the top-down approach that pursues short-term alliances with politicians who exchange political support for concrete and immediate benefits for union members. Although this strategy delivered gains to relatively privileged sectors of Boston's working class for decades, it has kept a core group of unions largely isolated from efforts to build a more radical labor movement committed to advancing working-class power and interests in a larger sense.[55]

Yet as the chapters in this volume attest, despite these obstacles, the city's labor movement has been visible and active since Trump's election. Workers are organizing particularly within the leading sectors of the post-industrial economy, in education, finance, medicine, and the low-wage service industries that meet the needs of the better-paid professionals who work in those sectors.

Strikingly, in New England "more than half of union members are doctors, lawyers, teachers, architects, and other white-collar employees."[56] Reflecting the public- and service-sector orientation of the state's unions, the largest unions in Massachusetts are the Massachusetts Teachers Association (MTA), the Service Employees International Union (SEIU), the Association of Federal, State, County, and Municipal Employees (AFSCME), and the Massachusetts Nurses Association (MNA). Nurses and teachers are now one dynamic epicenter of organized labor in Boston and Massachusetts.

Some unions are also reaching out actively to organize the lower sectors of the service economy. Some of the city's unions, perhaps most notably SEIU and UNITE HERE, are challenging old-style political unionism by focusing on organizing workers and workplaces that have been underrepresented within the house of labor. These campaigns came relatively late to Boston. Justice for Janitors, which began in Denver, Pittsburgh, and Los Angeles at the end of the 1980s, did not reach Boston until the new century. By 2016, after more than a decade of organizing, SEIU Local 32BJ was representing sixteen thousand janitors in the Boston area, or about 90 percent of the workforce. These workers were earning between $17 and $25 an hour, with benefits.[57] Similar gains were sought at area universities. In October of 2016, three thousand five hundred graduate students at Harvard organized through the UAW and voted in the union in the largest NLRB election in a decade.[58] As Carlos Aramayo's chapter in this book highlights, this effort was preceded by UNITE HERE's success in organizing over one thousand low-wage workers at area universities between 2012–2014 and was then followed by a successful strike in the fall of 2017 by food service workers at Harvard. Similarly, as Amy Todd explores, adjunct faculty at area campuses have also gotten the union bug.

The new century also saw considerable labor-related activism outside of traditional union structures. The expansion of worker centers is perhaps the most conspicuous example of attempts by nonunionized, low-wage, and largely immigrant workers to improve conditions both at and beyond the workplace. A total of five worker centers existed nationally in the early 1990s, a number that exploded to over 150 by the mid-2000s,[59] and to around 230 by 2018.[60] Many are now loosely organized through a number of umbrella networks, including the National Day Laborers Organizing Network (NDLON), the National Domestic Workers Alliance (NDWA), the Restaurant Opportunities Center United (ROC), the National Guestworker Alliance, the Food Chain Workers Alliance, and the National Taxi Workers Alliance. As Aviva Chomsky explains, worker centers have a social-movement orientation that focuses on economic and immigrant rights while trying to establish alliances with a wide range of groups, including religious actors, state agencies, labor unions, and other progressive organizations.

Although worker centers are typically not rooted in the workplace, and generally do not attempt to organize workers with the purpose of establishing unions and seeking collective bargaining agreements, they do target employers and have had considerable success in acquiring back wages. They have also pressured local and state governments to enforce labor laws and improve conditions for workers. Although their relationship with labor unions has at times been uneasy, the AFL-CIO has now established partnerships with worker centers throughout the country in an effort to reach more deeply into working-class communities.[61] These types of alliances, in turn, have laid the groundwork for broader campaigns around issues including immigrant rights, wage theft, and the Fight for $15 that attempt to expand the labor movement beyond work and unions, Gruman argues in his chapter. In his interview with Chomsky, Jeff Crosby shows how organizing marginalized groups within and outside of unions and building coalitions with progressive community organizations grew out of and contributed to one union local's more radical political orientation. We have also included two chapters (by Eric Larson and by Bella Robinson and Elena Shih) on innovative organizing in Providence, Rhode Island, the major metropolitan area closest to Boston, both because of the social and economic linkages that make it part of the greater Boston area, and because of the significance of these organizing efforts that directly address some of the major themes of the book.

Community-union alliances are exploring new, more radical ways of transcending unions' traditions of political bargaining. They are fighting to bring a larger working-class agenda into city and state politics, organizing inside and outside of the workplace particularly with respect to the minimum wage, sick leave, and wage theft. Gruman's chapter traces how the Raise Up Massachusetts coalition has used legislative initiatives and, when those failed, successful ballot initiatives to raise the minimum wage and to make Massachusetts the first state to require employers to provide paid sick days. Raise Up Massachusetts falls under the umbrella of the SEIU's national strategy beginning with the Fight for a Fair Economy in 2011, and the Fight for $15 in 2012. Both of these campaigns sought to grapple with the twin issues of a hostile political environment and declining membership—despite massive organizing campaigns—through alliances that mobilize working-class communities to press for political change beyond unions' traditional work with the Democratic Party. In Massachusetts, as in California and some other states with robust ballot initiative processes, the initiative has proven a fruitful arena for mobilizing coalitions and achieving concrete gains, as well as for pressuring politicians from the grassroots rather than the backroom.

Other groups, such as the Policy Group on Tradeswomen's Issues (examined here by Susan Moir and Elizabeth Skidmore), have led the fight to give women better access to jobs in the (higher paying) building trades. And as Enid Eckstein writes, some initiatives, such as the "No on 2" campaign led by the Massachusetts Teachers Association to thwart the push for charter schools, have shown how a particular group of workers and the working-class public share common interests in the struggle to insure that "common goods" such as education remain in the public domain.

The chapters collected here show that Boston's labor movement is taking an all-of-the-above approach to confronting the crisis facing both organized and unorganized workers. As Erik Loomis's insightful conclusion reminds us, the challenges arrayed against workers in the twenty-first century are steep. The region's unions must find ways to build and utilize political power in more effective and coherent ways, advancing their own short-term interests while also working with a wide range of groups to build power for the labor movement as a whole. To revitalize the labor movement, we must continue to work to organize new sectors and new workers, to re-energize existing unions, to form coalitions between unions and community organizations, to push a working-class political agenda in state and local government, and to fight for rights for unorganized workers and immigrants. Workers in the blue city of Boston and the blue state of Massachusetts face many challenges that are common to workers nationwide, and others that arise from the particularities of local history. As Boston's working people struggle to meet these challenges, new leadership, new organizations, and new ideas reveal a still-thriving working-class culture and potential that is continuing to unfold.

PART I

Labor, Power, and Inequality in Boston

CHAPTER 1

Unshared Growth

Earners and Earnings Inequality in Boston Before and After the Great Recession

Randy Albelda, with Aimee Bell-Pasht, MA,
Urata Blakaj, MA, Trevor Mattos, MA

B oston is the economic hub of New England, led by its world-renowned educational institutions, hospitals, high-tech and biotech companies, and large financial sector. Boston's current industrial mix is relatively new. James Green and Hugh Donahue foresaw these changes forty years ago, when they argued that the city was starting to transform for working-class Bostonians by the late 1970s. As the city lost manufacturing jobs, it saw a rise in lower-waged office and service work in the financial and health-care sectors.[1] Boston is a global city, and its growth is consistent with that of other such cities, as described by Saskia Sassen: thriving financial, health, and knowledge service industries, employing a class of highly paid professionals and managers that is undergirded by a substantial sector of low-wage service sector workers.[2] This is a recipe for strong growth but also for economic inequality. The severe Great Recession in the first decade of the 2000s, characterized by a financial crisis followed by cuts to the public sector (including education and health), had the potential to disrupt Boston's growth and inequality trajectory. Comparing data from before the recession (2005–2007) to the 2013–2015 period, it is clear that Boston has weathered this storm in terms of overall growth in economic state activity, employment, and inflation-adjusted earnings. But as has been the case since the late 1970s, this growth has not been shared equally within Boston or across the state.

In this chapter, we provide a snapshot of employed workers that live in Boston compared to those that live in Boston suburbs and the rest of Massachusetts in the period 2013–2015. Not surprisingly, Boston's wage earners are much more diverse in terms of race, ethnicity, and nativity than those in the Boston suburbs and the rest of Massachusetts. We then compare earnings levels and earnings shares before and after the Great Recession by lower-wage, median, and higher-wage workers (at the 20th, 50th and 80th percentiles). We find that, while on average, workers that live in Boston and its suburbs saw their real (inflation-adjusted) earnings increase over these two periods, that growth was very uneven, with the top 20 percent seeing the most growth and those in the middle losing earnings shares.

We then turn our attention to Boston's most vulnerable workers by exploring the percentage of workers that are low wage (defined here as those earning two-thirds of median hourly wages in the state) and low income (defined as those earning 200 percent of the federal poverty line income threshold). We find that almost one out of every three workers who live in Boston earns low wages and one in five is in a low-income family; beyond this, 36 percent of workers either earn low wages *or* live in low-income families. In spite of the economic growth that took place during the recovery from the Great Recession, we find that these percentages have not changed since the crisis of 2007–08, reaffirming the early findings that the lion's share of increased post-recession earnings went to those workers at the top of the earnings ladder.

Finally, we take a look at the change in the job and demographic characteristics of working-class workers living in Boston before and after the recession. Here, we use "working class" to describe workers over twenty-five years of age with less than a bachelor's degree.[3] Under that definition, we find that this group of workers has shrunk in Boston. However, there has been a shift in its composition. The number of construction and manufacturing workers has declined as has sales and administration workers, but there was an increase in the number of service workers. The working class living in Boston is also less white than it was in 2005–2007 and also older.

Boston is a highly unequal city, with the top 20 percent of earners holding the majority of earnings, and the Great Recession has not put a damper on that. And because the top 20 percent of earners garnered the majority of the income gains between the 2005–2007 and 2013–2015 period, the city's inequality has only increased. The majority of Boston's working-class workers are people of color and about half work in services, as opposed to the traditional blue-collar (manufacturing, transportation, and construction) or pink-collar (retail trade and administrative support) occupations described by Green and Donahue. These changes represent new challenges but also point to the direction of the types of organizing and organizers that will be most effective. Stemming the tide of inequality will require promoting wage growth in service jobs and leadership and organizing strategies that reflect that Boston's working class is majority minority.

Boston's Workers: A Snapshot

Most of the data in this chapter come from three-year samples of the US Census Bureau's American Community Survey (ACS), using 2013–2015 for the post-recession period and 2005–2007 for the earlier period. We chose these two time periods in order to compare workers at comparable peak economic periods.[4] Specifically we look at workers eighteen years and older who reside in Massachusetts, as represented in the Public Use Micro Sample (PUMS) data from 2005 to 2007 and 2013 to 2015. These combined data sets allow us to get a large enough sample of workers living in Boston to confidently make comparisons across the state and over time.[5]

In exploring worker characteristics, we look only at residents of the geographic area we explore. So, all data presented for Boston are for workers who live in Boston, regardless of where they work. We compare characteristics over these two time periods as well as across three geographic areas of Massachusetts: the city of Boston, the Boston metro region (which we refer to as the Boston suburbs), and the rest of the state which includes both rural areas as well as many cities, notably Fall River, Holyoke, Lowell, Lawrence, New Bedford, Pittsfield, Springfield, and Worcester. In the 2013–2015 period, just under 10 percent of all Massachusetts workers lived in Boston, 49 percent lived in Boston's suburbs, while 41 percent lived in the rest of Massachusetts.

The ACS data are cross-sectional, meaning they only explore a sample of the population at a point in time. That means we are not comparing the same individuals over the two periods. Therefore, we do not know if the changes in earnings we find are due to a change in the composition of workers residing in Boston or a change in the level of earnings of workers who lived in Boston in the earlier period. For example, the percentage of Boston workers with a college degree increased over the two periods. However, we do not know if this is because more workers who lived in Boston in 2005–07 earned their college degrees, if more people with college degrees moved into Boston after 2007, or if those without a college degree moved out. Cross-sectional data are useful, however, in delineating the trends in inequality and how the composition of workers, the jobs they hold, and earnings they receive have changed over time.

Finally, we primarily look at workers' annual earnings, the amount of wages, salaries, or income from self-employment workers reported over the twelve months before they were surveyed by the ACS census takers. We only include workers with non-zero earnings, which means we exclude people who report that they had no earnings in the previous twelve months. We do, however, include those that report having negative earnings.[6] We adjust all earnings to 2015 price levels.

The Demographic and Employment Characteristics of Boston Workers

Between the two time periods under investigation here, the number of workers who lived in Boston grew 9 percent, from 286,078 in 2005 to 314,520 in 2013, while the total number of workers in the state has grown 3.4 percent over the same period, from 3,142,022 to 3,265,783. Table 1 provides a demographic profile of workers in Boston across the two time periods, along with workers living in Boston's suburbs and the non-metro region in 2013–15. The sex composition is not depicted because it is unchanged and does not differ much across the three regions: 48 percent of all Massachusetts workers are female.

The racial, age, and education composition of workers who live in Boston has experienced some notable changes between 2005 to 2007 (column 1) and 2013 to 2015 (column 2). There are a larger percentage of Black and Latino workers and smaller percentages of white and Asian workers now than before the recession. A higher share of earners have higher levels of education: 46.8 percent of workers living in Boston have at least a bachelor's degree in the 2005 to 2007 period while 53.6 percent do in the 2013 to 2015 period. The percentage of immigrant workers has decreased slightly, with just under one out of every three workers born outside the United States. There are higher percentages of workers ages

55 and older as well as ages 25-34 who lived in Boston today than in 2005 to 2007.

Workers who lived in Boston in 2013 to 2015 (column 2) were much more diverse in terms of race, ethnicity, and nativity compared to those who lived in its suburbs (column 3) and the rest of the state (column 4). Workers who live in the suburbs are only slightly more likely to have higher education levels than those in Boston, while those who live in the non-metro regions have the lowest levels of educational attainment. Almost two-thirds (64.3 percent) of non-metro workers do not have a bachelor's degree. Boston is the home to a much higher percentage of workers ages 25–34 than the suburbs and almost twice as many as in non-metro regions. Conversely, older workers (55 and older) are a considerably smaller share of workers in Boston.

Table 1: Demographic and Educational Characteristics of Workers Residing in Boston (2005–2007 and 2013–2015) compared to Those in Boston Suburbs and Non-metro areas (2013–2015)				
Race/Ethnicity*	2005-07 Boston (col 1)	2013-15 Boston (col 2)	2013-15 Suburbs (col 3)	2013-15 Non-metro (col 4)
White, not Hispanic	56.3%	52.2%	79.2%	81.2%
Black, not Hispanic	19.1%	21.3%	5.3%	3.9%
Asian, not Hispanic	14.5%	8.4%	8.0%	4.0%
Hispanic, any race	7.5%	16.4%	6.6%	9.9%
Nativity				
Native born	67.3%	68.7%	79.0%	86.3%
Foreign born	32.7%	31.3%	21.0%	13.7%
Educational Attainment				
HS diploma or less	35.9%	28.6%	25.1%	36.2%
Some college, no bachelor's degree	17.3%	17.8%	21.5%	28.1%
Bachelor's degree	26.2%	30.5%	29.2%	21.6%
Masters, prof. or doctoral degree	20.5%	23.1%	24.2%	14.1%
Age Category				
16–24	9.1%	8.2%	6.0%	7.7%
25–34	30.1%	36.5%	20.0%	18.9%
35–44	27.5%	20.0%	21.0%	20.4%
45–54	20.9%	18.8%	27.5%	27.5%
55–64	9.2%	11.9%	17.4%	18.2%
65 & older	3.2%	4.6%	8.0%	7.4%

*Does not include those identifying as "Other"

Source: ACS 2005–2007 and 2013–2015, by authors

Table 2 depicts the distribution of workers by occupation, industry, and class of work. The distributions of workers who live in Boston over the two time periods are in columns 1 and 2 while those in Boston suburbs and the non-metro region are in columns 3 and 4. Occupation refers to the type of work performed, regardless of employer; industry classifies workers by product produced by their direct employer; class of work refers to the ownership classification of a worker's direct employer. For example, a clerical worker who works for Massachusetts General Hospital in Boston would be classified under the occupation of administrative support, in the health-care services industry, and as an employee of a nonprofit.

Boston (and the immediate surrounding area) has well-developed and relatively high-paying financial, medical, and knowledge industries. And as Sassen argues, workers in these higher-paying industries demand and rely on a host of paid services, especially in low-wage food, hospitality, care, cleaning, and protective service industries and occupations.[7] We would expect to see the shares of employment of professional and service workers rise (or fall) together. However, looking at the change in occupational characteristics over the two time periods in Boston, there has been a large increase (7 percentage points) in the portion of workers who are white-collar managers or professionals, with declines in blue-collar jobs in construction, production, maintenance, and transportation as well as in pink-collar jobs in retail and administrative support, with the share in service occupations staying at about 22 percent. This trend is somewhat mirrored in the industry distribution, with the largest growth in workers employed in high-wage services (professional, scientific and educational services) industries and the largest decline in workers employed in construction and manufacturing industries. Because the proportion of service workers across the state has increased slightly, the lack of growth in Boston's low-wage service jobs could signal that service workers no longer live in the city. Finally, in terms of class of worker, there has been a slight increase in the percentage of workers living in Boston who work for nonprofit employers, mostly educational and health-care institutions in the city.

Despite new attention to the so-called gig economy, the percentage of Bostonians that report being self-employed in their primary job is small (7.7 percent) and has actually shrunk over the two periods.[8] This suggests that while more workers may feel or be economically insecure, it is not because they do not have a formal employer. The decline of self-employment may instead reflect the city's loss of construction workers, who are typically self-employed.

Comparing workers who live in Boston to those residing in the suburbs and beyond the Boston metro region, we see that Boston workers are much more likely to be employed in service occupations and industries as well as for nonprofit employers. This is not surprising given the concentration of nonprofit health-care and educational service industries and occupations in the city. Outside of the larger share of service workers (both in service occupations and in health-care services industry) and the lower share of blue-collar occupations and industries, workers in Boston and its suburbs have similar occupational and industrial composition. The areas outside the Boston metro region have a higher share of workers in pink- and blue-collar jobs and a considerably lower share of managers and professionals.

Table 2: Employment Characteristics of Workers Residing in Boston (2005–2007 and 2013–2015) Compared to Those in Boston Suburbs and Non-Metro Areas (2013–2015)

	2005-07 Boston (col 1)	2013-15 Boston (col 2)	2013-15 Suburbs (col 3)	2013-15 Non-metro (col 3)
Occupation				
Managers & professionals	40.6%	47.5%	50.3%	38.6%
Services*	21.9%	21.7%	14.5%	18.2%
Sales & administrative support	23.1%	19.1%	20.8%	21.9%
Construction, production, maintenance & transportation	14.3%	11.8%	14.4%	21.4%
Industry				
Construction, nat'l resources & manufacturing	11.1%	8.7%	14.8%	19.8%
Trade, transportation & utilities	13.5%	12.5%	15.5%	17.8%
Financial, insurance, information, real estate	13.3%	12.2%	11.5%	8.1%
Services: professional, scientific & educational	18.8%	23.1%	23.3%	16.6%
Services: health care & social services	17.6%	18.9%	15.4%	16.5%
Services: all other (management, waste, entertainment, food, personal)	21.0%	20.2%	15.7%	16.7%
Public administration	4.7%	4.4%	3.9%	4.4%
Class of Worker				
Employee of a private for-profit	65.5%	64.0%	65.0%	66.2%
Employee of a private nonprofit	14.9%	17.0%	12.7%	10.0%
Local, state, or federal government employee	11.9%	11.0%	11.4%	13.8%
Self-employed	7.7%	6.8%	10.8%	10.0%

*Includes health-care support, protective, cleaning, food prep, hospitality, and personal care services.

Source: ACS 2005–2007 and 2013–2015, by authors

Earnings and Earnings Inequality

Overall, Massachusetts and the Boston metro region have experienced strong inflation-adjusted economic growth between 2005 and 2015, as measured in terms of state gross domestic product (GDP). Total Massachusetts GDP grew by 16.3 percent over this period, above the US average state growth rate of 13.3 percent. At 16.9 percent, the Boston metropolitan area saw an even higher GDP growth than the state as a whole and more than the 13.1 percent average increase in metro areas nationwide.[9] Turning to earnings growth using ACS data, we find that total inflation-adjusted annual wages, salaries, and income from self-employment across the state grew by 10.3 percent from the 2005–2007 to the 2013–2015 period. Earnings of workers in Boston in 2013-2015, however, were almost 20 percent higher than in 2005–2007, compared to an 8.9 percent increase in Boston suburbs and a 10.1 percent increase in earning in the rest of the state. This suggests that all workers in the state have seen inflation-adjusted rise in earnings, but Boston workers' earnings growth has been twice that of workers elsewhere in the state.

Of the state's 3,266,000 workers, 314,515 (9.6 percent) live in Boston, while 49.2 percent live in Boston's suburban area, with the remaining 41.2 percent outside the Boston metro region. Boston workers garnered 9.6 percent of all earnings in the state in the 2013–2015 period, matching their worker population share. However, suburban workers received 56 percent of all earnings while non-Boston metro areas had 34 percent. Not surprisingly then, workers living in Boston's suburban areas had higher levels of earnings than workers living in Boston or outside the Boston metro region. On average, workers in Boston earned $60,500 annually, while those in the suburbs had an annual average of $69,200, considerably more than the non-Boston metro average of $50,300. Regression analysis indicates that after adjusting for age, race, gender, education level, nativity, industry, occupation, and weeks worked, Boston workers earned slightly more than workers in the suburbs and much higher than those outside the metro area.[10] This means that workers in Boston actually have a slight wage premium over those in suburban areas, once controlling for their demographic and employment differences. So, earnings differences are largely explained by the composition of Boston's workers compared to those in the suburbs.

And while average earnings grew over the two time periods, that growth was not shared equally among workers. Figure 1.1 depicts the earnings levels at the 20th, 50th (or median), and 80th percentile of earners[11] in the pre- and post-recession periods in each of the three areas of the state.

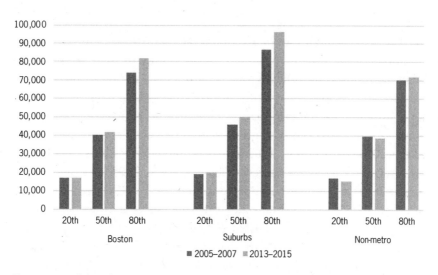

Figure 1.1: Annual earnings at 20th, 50th, and 80th percentile by area, pre- and post-recession

Focusing on changes over time, while workers in Boston and its suburbs saw increases at all three levels of earnings depicted in Figure 1.1, the highest percentage increase occurred at the 80th percentile. Workers at the 20th and median levels of income in the non-metro area actually experienced decreases in earnings levels. And while the earnings growth of workers in Boston has kept pace with those in the suburbs, that is not the case with workers outside metropolitan Boston. Workers residing in the suburbs earned slightly more than workers in Boston and elsewhere in the state at all three income percentiles in both time periods.

Growth in Earnings Inequality

To measure earnings inequality, we look at the share of total earnings held by workers at each quintile (that is, each 20 percent) over the two periods.[12] Figure 1.2 depicts the total share of earnings held by each quintile in 2013 to 2015 for each of the three areas in Massachusetts. Focusing on Boston, the top 20 percent of earners (those in quintile 80-

100) that reside in Boston hold 54 percent of all the earnings generated by Boston workers. That is, the top 20 percent earn more than the bottom 80 percent combined. Meanwhile, those in the bottom 20 percent of earners hold just under 3 percent of all the earnings made by Boston workers. The level of inequality, measured by the share of earnings at the top of the earnings scale, is highest in Boston and lowest in the non-metro region.

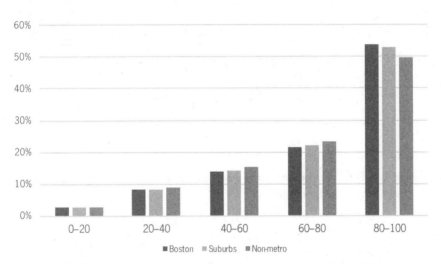

Figure 1.2: Share of total earnings by earnings quintile in 2013–15 by geograpical area

To measure the change in earnings inequality over time we look at the difference in earnings shares by quintiles between the two periods, depicted in Figure 1.3.[13] The graph starkly shows that the top 20 percent of earners in all three areas hold a larger slice of the earnings pie in 2013 to 2015 than they did just eight years earlier (2005–2007) by about 1.5 percentage points. So even though the pie grew (that is, total earnings increased), the slices going to those in the bottom 60 percent got smaller, with the 2nd quintile (those in the 20–40 percent range) and 3rd quintile (the 40–60 percent range) seeing the largest reductions in earnings share. The largest shift of earnings to the top decile occurred in the non-metro region, while the smallest was in Boston (where the levels of inequality remain highest).

In summary, workers who live in Boston have experienced an increase in earnings since the last business cycle peak (the pre-recession years

2005–2007), but most of those earnings gains have been captured by the top earners, increasing inequality among Boston workers.

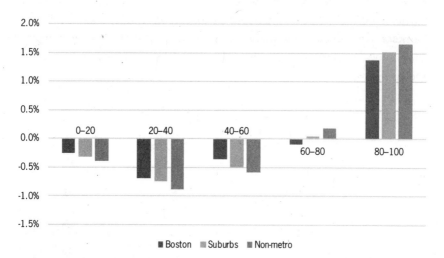

Figure 1.3: Percentage point change pre- and post-recession in earnings share by quintile by by geographic area

Low-Wage, Low-Income and Working-Class Workers in Boston

We now turn our attention to the most vulnerable workers, those who earn low wages or live in a low-income family. In addition to not earning much, low-wage workers are most likely to lack employer benefits. Low-income workers live in a family whose total income may make it hard to secure basic needs that make working possible, like housing, food, and transportation. We define low-wage workers as those earning an hourly wage of no more than two-thirds of the median hourly wage in the Commonwealth.[14] In 2015 adjusted prices, the Massachusetts median wage in the 2013–2015 period was $23.25 an hour and in the 2005–2007 it was $22.75 an hour. Workers in the post-recession period are considered low wage if they earn no more than $15.83 an hour.[15] We define a worker as low income if they live in a family whose total income is at or below 200 percent of the federal poverty line, a nationwide measure based on family size that is adjusted annually for inflation. In 2015 dollars, the low-income threshold for a worker in a family of three is an annual family income of $37,742, and for a single adult it is $24,164.

Given the high cost of housing in the state, especially in Boston and the metro region, these levels of income could make it hard to cover even the basic costs of living. A worker could be low income but not low wage (i.e., someone with a high wage but who is the sole earner in a large family or someone who works few hours). Similarly, a worker could be low wage but not live in a low-income family (i.e., someone who lives with other workers who pull family income over the low-income threshold).

Table 3 depicts the percentage and number of workers in Boston, Boston's suburbs, and the non-metro areas that were low wage, low income, or one or the other over the two time periods. Almost one out of every three workers in Boston earns a low wage, while one out of five lives in a low-income family. Despite Boston's robust and growing economy, these percentages have remained more or less the same in both time periods. Workers in the suburbs are less likely to be low wage, low income, or either than workers elsewhere, and the percentages have also not changed much from the 2005–2007 period to the post-recession years of 2013–2015. Workers outside the Boston metro region, however, have seen a substantial increase in the percentages who are low wage and low income or either.[16] In the 2013–2015 period, the percentage of low-wage workers in the non-metro parts of the state surpasses that of workers in Boston, although Boston workers include the highest percentage of low-income workers.

Probing the data, we find that Boston's low-wage workers are much more likely to not be white, not have a college education, not be native born, and to work in a non-health-care or professionally-related service or retail industry than workers who are not low wage. Still, one-third of all low-wage workers are white, just under 30 percent have at least a bachelor's degree, and 22 percent are in a managerial or professional occupation.[17]

Table 3: Percent and Number of Low-Wage & Low-Income Earners Pre-& Post-Recession in Boston, Boston's Suburbs, and Beyond the Boston Metro Area				
	Pre-recession (2005–2007)		Post-recession (2013–2015)	
	Percent	Number	Percent	Number
Boston				
Is low wage	31.6%	90,181	31.1%	97,502
Is low income	21.1%	60,144	20.2%	63,265
Is either low wage or low income	36.8%	105,003	35.9%	112,690
Suburbs				
Is low wage	24.3%	394,254	24.8%	397,035
Is low income	10.6%	171,195	10.8%	173,695
Is either low wage or low income	27.0%	438,491	27.6%	442,092
Non-metro				
Is low wage	29.3%	358,745	33.9%	949,557
Is low income	13.5%	165,828	16.4%	456,567
Is either low wage or low income	32.6%	399,188	37.5%	503,855

Source: ACS 2005–2007 and 2013–2015, by authors

Shifting Middle: Change in the Occupational and Industrial Composition of Boston's "Working Class"

Green and Donahue described a changing industrial terrain for working-class people in the Boston area in the 1950s through the late 1970s. The shift away from manufacturing has continued even in the relatively short period of time we explore here. The percentage of Boston workers laboring in manufacturing industries is low and getting lower. As depicted in Table 2, the portion of workers in construction and manufacturing industries in Boston fell from 11.1 to 8.7 percent. While the continued decline of well-paying manufacturing jobs is probably one important change taking place, there are other occupational and industrial shifts as well.

In Boston from 2005 to 2007, there were 259,988 workers over age 25, and of those, 135,973 (52.3 percent) did not have a bachelor's degree. By 2013 to 2015, the number of workers over 25 had grown to 288,782, but the number without a bachelor's degree fell to 131,635. If we recall our working definition of "working class," we can see that the percentage of working-class Boston workers fell to 45.6 percent of the total of working-age adults over 25. In Table 4 we present the industrial and occupational distribution as well as the race/ethnicity and age distribution of workers that most likely represent the working class in Boston. Boston's current working class has seen a reduction in pink- and blue-collar jobs historically associated with the working class. A large percentage of the working class can now be found in typically low-wage service occupations and in services industries, including health care.

Table 4 also charts the transformations in the demographics of Boston's working-class residents since the Great Recession. Boston's working class was already majority minority in the 2005–2007 period and became even more so in the 2013–2015 period. In the earlier period, 37.4 percent of workers living in Boston were white and not Hispanic, but by the 2013–15 period, this dropped to 29.2 percent. The other noticeable change is the increase in the number and percentage of older workers ages 55–64. These trends point to why union organizing efforts in the services remain an important strategy but also speak to the importance of leadership that understand and address the racial, ethnic, and age cleavages among Boston's working class.

Table 4: Occupational, Industrial, Racial, and Age Distribution of Boston's "Working Class" (Those Without a Bachelor's Degree and 25 Years and Older)

	Boston Pre-recession 2005-07		Boston Post-recession 2013-15	
	Percent	Number	Percent	Number
Occupation				
Managers & professionals	15.5%	21,072	16.2%	21,320
Services	34.9%	47,444	39.0%	51,368
Sales & administrative support	25.1%	34,153	22.4%	29,488
Construction, production, maintenance & transportation	24.5%	33,303	22.4%	29,458
Total	100.0%	135,972	100.0%	131,635
Industry				
Construction, nat'l resources & manufacturing	15.8%	21,444	12.0%	15,788
Trade, transportation & utilities	16.8%	22,814	17.5%	22,988
Financial, insurance, information, real estate	8.1%	11,054	6.4%	8,425
Services: professional, scientific & educational	7.4%	10,012	8.4%	11,085
Services: health care & social services	17.4%	23,700	20.0%	26,308
Services: all other (management, waste, entertainment, food, personal)	29.7%	40,345	30.3%	39,928
Public administration	4.9%	6,603	5.4%	7,112
Total	100.0%	135,972	100.0%	131,635
Race/Ethnicity				
White, not Hispanic	37.4%	50,834	29.2%	38,387
Black, not Hispanic	28.9%	39,336	33.0%	43,473
Asian, not Hispanic	6.9%	9,413	8.2%	10,797
Other, not Hispanic	3.9%	5,331	2.7%	3,578
Hispanic, any race	22.8%	31,058	26.9%	35,400
Total	100.0%	135,972	100.0%	131,635
Age Category				
25-34	25.5%	34,678	27.4%	36,050
35-44	31.2%	42,440	24.4%	32,132
45-54	27.9%	38,002	25.8%	33,975
55-64	11.1%	15,111	17.2%	22,613
65 & older	4.2%	5,741	5.2%	6,865
Total	100.0%	135,972	100.0%	131,635

*Includes health-care support, protective, cleaning, food prep, hospitality, and personal care services.

Source: ACS by authors

Conclusion

Together our data paint a picture of an economically growing but increasingly unequal Boston. Some of the changes occurring are part of a long-term trend led by the reduction in manufacturing work. In the 2000s, growing inequality was in significant part driven by the loss of better-paying jobs in manufacturing. But this only tells part of the story, since the top 20 percent of wage earners have captured most, if not all, of the earnings growth. And while Green and Donahue noted that an important change in the composition of the working class in the 1970s was an increase in women's employment in Boston, in the 2000s the more noticeable demographic change was the rapid change in the racial and ethnic composition of Boston's workers, and the decrease in the white working class, at least as defined by education level. Finally, the data reveal the complementary economic relationship of Boston to its suburbs, as evidenced by their parallel earnings growth and similar occupational and industrial distributions. It is also clear, however, that workers in the rest of Massachusetts have not enjoyed overall economic gains.

CHAPTER 2

Boston's Public Sector and the Fight for Union Survival

Enid Eckstein

As labor historian James Green wrote in 1977, the "contemporary history of the Boston labor movement is difficult to write because the city's workers are still making it."[1] Boston's working people continue to shape their history today, but they do so in a very different world from the one Green described over forty years ago. The loss of union jobs, the fierce anti-union tactics, and other effects of globalization that date to the 1970s have brought steep declines in the ranks of unionized workers in the private sector. If workers in the public sector once may have felt insulated from these forces, the picture today is grim: in the intervening years many states and the federal government waged war against public sector workers and their labor unions, culminating most recently in June 2018 with the Supreme Court's *Janus v. AFSCME* decision.

Years of austerity, budget cutting, and relentless attacks on the public sector have taken their toll in state after state. Unions' traditional alliances with the Democratic Party have hindered their ability to confront these attacks, which have been led by national and state-level conservative Democratic as well as Republican administrations. Now public sector workers, often led by teachers, are on the front lines of a fight back to restore services, fight for the common good, and improve wages and working conditions. The spring of 2018 saw thousands of West Virginia teachers wage a victorious strike with overwhelming public support. Teachers took to the streets and led red-state rebellions in Arizona, West Virginia, Oklahoma, Kentucky, and North Carolina. Most of these states prohibit public sector strikes, but overwhelming public support demonstrated the power of solidarity. Many state governments gave in to teacher demands. Meanwhile, in May 2018, fifty-three thousand University of California employees took to the picket line in a fight against austerity and privatization in higher education, and to defend the very idea of public institutions.[2]

Massachusetts union members are on the front lines of some of the same fights in defense of public services against austerity. The state's labor movement looks very different from the one that Green described some forty years ago. Public sector workers are playing a key role in the labor movement's ongoing shift away from the business union model that prevailed during the Cold War in the second half of the twentieth century. Public sector unions' commitment to public services, their inclusion of large numbers of women and people of color, and their moves to include new categories of marginalized workers, like home health-care workers and child-care workers, has made public sector unions especially open to social movement unionism and alliances with progressive organizations.

A History of Public Sector Unionism

Despite having no legal standing before the 1960s, US public sector unions have organized, lobbied for civil service protections, and engaged in informal negotiations with public employers since the mid-1800s. Firefighters, railroad workers, letter carriers, health-care workers, teachers, and many others banded together to form voluntary associations to improve working conditions. Many engaged in work actions to press their demands. The National Education Association (NEA) was formed in 1857, the American Federation of Teachers (AFT) in 1911, and the American Federation of State, County, and Municipal Employees (AFSCME) in 1932.

The roots of public sector unionization in Massachusetts run deep. The 1919 Boston Police Strike has been well documented, but many lesser known struggles also linked better working conditions with improved public services. Boston Elevated Company (today's "MBTA") employees organized in the late 1890s and waged a lengthy, militant strike in 1912. Both the Massachusetts Teachers Association (NEA) and the Massachusetts Federation of Teachers had their start before 1900 and campaigned for improved salaries, professional advancement, and well-funded public education. Such negotiations, from the 1920s on, produced actual contract-like agreements in a number of cases, even though no law authorized collective bargaining. Boston firefighters organized with the International Association of Firefighters and won an eight-hour day in 1942.[3]

Public sector employment expanded nationally after World War II, as state and local governments added millions of jobs. Public sector unions developed in response to this enormous expansion, and they became a key growth area in the labor movement after public employees were granted legal organizing rights in the late 1950s. While cities such as New York granted union recognition earlier, Wisconsin was the first state to enact a comprehensive public sector collective bargaining law, in 1959. Other states soon followed, and President John F. Kennedy issued an executive order allowing federal employees the right to organize. The expansion of public sector employment and unionization coincided and intersected with the civil rights movement, which contributed to government expansion while opening new public jobs to Black workers. Throughout the South, sanitation and other workers inspired by the civil rights struggle took to the picket lines in a wave of militancy that won limited rights and brought many Black workers into union membership. Martin Luther King Jr. famously marched in support of AFSCME's campaign to organize sanitation workers in Memphis, which was just one of many new AFSCME locals organized by Black workers during this period.[4] Public employees' unions and the civil rights movement drew strength from each other, despite differences in approach. In the face of limitations on the right of public employees to strike, workers organized and engaged in work actions. In 1970, two hundred thousand postal workers staged a national strike in defiance of a ban on strikes and won major concessions. The struggle to organize and win collective bargaining transformed many diffuse worker organizations from professional employee associations to full-fledged unions willing to take on a fight.

Public sector unions became the labor movement's big success story during the late 1960s and 1970s. Multiple state legislatures enacted laws providing collective bargaining rights to public employees. Even California's governor Reagan signed California's collective bargaining law in 1968. In 1955, public employee unions had about four hundred thousand members nationwide in total; that figure rose ten-fold, to over four million, in the 1970s. By 1992, states provided some collective bargaining rights to at least a portion of public employees. Significantly, the rise in public sector unionism occurred as private sector union membership was in decline. The continual decline in manufacturing and construction jobs created a seismic shift in the overall balance between public and private unionization. In 1979, there were 15 million union members in the private sector and 7 million in the public sector. By 2009, the majority of US union members were government workers. In contrast, private sector union density continued to decline, and in 2019 it hovered at 6.2 percent.[5]

Massachusetts was no exception to these trends. Employment in Massachusetts' public sector grew from 243,952 jobs in 1960 (with over half in either state or local municipalities) to 367,078 in 1983, a number that remained roughly stable over the next decades.[6] In 1958 public employees in Massachusetts won legislation guaranteeing their right to belong to employee organizations, and by 1960 city and town employees won the right to bargain on limited matters. Several groups, including highway and corrections workers affiliated with AFSCME, organized and won improvements and a grievance procedure. By 1965, municipal unions had won the right to bargain over wages, hours, and working conditions. Several work actions followed. Boston welfare workers struck in 1968 for lower caseloads and better working conditions.[7] It was not until 1973, though, that most Massachusetts public employees won full collective bargaining rights. With the passage of Chapter 150E, the Massachusetts Labor Relations Commission issued standards for appropriate bargaining units affecting fifty-five thousand state employees in more than two thousand classifications. Ten statewide bargaining units were created, and employees voted for union representation. Shortly thereafter, in June of 1976, thirty thousand state workers, frustrated by the lack of progress at the bargaining table, took to the picket lines for three days, waging a statewide strike.[8] By November, the unions ratified a new contract with major wage and benefit improvements.

Massachusetts' rate of unionization has tended to be higher than the national average, but they followed national trends. In 1983, 23.7 percent of the Massachusetts workforce were union members. And although the private sector employed far more people, union density in the private sector was only 17.6 percent. In the much smaller public sector, 60.4 percent were union members. By 1983, 221,713 of the state's 603,187 union workers were employed in the public sector and 381,474 in the private sector. By 2016, the total Massachusetts workforce had grown by over half a million, to 3,162,374. Union membership had dropped precipitously, however, down to 12.1 percent of the labor force. The numbers and the percentages fell in both private and public sectors, but the fall was more pronounced for the former. By 2016, private sector employment had grown by over two hundred thousand, but a mere 6.4 percent of private sector workers were unionized. Meanwhile, public sector employment remained relatively stable, inching up only by about thirty thousand. Just over 50 percent of these workers belonged to unions, a fall from over 60 percent in 1990, as their ranks thinned under Republican governors William Weld, Paul Cellucci, and Mitt Romney. Still, today more than half of all Massachusetts union members are public sector workers.[9]

Challenges Facing Workers in Massachusetts

Workers in liberal Massachusetts face some of the same challenges confronting the labor movement nationwide. First, the problem of overall union decline: How does labor organize the unorganized within a changing private sector that has lost so much union density and has increasingly created part-time contingent work? Organizing the private sector remains key for the future of the labor movement and working people for a simple reason: it is where the vast majority of jobs still are. A second, rather different problem involves expanding unionization within the public sector: How does labor recover, retain, and perhaps even expand the relatively high levels of unionization among public employees when their unions and the services they deliver are also under attack? And how do public sector unions build strong effective organizations in an increasingly hostile political environment?

Unions in both sectors are seeking ways to overcome public perceptions that they are engaged in a rearguard battle to defend the privileges of a shrinking proportion of workers. Progressive voices in the union movement are finding ways to reach beyond their organized constituencies and fight for the interests of the working class more broadly, especially the growing sectors of low-wage, immigrant, and contingent workers. Public sector unions are well positioned to lead this movement. Public workers reside in every community, deliver critical services, and can use their position to advocate for high-quality services.

In analyzing the prospects for a besieged union movement in the United States, Jake Rosenfeld has argued that "government is not the answer." In a supportive political climate, public sector unions tend to be successful and win strong contracts, but the political climate has become increasingly adverse, even in blue states like Massachusetts. Rosenfeld argues that public sector workers tend to be better educated and enjoy better working conditions than those in the private sector, with or without unions. To the extent that unions have come to represent the public rather than the private sector, they have shifted away from their historic mission of representing and fighting for the most vulnerable workers, who toil in private businesses.[10] Yet public sector union activism in Massachusetts is critical to the future of the Massachusetts labor movement. A healthy labor movement needs strength in both the private and public sector. But public sector unions have a unique opportunity to be in the forefront of the struggle to win the "common good" and envision a better future. While it is true that public sector workers hold a relatively privileged position among the working class, the rise of relatively secure public sector jobs with good benefits has been particularly important for low-wage workers, women, and people of color, all of whom found access to public sector employment easier than in many private sector industries. Because public sector expansion coincided with civil rights victories that opened the workplace to women and workers of color, public sector unionism brought more women and people of color into the labor movement.

However, Boston's racial divides have complicated the opportunities that new public sector employment, and unions, have opened for workers of color. The expansion of the public sector coincided with the city's demographic shift from a majority-white city to a majority-minority city. But new opportunities were structured by existing racial inequalities. Nationwide, Blacks and other people of color tend to be concentrated in the lower-wage sectors of public employment, and Boston is particularly egregious in this regard.[11] The city became majority-minority both because of immigration and because of white flight—especially in the era of school desegregation, which came relatively late to Boston in the mid-1970s. A former City Councilor estimates that Boston lost about 10 percent of its population during the early- to mid-1970s. In an attempt to keep white middle class workers in the city, Boston passed ordinances in 1976 and 1994 requiring that city employees reside there. Residency requirements have kept white middle class employees in the city, but they have resulted in limited career mobility for workers of color, since they are disproportionately burdened by Boston's high cost of housing. A 2014 *Boston Globe* investigation found that about two-thirds of the city's eighteen thousand employees actually resided there, with higher-paid workers more likely to reside in the suburbs. As the city's housing market boomed in the early 2000s and again after the 2008 crash, many found the regulations anachronistic, with low-wage workers forced to pay the city's high rents in order to keep their jobs, while their higher-paid colleagues were able to decamp to cheaper suburban locales. Several public employee unions battled the ordinances: teachers' unions successfully fought for state legislation exempting them from the requirement, and some public safety unions have bargained for the right to move out of the city after ten years on the job.[12] (The residency requirement played out somewhat differently in the construction industry, as described in the following chapter by Aviva Chomsky, on Black workers in Boston.)

But these structural fault lines have also opened up opportunities for unions eager to reach out to low-wage workers and workers of color. Public sector unions are important to the larger labor movement because of their unique role in defending public services and the "common good" more generally, strengthening unions' relations with other progressive movements. Given the demographics of public sector unions, they also play a critical role in the development of new leaders of color and women leaders. Although a well-organized public sector will not solve all of labor's problems, the loss of density in this area would be devastating for the labor movement as a whole as it tries to make strides in organizing the private sector. It is also important to note that as the structure of work has evolved, some unions have created locals that are made up of both public and private employees. For example, SEIU Local 1199, traditionally a union of private-sector health-care workers, has recently organized publicly funded home-care workers. On the other hand, SEIU Local 509, founded as a union of state employees, now include private-sector human services workers, some of whose work had previously been in the public sphere.

Public sector unions in Massachusetts and elsewhere are confronting the challenges facing labor unions across the country through intensive organizing that links members' interests to the larger public good. They are leading campaigns supporting public services, and winning recognition of low-wage workers, like home health-care and child-care workers, as public sector employees eligible for collective bargaining rights. Nevertheless, the challenges they face are steep.

The Attack on the Public Sector

Organized opposition to public sector union power had its roots in the changing economic and political climate of the 1970s. Despite enjoying a Democrat-controlled Congress that passed pro-worker legislation like that which created OSHA, the Occupational Safety and Health Administration, President Jimmy Carter adopted a supply-side economic agenda, deregulating key industries like railroads, airlines, and trucking. The 1970s also saw the rise of a virulent anti-union agenda in the private corporate sector. In the public sector, the attack was less direct, and began with cutbacks and privatization. California's Proposition 13 in 1978 signaled the start of the anti-tax revolt.

The subsequent election of Ronald Reagan brought massive tax cuts for the wealthy, and further deregulation of the economy. In 1981, President Reagan fired an opening shot against public sector workers when he terminated several thousand PATCO air traffic controllers for engaging in a strike. Reagan and his team touted privatization as a critical element in the administration's effort to reduce the size of government and balance the budget. In state after state, governors contracted out human services, health-care, and public-works departments, and experimented with privatization of transit systems. Governors and municipal leaders embraced small, "lean" government and touted free market competition as a solution to the fiscal woes. A 1987 survey of state, city, and county executives cited cost savings as one reason for privatization, but the second was "to solve labor problems with unionized government employees."[13] State government officials attacked union contracts for imposing higher costs and burdensome rules, but did not directly attack collective bargaining rights.

As state revenues continued to decline and elected officials were not willing to raise taxes, legislatures around the country balanced budgets on the backs of public employees and contracted out services previously performed by state employees. Massachusetts' governors and municipalities followed the national trend to reduce the state payroll. By the late 1970s there was a growing anti-tax sentiment, and in 1980 the Massachusetts electorate, following California's example, voted to pass Proposition 2 ½. The Proposition limited property tax growth, causing considerable strain to towns and cities, which relied heavily on these taxes. With the state's economic downturn in the late 1980s, state tax revenues declined. Faced with a fiscal crisis, the executive and legislative branches of state government cut back on social services and welfare funding, resulting in layoffs.[14]

The right wing has been targeting state services and the workers who deliver them for several decades now, even in supposedly blue Massachusetts. Faced with severe budget shortfalls, a succession of Republican and Democratic governors have cut or privatized thousands of state jobs and services. In 1990, the anti-tax forces sought to further cut state funding for the state's safety net when it tried to pass Question 3, which the voters soundly defeated. Despite the successful movement to defeat Question 3, in 1991 Massachusetts elected the Republican Bill Weld as governor. Weld's opponent, Boston University President John Silber, was a combative, anti-union social conservative. Many Democrats, including some local unions, turned their backs on him. Weld and his Republican successors, governors Cellucci, Romney, and Baker, relied heavily on policy support from the Pioneer Institute, a conservative think tank supported by the Koch brothers, the notorious right-wing philanthropists. The Institute provided the intellectual underpinnings of a multiyear attack on public employees' pensions and benefits, which took several forms, including the privatization of multiple state services, expansion of charter schools, and support for multiple free-market reforms.[15]

Predictably, then, Weld launched a full-scale attack on state employees. He slashed services, laid off thousands of workers, introduced furlough days, and sought to privatize a number of state services, including state mental services, highway maintenance, public transit, and the prison health-care system. The unions fought back, protested, took their fight to the public, and had some victories along the way, but Weld successfully cut or contracted out some state services. During the same period, several Massachusetts municipalities engaged in their own belt-tightening and cut services. One signature case in Boston involved the public Boston City Hospital. Like other public institutions, the 1964 Civil Rights Act opened up employment there to Boston's Black and Puerto Rican populations. According to AFSCME organizer Meizhu Lui, "It was the Black struggle that drove large gains in union membership at that time, demonstrating the importance of the participation of people of color in the labor movement."[16]

In 1994, Boston mayor Thomas Menino, faced with declining city revenues, followed the lead of other big-city mayors and announced the merger of the public Boston City Hospital with a private entity to create the new Boston Medical Center, a private institution. Other municipalities closed public hospitals or spun them off. Public employees, with public employee benefits, now became private sector employees, with weakened benefits and without a union. SEIU and AFSCME represented the majority of Boston City Hospital employees. The unions aggressively campaigned to maintain the public mission of the hospital in the new private hospital and succeeded in maintaining the union, jobs, and benefits for the thousands of members in the new institution. SEIU then went on to organize the remaining nonunion employees in the Boston Medical Center.

The 2008 Recession and the Escalating Attack on Unions

The 2008 recession accentuated ongoing trends of cutbacks and privatization. Nationally, total government (state, local, and federal) jobs have decreased by over five hundred and eighty thousand since the end of the recession, the largest decrease in any sector since the recovery began in 2009.[17] Women and people of color were hit especially hard as states reduced their budgets and privatized or cut jobs. Conservative legislators used this opportunity to introduce legislation designed to roll back existing labor protections. The stability and future of public sector unions, along with the services they provide, is under threat in state after state. Budget cuts and privatization are only a part of a full-fledged attack on the fundamental rights of collective bargaining in general, and those of public sector workers in particular. Not content to privatize and downsize government, the current anti-labor campaign aims to roll back private sector unionism. This round of attack threatens the very foundations of collective bargaining and has its roots in the so-called "right-to-work" laws that originated in the South following World War II. In these states, even if a union was certified by a majority of the workers, the workers did not have to belong to the union or support its work. States that enacted these laws in the 1950s still have low rates of private sector unionization. Absent state-level right-to-work legislation, unions may collect dues from workers in a bargaining unit who elect not to join the union, since these workers would still receive the services of improved pay, benefits, and working conditions made through collective bargaining. To survive in this environment, unions need to build strong continuous organization to build and maintain membership. To solve the "free-rider" problem, unions negotiate "fair share" or agency fees that require nonmembers to pay their share of the costs of union representation.

This policy did not exist in the public sector until 1977, when the US Supreme Court ruled in the case *Abood v. Detroit Board of Education* that the right to collect agency fees also applied to the public sector. With the institution of agency fees, many public sector unions neglected to build strong member-driven organizations. With the Court's *Janus v. AFCSME* decision in June of 2018, which overturned the 1977 precedent, public sector unions lost the ability to collect agency fees.

The *Janus* decision is part of the broader right-wing campaign to lower wages and labor standards across the country. Because unions—especially in the public sector—had developed sophisticated lobbying and electoral power, the right's electoral, legislative, and economic strategies dovetailed: in order to implement their economic agenda, conservatives had to undercut unions' political influence and workplace strength. As early as 2004, the Republican consultant Grover Norquist identified public employees, labor unions, and trial lawyers as three "pillars" of the Democratic Party—unions and lawyers provide campaign funds, he reasoned, and public employees provide an army of volunteers making phone calls and knocking on doors in support of "big government."[18] In accordance with this view, Republicans have sought to cut off union contributions and volunteers, and therefore limit support to the Democratic Party.

The post-recession round of anti-labor mobilizations are spearheaded by traditional anti-union forces, such as chambers of commerce and the Koch brothers, the right-wing benefactors who fund policy-making organizations like the State Policy Network (SPN), an alliance of 66 state-based think tanks, two of which, the Pioneer Institute and the Beacon Hill Institute, are based in Massachusetts. "Big government unions are the biggest sources of funding and political muscle for the left," wrote SPN President and CEO Tracie Sharp. "To win the battle for freedom, we must take the fight to the unions, state by state." SPN devised a 2017 plan to "defund and defang" government unions and ensure "the permanent collapse of progressive politics" to construct "right wing hegemony." The SPN and its members aim to strike a "mortal blow" to the Democrats by depriving their candidates of funding from "dues extracted from unwilling union members."[19] This is at the heart of the *Janus* case, as well—an attempt to bankrupt public sector unions.

Another escalation of the right's anti-labor offensive began when Wisconsin governor Scott Walker was elected in 2010. Despite massive protests by union members and their allies, he successfully passed his Budget Repair Bill, Act 10, an out-and-out attack on union rights for one hundred and seventy-five thousand Wisconsin public sector workers. Act 10 required all public sector bargaining units to take an annual vote to maintain certification as a union, outlawed dues check-off and fair-share fees, and limited union bargaining to wages alone, and then only to adjust for inflation.

Significantly, Governor Walker exempted police and firefighters from these new restrictions, creating a division among the unions. His actions sent a chilling message to public employees and their respective unions across the nation. As of 2019, the rate of union membership in Wisconsin's workforce has dropped to 8 percent, from 14 percent in 2010.[20]

Wisconsin is just one of about two dozen states where members of Republican-led majorities in one or both chambers introduced measures intended to limit public sector collective bargaining, like right-to-work bills or a rollback of prevailing-wage laws that establish workers' pay on public projects. Within a five-year period, several additional states enacted some form of right-to-work legislation, and fifteen other states passed other limits on collective bargaining in the public sector. Right-to-work was now the law in former union strongholds such as Michigan, Wisconsin, and Indiana.[21] Missouri's legislature passed similar legislation, but the public overwhelmingly defeated it in a referendum in 2018 before it could even take effect. New Hampshire tried multiple times, but union members there and in Massachusetts organized to defeat this effort. Right-to-work has many serious implications for workers and the general public. A recent Economic Policy Institute study reports that wages in right-to-work states are 3.1 percent lower than those in states without these restrictions, meaning that for a typical full-time, full-year worker, right-to-work states offer annual wages that are $1,558 lower than those in a state without these laws.[22] Right-to-work states also have less overall worker protections. Right-to-work targeted private sector workers and various court cases targeted public sector unions. The right wing was on the offense.

At the heart of the Wisconsin campaign was a common message, that public sector workers were not sharing the pain that private sector workers experienced during the 2008 recession. The recession created an opening for renewed criticism of public sector unions, as anti-union advocates raised taxpayer concerns about union compensation and unfunded pension liabilities. Elected official after elected official railed against fat state budgets, pension liabilities, and entitlements. Former Massachusetts Republican governor Mitt Romney reflected this resentment when he stated, "I don't think government workers should be paid a better deal than taxpayers who are paying for them."[23] The overall right-wing strategy reflected what some have called a "politics of resentment" aimed at culling the benefits won by union workers.[24]

In 2014, this campaign moved to the Supreme Court, when the justices heard *Harris v. Quinn*. In this case, the National Right to Work Legal Defense Foundation funded a claim on behalf of Pamela Harris, an Illinois home-care worker represented by SEIU, who alleged that the state's Public Labor Relations Act violated her First Amendment rights of free speech and association. The court ruled in favor of Harris, agreeing that the union's collection of agency fees violated her free-speech rights. Although the decision was narrow, the *New York Times* reported, its language "suggests that this may be the court's first step toward nationalizing the right-to-work gospel by embedding it in constitutional law."[25] The Harris decision presented challenges to home health-care unions. Despite the obstacles, Massachusetts 1199SEIU had prepared for this decision and anticipated future attacks designed to erode the power of home health-care workers (Personal Care Attendants) . In the last few years, the 48,000 Massachusetts home-care union members have had to reaffirm their union membership and agree to an alternative dues collection process. During the same period the union successfully won pay increases and created a training program for PCAs and other benefits.[26]

The following year the court heard the case of *Friedrichs v. California Teachers Association*. Labor dodged a bullet here, when Justice Antonin Scalia died suddenly and the court split 4-4, leaving the precedent in place. The National Right to Work Committee, not to be deterred, continued to push other similar cases forward. It is quite possible that the *Janus* decision will further erode public sector union strength in Massachusetts, devastating some unions and depriving the public of strong advocates for quality public services. Massachusetts unions will need to learn from their brothers and sisters in right-to-work states how to operate in an environment where unions must continuously campaign to maintain union membership and build strong alliances to defend public services.

Massachusetts Public Sector Unions Fight Back

The fight to defend the public sector is being waged on multiple fronts: within unions, the Massachusetts AFL-CIO, union-community coalitions, and in the electoral arena. The Massachusetts AFL-CIO formed the Public Sector Task Force in 2017, which brought together all public sector unions to prepare for the *Janus* decision. Its purpose was more than defensive, and sought to "unite public and private sectors to defend public services and campaign for sufficient revenue to fund the 'public good.'"[27] The Task Force held training sessions, studied experiences in other states, held several large rallies, and worked on potential legislation to respond to an adverse decision. Unions are developing organizing plans to prepare for resisting right-to-work and to build new member activism. Union locals are working with their international affiliates to build one-on-one organizing campaigns to reach out to union members. The Massachusetts Teachers Association (MTA), for example, launched their "All-In Campaign" in which members are "going all in" to protect public education and the power of their union to defend services. SEIU members in multiple locals launched "Together We Rise," an effort to conduct one-on-one conversations, develop new leaders, and build stronger local unions to fight for better services. The state and municipal workers' union launched AFSCME Strong to organize member-to-member and build political capacity. Multiple unions are asking members to recommit to the union by signing new membership cards.

After *Janus*, public sector unions will be challenged even more to create a new culture of activism and struggle, which has been lacking for many Massachusetts public sector unions. The unions have relied on their ability to win ongoing improvements for members and have enjoyed reasonable labor relations with employers. Dues collection has become automatic, requiring few one-on-one conversations with members about the need for the union. Currently, few public sector unions have significant internal organizing capacity, but several are starting to build it. Many unions now need to recruit and train a new generation of leaders, build ongoing steward structures, and strengthen the union. They will need to instill in members a reason to belong to the union. Unions will need to shift resources and make member activism a priority. Without this culture shift, unions will lose membership, revenue, and strength.

In Massachusetts, public sector unions have dug in for the long haul and are building alliances to defend state services. In the face of accusations that the pension and benefit plans of public sector workers are draining taxpayer-funded state coffers, unions have argued that teachers, transit workers, and other public servants provide critical services and are allying with the poor and working class communities that rely on these services to defend them from cutbacks. Massachusetts unions have long advocated for the responsible use of public dollars and been watchdogs against corporate giveaways. In 1990, when newly elected Governor Weld declared war on public sector unions and aggressively sought to privatize state services, labor fought back by securing passage of the Taxpayer Protection Act. The law, passed in 1993 over the governor's veto, was the strongest anti-privatization law in the country.

The state's unions have also sought innovative ways to defend the interests of the state's lowest-paid workers. The SEIU successfully fought to have the state classify Medicaid-reimbursed home health-care workers as publicly funded independent providers and has negotiated wage increases and other benefits for them. SEIU has 509 organized family child-care providers. The MTA and AFT organized paraprofessional workers and charter school employees. Several unions organized graduate student teaching assistants and adjunct professors. Public sector unions have also been prominent in the state's fight to raise the minimum wage. (See Harris Gruman's essay on Raise Up Massachusetts and Aviva Chomsky's on worker centers in this volume.)

In 2014, the election of Republican governor Charlie Baker ushered in a new era of "free market" economics and privatization in Massachusetts as he sought to overturn the anti-privatization protections labor won against the opposition of the Weld administration. Partnering with the conservative Pioneer Institute, Baker supported the expansion of charter schools and won an exemption for the Metropolitan Boston Transit Authority under the Taxpayer Protection Act, which facilitated the privatization of mass transit services. The state's unions fought Baker's plans, however, and handed him significant defeats along the way. For example, Baker strongly supported Question 2, a 2016 ballot question that sought to lift the cap on charter school expansion. The initiative was funded mainly by out-of-state, pro-charter organizations, and it was opposed by the Save Our Schools campaign, a coalition of organizations like the MTA, the Massachusetts AFT, the AFL-CIO, and the NAACP. The defeat of Question 2 showed the power of public sector unions to defend public education and defeat deep-pocketed adversaries, including $15 million in dark money contributions, much of it illegal.[28] The MTA and AFT joined forces and worked to build a strong coalition against charter school expansion, where they were joined by the NAACP, the Massachusetts AFL-CIO, Jobs with Justice, the Massachusetts Building Trades and other private sector unions, as well as school committees in over two hundred communities in the state. Baker and the charter-school allies outspent the unions, but the Save Our Schools forces prevailed—62 percent to 38 percent.

While the governor and his allies outspent the supporters of public schools, the Save Our Schools team invested in building a grassroots movement that contacted more than 1.5 million voters in the state by knocking on doors, making phone calls, or talking one-on-one with family, friends, and neighbors. The question was defeated soundly in most every Massachusetts city, across every demographic group. The success of the Save Our Schools campaign demonstrates that the general public, when organized and mobilized, did not buy the narrative spun by the governor and the backers of privatized education.

Likewise, the Massachusetts AFL-CIO brought together transit unions in a campaign, "Invest Now," to not only fight privatization but to demand enhanced services and the funding necessary to improve the state's transportation system. The Invest Now campaign exposed the poor performance and safety records of private companies bidding on transit services and united riders, workers, community groups, non-profit organizations, businesses, elected leaders, and municipalities in support of public transit. The International Association of Machinists successfully fought back Baker's plans to privatize bus maintenance services, slowing down the governor's privatization schemes. The ongoing work to fight privatization and build key community alliances against Baker's agenda have helped create a broad campaign to support the common good, and consequently the services union members deliver.

Finally, in January 2018, public sector union members took on a different kind of fight and won, in response to an unexpected cutting of benefits. The Group Insurance Commission, which includes several Baker appointees, voted 8–5 to eliminate more than half of the insurance carriers used by over four hundred thousand public employees and retirees who receive health insurance through the Commission. Union members packed public hearings, attended rallies, and called legislators and the governor. Within a few weeks, the Commission relented, restoring the carriers and members' health benefits.[29] In the aftermath of the dispute, unions filed several pieces of legislation to protect employees' benefits for the future.

The survival of public sector unions is ultimately about the survival of all Massachusetts unions. A radical decline in union membership undermines the strength of all unions. In Wisconsin, Governor Walker successfully divided the unions and played on taxpayer resentment against public sector workers. Private sector workers, by actively supporting public sector campaigns, have an important role to play in the defense of both government services and public workers. Private sector union leaders must continue to educate their members to recognize the attacks on state services and public unions as threats against the future of the labor movement as a whole. Private sector union members, as well as nonunionized workers everywhere, have an equal stake in good public schools, public transportation, and a fair tax structure that ensures strong services of all kinds. It will take the unified efforts of both public and private sector union members and their leaders to reverse this downward slide of union membership with a collective vision of a better society organized for the common good.

In Roman mythology, the two-faced Janus was the god of gates and doors, representing gateways between what was and what is to come. *Janus* is a similar sort of threshold for public sector unions. Those unions that remain complacent, resting upon the gains of the past, and do not transform into strong fighting organizations will be challenged to survive. Those that look to the future and build strong fighting unions will endure and write a new chapter in Massachusetts labor history.

Postscript

Two years after the Supreme Court decision, which face of Janus prevailed? The attack on public sector union rights continues, led by the National Right to Work Committee and its myriad state partner organizations. If the right wing thought the *Janus* decision would be the deathblow to public sector unions, it thought wrong. A *Politico* review of ten large public-employee unions indicates that they lost a combined 309,612 fee payers in 2018, but they also reported a gain of 132,312 members—and all but one reported more money in the union's treasury than in the year prior.[30]

In a number of states, anti-union activists filed suits for the retroactive return of union dues collected under legal agency fee agreements. Mark Janus, the former AFSCME childcare worker who sued for return of his dues, is now a Senior Fellow at the Liberty Institute, an anti-union think tank. There have also been challenges to the right to exclusive representation—the right of a union, chosen by a majority of the employees of an employer, to represent all the employees in the unit. So far, the courts have ruled against these initiatives.[31] Meanwhile, the right-wing organizations that have led the anti-union fight in recent years have been aided and abetted by the Trump administration, which signaled its support for a national right-to-work law and a rollback of many labor protections.

Immediately following the *Janus* decision, a number of anti-union organizations ran a campaign to persuade union members to drop their memberships. Massachusetts teachers received letters outlining the steps to do so. But unions have successfully beat back many of these attacks. Prior to *Janus*, many Massachusetts unions initiated strong member-to-member outreach programs. The *Janus* threat forced many local unions to update membership lists and conduct concerted outreach to members. In 2019, the Bureau of Labor Statistics reported that 51.2 percent of Massachusetts union members were public employees, while 53.2 percent of the workforce were public employees covered by union contracts. This 2 percent difference is a cautionary note that some eight thousand public employees may be using the *Janus* decision to avoid dues.[32]

In the fall of 2019, the Massachusetts AFL-CIO Public Sector Task Force successfully won passage of state legislation to strengthen public-sector union rights, despite Governor Baker's veto. The new law gives unions access to employee contact information, strengthens the ability of the union to meet employees at the work site, and enables unions to charge a nonmember reasonable costs and fees for grievance representation. Not all of labor's fights have been defensive, however. In fall 2019, Dedham teachers waged a successful strike and won major concessions. In this same period, teachers' unions and their allies mounted a successful broad-based campaign to reform the state education funding system to provide greater equity in educational funding with passage of the Student Opportunity Act. In short, while many predicted the demise of public sector unions, they are alive and well, fighting for the common good.

Many of these unions have been on the forefront of the fight against the Covid-19 pandemic and the fight for racial justice. Several unions are partnering with housing rights organizations in support of a ban on evictions. Other unions are working with Raise Up Massachusetts to advocate for emergency paid sick leave. Teachers' unions and others have embraced the Black Lives Matter movement against systemic racism. Health-care workers, home-care workers, transit employees, and teachers and school staff have been engaged in the struggle for a fair and equitable recovery from the pandemic. Workers in the state's universities and other institutions of higher learning who are facing significant cuts are fighting back. Members continued to work to deliver vital services, sometimes at great personal sacrifice to their health and families. Boston and Massachusetts workers continue to write their history.

CHAPTER 3

A Tangle of Exclusion

Boston's Black Working Class and the Struggle for Racial and Economic Justice

Aviva Chomsky

I really feel that the area where we haven't done enough is a collective struggle around jobs and salaries and income. You know, we can look to unions to do that, but unions have been historically controlled by others, they haven't been controlled by ourselves. And I don't think we've done enough during our years here to build an economic strength among ourselves as workers, and really demanding our rights, our opportunities.[1]

—*Chuck Turner, community activist
and former Boston city councilor*

B oston's Black workers have fought intertwined struggles for racial and economic justice over many decades. Such struggles have often taken place in the workplace, but they are also found in the fight for the right to access to work, as well as rights to housing and schools, safe neighborhoods, freedom from police brutality, and fair treatment by government and private institutions. Sometimes these struggles aimed at integration and access; other times they emphasized autonomy and community control. Not all of these issues necessarily fit the common perception of what constitute "labor" issues, but the activism of Black workers in Boston and elsewhere reveal the extent to which race and class have been tightly braided together under the system of racial capitalism. Racial exclusion has kept Boston's Black population disproportionately working class, disproportionately employed in marginal positions, and disproportionately unemployed. Late twentieth-century industrial decline and public sector cutbacks, as well as attacks on unions, in some ways brought more of Boston's white working class face-to-face with conditions long affecting Black workers. While many of Boston's unions had historically resisted Black advancement as a threat to their own members, the crisis of the working class in the twenty-first century also encouraged some historically white unions to develop a more radical, structural analysis, and opened some doors to increased collaboration between these unions and the city's growing communities of color.

Black organizing in Boston has ebbed and flowed over the past century, sometimes in synchrony with national trends and sometimes by its own logic. Despite Boston's reputation as a liberal, Democratic Party stronghold, its history of Black exclusion and marginalization runs deep. Boston's emergence from its mid-twentieth-century stagnation into a thriving, multicultural, knowledge-based economy at the end of that century into the next did not bring concomitant opportunity for the city's Black population. During the city's decline, Black communities confronted urban renewal, white flight, disinvestment, job loss, and failing schools. Its renaissance after 1980 brought new problems like gentrification and a rising cost of living, along with foreclosures, continued disinvestment in Black neighborhoods, unemployment, and consignment to segregated and underfunded schools.

Black workers' relationship with Boston's organized labor movement has been complex and sometimes tense. Black labor struggles in the city have tended to be as much about *access* to jobs as for better rights *on* the job. In some cases, especially in the construction industry, unions have served as gatekeepers that have excluded Black workers from access to jobs. Union seniority systems, designed to reduce arbitrary discrimination, frequently worked against Black workers who gained access to unionized jobs in the 1970s just as both manufacturing and the public sector were on the cusp of contraction. Yet Black workers with secure employment by the end of the twentieth century tended to be concentrated in sectors that were heavily unionized, especially in the public sector. Thus Black workers benefited disproportionately from these high rates of unionization, but this came just as union density was shrinking after years of concerted right-wing attacks.[2] In some cases, Black workers formed caucuses in their unions like the Black Educators Alliance of Massachusetts (BEAM) in the Massachusetts Teachers Association (MTA), the Massachusetts

Association of Minority Law Enforcement Officers, the Boston Society of Vulcans (firefighters), and AFRAM Massachusetts, the state branch of the National African American Caucus in the SEIU.

At the end of the 1970s, optimism about the potential for Black political organizing in Boston was high. Organizations proliferated and radicalized, fighting for diverse yet interconnected causes including school desegregation, access to political power and representation, separation from the city to create the Black municipality of Mandela, the creation of Roxbury Community College, welfare rights, and access to jobs. The latter led to a boycott campaign for jobs at Wonder Bread, the creation of United Community Construction Workers and Boston Black United Front, and political projects for Boston Jobs for Boston People and a Boston residency requirement in construction hiring. These were working-class struggles, many of them about access to the basic goods of society that had generally been won by unionized workers—from whose ranks many Black workers were still excluded. But most of them took place outside of the workplace. Even those that focused specifically on labor rights were more about the right to a job, rather than rights on the job. Thus, most of these campaigns were waged outside of unions.

But the dynamism of this organizing could not stem the larger structural transformation of the city and its devastating impact on Black workers. In 1960, almost half of Boston's jobs were blue collar; by 2014, fewer than one-fifth were. The National Urban League reported in 1980 that "more blacks have lost their jobs through industrial decline than through job discrimination."[3] The report could have added the role of public sector cutbacks. Once again, race and class issues were so deeply intertwined as to be inextricable: the sectors in which Black workers had most successfully gained access were the ones that suffered the worst contraction.

Boston's 1980s renaissance brought a bifurcated job market, creating great opportunity for high-technology, educational, and medical professionals. The low-wage economy that serviced the renaissance increasingly employed new immigrants from Latin America, Asia, the Caribbean, and Africa, rather than the city's native Black population. Young professionals flocked to the city's shiny new developments, as low-wage workers were pushed further from the city's center.

This residential, and its concomitant educational, segregation played an important role in labor opportunity in Boston. Barry Bluestone argues that Black workers' low and sporadic labor market participation stems primarily from "pre-labor-market" discrimination. Isolation in transit-poor, segregated neighborhoods, poor schools, lack of access to health care, and lack of experience consign a significant portion of Boston's Black population not to joblessness, but to short-term, unstable employment opportunities. Young single mothers in particular have low rates of labor force participation. Black students in Boston continue to attend segregated, and inferior, schools. The school-to-prison pipeline and the criminal records it generates severely hinder access to stable employment; Black students in Massachusetts are four times more likely than white students to be suspended, and while Blacks comprise 7 percent of the state's population, they number 28 percent of those incarcerated statewide.[4] Thus it should come as no surprise that these broader Black working-class issues, including access to jobs, have shaped Black Bostonians' labor history and their sometimes contentious relations with the city's generally white-dominated unions.

This chapter traces what I call the "tangle of exclusion" that has confronted Boston's Black working class and shaped its relationship to the labor movement. It begins by examining the creation of the city's Black working class through different streams of migration and traces how the city's political and economic development have conspired to marginalize its Black population. It then examines the growth of Black political organizing in the 1960s and how the struggle for labor rights was tied to the movements for Civil Rights and for Black Power, combining demands for access with those for autonomy and self-determination. I look at Boston's notorious school desegregation battles of the 1970s in the context of the city's manufacturing decline and the rise of affirmative action. Attacks on the public sector and on unions since the 1990s have brought many of Boston's unions from recalcitrance to an embrace of racial and economic justice. Black organizations have long had a deep understanding of the tangle of exclusion confronting the Black working class. By the twenty-first century the mainstream labor movement was coming to realize that it had a lot to learn from that history.

Background and Characteristics
of Boston's Black Population

Although Boston was home to a small Black population prior to the twentieth century (the city's fabled "Black Brahmins"), most of the city's Black population came in several overlapping migrant streams from the US South and, to a lesser extent, Cape Verde and the West Indies, followed by a truly global influx that came from Africa, Brazil, and the Caribbean at the end of the twentieth century.

African Americans moved from the rural south to the urban north and west in two periods. The first million and a half migrants came during the period between the decline in European migration during World War I and the Depression. The second, larger wave of about five million migrants arrived during World War II. Another wave of migrants came from Cape Verde, a Portuguese colony off the west coast of Africa. Cape Verdeans, many of whom identified more as Portuguese than as Black immigrants, began to migrate to southeastern Massachusetts in the early 1800s, first working in maritime trades like whaling and later in the cranberry fields. After Cape Verde's independence from Portugal in 1975, larger numbers arrived in Boston. Some eighty-five thousand West Indians came to the United States between 1900 and 1924, when the US government imposed immigration restrictions. A second wave of West Indian migration began after the US reformed its quota system in 1965, just as Britain imposed new restrictions on West Indian migration. By 2014 there were four million immigrants from the Caribbean in the United States.[5]

Boston experienced these migrant streams in unique ways. The city's lack of heavy industry made it an unpopular destination for southern Blacks. Those that did choose Boston tended to come from the Upper South (especially the Richmond and Charleston areas), and to be more literate and more likely racially mixed than those migrating to other northern cities. Still, they were often not welcomed by the city's established Black population. Meanwhile, Boston's close ties with the Caribbean, as a sugar port and as the headquarters of the United Fruit Company, made it a popular destination for West Indian migrants. Compared to other northern cities, Boston's Black population has therefore been relatively small, but heavily foreign-born.

Because of the high cost of migration from the West Indies and the literacy requirements the US government implemented in 1917, West Indian immigrants have generally come from wealthier and better educated populations in their nations of origin. Mary Waters's observations about the late twentieth century likely also held true earlier: that West Indian workers' particular history shaped their labor market engagement and also their politics. "While blackness is stigmatized to some extent in all of the former European colonies," writes Waters of the racial politics of the Caribbean, "the reality of black political power, numerical dominance, and relative cultural and social freedom contrasts sharply with the American black reality of minority status, political and social domination by a white majority, and relative lack of political power." West Indian workers also tended to come with a strong organizational culture, growing from their interactions with Garveyism, labor unions, and anti-colonial movements in their home countries. Boston's West Indians created an active UNIA chapter, welcomed Eric Williams to the city in the late 1930s, and supported the Jamaican labor rebellions in 1938.[6]

The Black population in Boston was distinctly multi-class in the first half of the twentieth century. From the perspective of a young Malcolm X, arriving in Boston from Mason, Michigan, in the late 1930s, the Black elite of Roxbury were "acting and living differently from any black people I'd ever dreamed of in my life. This was the snooty black neighborhood; they called themselves the 'Four Hundred,' and looked down their noses at the Negroes of the black ghetto," especially the "Southern strivers and scramblers, and West Indian Negroes, whom both the New Englanders and the Southerners called 'Black Jews.'"[7]

Black migrants from the US South continued to be numerically dominant as the twentieth century progressed, but they and the growing West Indian and Cape Verdean communities were joined later in the century by migrants from other African countries, Haiti, Brazil, and elsewhere in Latin America and the Caribbean. Despite these cultural and ethnic differences, race created certain commonalities in racially bifurcated Boston. New arrivals, whether domestic or international, tended to accept the myth of the American dream and accept discrimination and harsh conditions, believing that with hard work and sacrifice, their children would be more successful. Subsequent generations were often less sanguine. Their disillusionment could lead to political organizing and protest, or it could lead to despair. Malcolm X, who said that the "streets of Roxbury" served as his high school, gave a first-hand explanation of the generational shift that so many sociologists have identified. "These ghetto teenagers see the hell caught by their parents struggling to get somewhere, or see that they have given up struggling in the prejudiced, intolerant white man's world. . . . So the ghetto youth become attracted to the hustler worlds of dope, thievery, prostitution, and general crime and immorality."[8] This trajectory was especially true of the generations born into late twentieth century urban crisis and industrial decline, although the deteriorating conditions and hopes could also lead to political mobilization and protest.

Boston's unions, as Jim Green has shown, were historically hostile to Black workers. Violet Johnson called Boston's Irish-immigrant dominated Central Labor Union "one of the foremost Jim Crow institutions" in the city in the early twentieth century. A 1914 study estimated that "with respect to the labor unions, it is a fact that the number of Negroes found in their ranks is not large. Probably not over one in ten counts half a dozen or more of this race on its rolls. . . . The unions are . . . fewest in number and weakest in strength in the field of menial and common occupations. This means that for the great mass of Negro laborers there are no unions at all to join." Though this phenomenon was not unique to Boston, the lack of heavy industry meant that CIO-style, race-conscious egalitarianism was weaker in Boston than in many other US cities as the century progressed. The small size of Boston's Black population (also due to the small scale of mass manufacturing) also meant that white ethnic—especially Irish—Bostonians had less need to create political alliances with the city's Black working class.[9] Thus both economically and politically, the Black population was more marginalized from Boston's institutions than was the case in other major cities.

Mel King, Immigrants, and Boston's Black Movement in the 1960s and 70s

Long-time activist and then state representative Mel King emerged as a leader in the Black community's growing mobilization in the 1960s and 70s around jobs, schools, and economic and racial justice. His career and activism exemplify both the tensions and the identification between West Indians and African Americans, and the ways in which labor and other social issues were indelibly intertwined in twentieth-century Black political organizing.

The son of early twentieth-century West Indian migrants (his parents hailed from Barbados and Guyana), King grew up in an activist milieu. His father worked unloading sugar boats on the waterfront and was the secretary of his union local. "I used to overhear them talk about the importance of organizing, some of the struggles, like fighting management, the poor work conditions, and striking," King recalled. King shared this family history of activism, uniting immigrant, racial, ethnic, and labor-based issues with other local Black activists of his generation. Ruth Batson, a leader in the school desegregation struggle, recalled growing up in Roxbury in the midst of her West Indian migrant mother's involvement in Garveyism. David Nelson, the state's first Black federal judge, "still recalled his Jamaican-born father's activities as union organizer for the Amalgamated Clothing Workers of America."[10] King poignantly articulated the complexities of race and ethnicity as a Black immigrant in a racist society:

> I grew up on the one hand feeling positive about being a West Indian and Black, but on the other hand, I had to grapple with the negative imagery of being a Black child in the United States, not wanting to identify with people who were slaves. . . . As far as white teachers and white students were concerned, people who were Black were considered Negro or Colored, but white people were of American or Italian or Irish descent. We resisted that by insisting that we were West Indian. . . . A lot of the Europeans went to a cultural maintenance program after school. Most of the Black kids went to Settlement Houses. So while they were learning their cultural traditions, we were pushed into becoming Anglo-Saxon Americans. The church was central in shaping our identity as Negroes or Coloreds.[11]

King's later activist career centered on the issue of Black worker rights, in particular, the discrimination and structural factors that led to structural Black unemployment. Yet like many Black leaders and organizations in Boston and nationwide, King's work combined demands for access with struggles for self-determination and autonomy, including community control of schools, resources, businesses, and even land.[12]

One of King's early jobs initiatives was the Boston Action Group, founded in 1962. The organization drew inspiration from ministers in Philadelphia and students in New York to bring together local students with the St. Mark Social Center in Dorchester to organize a boycott of local businesses that refused to hire Black workers. After months of research and popular education, BAG decided to target the Wonder Bread bakery in Dorchester. The factory, and 12 percent of the company's sales, were in Black areas of the city, but only eight of its two hundred and fifty workers were Black. BAG demanded that the company hire twelve new Black workers and, when it refused,

> ministers throughout Roxbury, the South End and Dorchester . . . urged their congregations to boycott Wonder Bread; leaflets were distributed through the neighborhoods asking people not to buy "Jim

Crow" bread; letters were sent to all the block captains asking them to notify their neighborhoods of the boycott and urge them to join; ministers, students, housewives, social workers, and others joined a Saturday picket march through the community to raise consciousness about the boycott; store owners were asked to cancel their Wonder Bread orders and were picketed if they refused; press releases were used to tell the BAG story across the city.[13]

Within a month Wonder Bread ceded to BAG's demands, and subsequent boycott campaigns followed against other businesses.

By the middle of the 1960s, King recalls, there emerged "more comprehensive efforts at internal economic development." The goal was "to stop leakage of Black capital from the Black community." These new initiatives "recognized the interconnectedness of jobs, housing, and education, as well as the social and cultural structure of our community." As federal construction and urban renewal funds poured into the city in the later part of the decade, "it was clear that one of the major barriers impeding the change necessary for successful development lay within the unions, particularly Boston's building trades," which had developed long-standing partnerships with contractors' associations. Furthermore, many of the developers were at the same time slum landlords who exploited their tenants. The answer was the creation of the United Community Construction Workers, "the first Black construction workers' union since Reconstruction," King wrote. "These men were united in the common interest of Black workers in all crafts and in the welfare of their community rather than in one particular trade area." While the UCCW combined ideas about access and autonomy, in 1968 the Boston Black United Front openly promoted a Black nationalist agenda, calling for community control of "Our Land" and "Our Politics," as well as power over security, justice, education, the economy, and housing.[14]

Black organizations also fought for access to jobs and rights in the rapidly expanding public sector in the late 1960s. In Boston, the integration of the public sector has been a protracted and still-incomplete process. Lawsuits brought by the NAACP and other organizations resulted in court orders implementing affirmative action policies in the city's police and fire departments. The small numbers of Blacks hired through these initiatives formed their own organizations to promote their interests within the departments and to fight for greater access for people of color. The Massachusetts Association of Afro-American Police (MAAAP) was founded in 1968 with the goal of "improvement of relations between police officers and the community, recruitment of minority personnel to serve as law enforcement officers and to assist in establishing a nationwide communication network to improve police performance through education and the sharing of experiences."[15] The Boston Society of Vulcans was formed the following year by Black firefighters after several participated in the founding meeting of the International Association of Black Professional Fire Fighters in New York. At the time the 2,100-member department employed seventeen Blacks and one Hispanic.[16]

Pre-labor Market Discrimination: Residential Segregation and Class

Residential segregation played a fundamental role in excluding many Black workers from the mid-twentieth-century rise to the middle class that white workers experienced. Federal, state, and local laws, policies, zoning, and redevelopment priorities, along with private real estate and financial policies, combined to segregate cities like Boston in ways that had both racial and class implications. Access to publicly subsidized home ownership was a major factor pulling second-generation white immigrants into the suburbs and into the middle class, while segregationist zoning regulations and public mortgage financing precluded Black access to the suburbs. As housing prices rose, so did net worth, while Black renters and homeowners were consigned to decaying urban cores whose tax bases were depleted by capital flight, and subject to increasingly suburban-dominated state legislatures more committed to tax cuts than to social services.[17] Thus the Black population has been disproportionately victim to evictions and foreclosures.

Segregation in Boston was created and enforced in multiple ways and at multiple levels. Martin Luther King Jr. described his experience of seeking housing in Boston in the 1950s: "I remember very well trying to find a place to live. . . . I went into place after place where there were signs that rooms were for rent. They were for rent, until they found out that I was a Negro, and suddenly they had just been rented."[18] During the 1950s, integrated working-class neighborhoods like Boston's South End were slated for demolition and "redevelopment." Public investment included highway projects like Boston's Route 128, which circled the city and promoted suburban development and drew white residents, commerce, and new employment in the growing high-technology sector out of the city. Some termed Route 128 "Boston's Road to Segregation."[19]

A 2015 study on "The Color of Wealth in Boston" found that household median net worth was $247,500 for whites, and $8 for US-born African Americans. (Black Caribbean immigrants fared slightly better than African Americans with $12,000 in assets.) The fact that 80 percent of white households and only one-third of Black households owned a home constituted a major factor in the difference. Black households were also significantly more likely to be encumbered with medical and student debt.[20]

Segregation, Schools, and Busing

Perhaps no symbol of racism in Boston is as deeply imprinted in the nation's consciousness as is the bitter struggle for the desegregation of the city's schools in the 1970s, years after the battles over desegregation in the South. Although Boston's schools were officially desegregated in the 1850s, de facto segregation actually increased in the twentieth century, both before and after the court-ordered desegregation ("busing") of the 1970s. The city's small Black population in the 1920s and 30s—about twenty thousand—was not large enough to sustain segregated schools. With the influx of Blacks from the South in the 1940s, residential segregation that concentrated the new Black population in the South End and Roxbury turned neighborhood schools into segregated schools.

Inadequate schools, along with residential segregation, comprised two pillars of what Bluestone called "pre-labor market" discrimination that contributed to Black unemployment. Black neighborhood schools were severely under-resourced, and their teaching and administrative staff was 95 percent white.[21] Mid-century civil rights struggles in Boston's public education system were not specifically for *integrated* schools, but rather for greater equity in resources and hiring. The struggle for educational justice evolved on dual tracks through the 1960s and 70s, into demands for resources and community control of Black neighborhood schools, as well as for access to better-resourced white schools.

King and the community control movement and the Freedom School movement fought to increase community control and improve Black schools. This approach combined a cultural/Black nationalist perspective with a class analysis that focused on unequal resources. The integrationist position, by contrast, focused more on racial rather than economic redistribution, demanding equal access to primarily white schools. The community control movement argued that schools in Black neighborhoods must "move to Black control of hiring, jobs, curriculum development." Activists established new Freedom Schools that tried to make this dream a reality. King critiqued the integrationists' narrow focus on racial imbalance because "it did not alter the power relations between parents, community, and the administrators and teachers in the schools." Nor did integrationism address the under-resourcing and decay of the schools in Boston's Black neighborhoods. "People began to recognize and proclaim that their own neighborhoods, not just white areas, could be healthy, livable sections of the city," King wrote, describing the atmosphere in the late 1960s. "Our approach for community control of schools was that hiring, firing, planning curriculum development, programming, would be based on needs as we assessed them. We believed that we should get a proportional share of education money."[22]

The community control movement and the integrationist movement could be complementary and intertwined: activists sought better schools, community control, and access to educational opportunity. But it was integrationism alone that came to be implemented. In 1972, after almost a decade of protest and direct action, the Boston NAACP and Black parents filed a lawsuit challenging Boston Public Schools' failure to comply with the state's 1965 racial imbalance law. In his 1974 decision, US District Court Judge W. Arthur Garrity placed the city's schools under court control and imposed a system of compulsory busing to remedy the imbalance. It wasn't precisely the solution anyone wanted. At Freedom House, "as we discuss the decision, we are apprehensive about the order to bus some children to South Boston. Those of us who were born in Boston know of the experiences black people have endured when they've 'found' themselves on the streets of that community," wrote NAACP education activist Ruth Batson. "While we in the black community feared the worst, we hoped for the best," she reported.[23]

But it was the worst that followed, as anti-busing forces gathered to oppose Black children's entry into white schools and the city exploded into violence. Because the desegregation order applied only to the city of Boston, it contributed to white flight to the suburbs. The court oversaw Boston's schools until 1988, but inequality, segregation, and conflicts over busing continue to plague the system and spur protest until the present.

The Boston Teachers Union and the Black Educators Alliance of Massachusetts

One further class and labor dimension of the schooling issue had to do with employment in the school district. Like so much of the Boston labor market, the teaching profession was overwhelmingly white. In 1965, a group of teachers founded the Black Educators Alliance of Massachusetts which sometimes found itself at odds with the white-dominated Boston Teachers Union, a familiar pattern in the Boston labor movement. Whether protesting the failure to hire Black teachers, advocating greater community control and resources for predominantly Black schools, organizing "Freedom Schools" and pressing for a more multicultural curriculum, or pushing for desegregation, BEAM frequently clashed with the BTU. During the desegregation struggle, BEAM pressed successfully for a court-ordered requirement that the city schools achieve a 10 percent "other minority" (which at the time primarily referred to Puerto Ricans) and 25 percent Black staffing levels, to match the racial makeup of the city at the time. The organization challenged seniority in the 1980s when Black teachers hired in the 1970s found themselves targeted to be the "first fired" after 1980's Proposition 2 ½ limited property taxes and led to a decade of school budget cuts.[24]

The BTU continued to oppose federal oversight on both student assignment and teacher hiring through the 1980s, through a series of court appeals that placed it in opposition to the city's Black organizations.[25] The BTU sued the school committee in 1981 to defend seniority over affirmative action in layoffs, losing three times in the next two years as the courts consistently ruled that minimum minority representation superseded seniority. By 1983, the union dropped the case, and the new BTU president Edward Doherty announced that "the issue is behind us."[26] Doherty stated that 710 white teachers lost their jobs in the 1981 layoffs. Yet in 1985, the union again fought (and lost) against the court-ordered affirmative action plan for Black and "other minority" staff. In 1990 Judge Garrity issued "final orders" announcing the federal government's withdrawal from the desegregation case, but he mandated that the 375 layoffs then projected must still give the court-ordered affirmative action plan precedence over seniority. 23.8 percent of Boston's 4,700 teachers at the time were Black, meaning that if affirmative action was prioritized, almost all of those laid off would be white. Once again, the BTU stood against the NAACP and other Black organizations fighting for affirmative action goals. As *Education Week* explained, lawyers defending affirmative action argued that "seniority is not a 'racially neutral' criterion for laying off teachers, because of the city's history of discriminatory hiring practices. If teachers were laid off according to seniority, the school district has estimated, 260 of the 375 teachers facing termination would have been members of minority groups."[27]

In 1990, the 35 percent "minority" goal may have still seemed reasonable. Two decades later, the 1974 goal was sorely outdated. In 2015, 87 percent of the system's students were youth of color (35 percent Black and 40 percent Latino), while 38 percent of the teaching staff was. 21 percent of teachers were Black—below the old court-mandated minimum. And the Black teachers hired in the wake of the 1974 decision were retiring at a rate three times faster than new recruits of color could replace them.[28]

As school "reform," charter schools, high-stakes testing, performance evaluation, and the 2001 federal No Child Left Behind law created increasingly punitive conditions for teachers after the 1990s, the BTU, like many other unions, began to rethink its position in Boston's landscape, including its stances on race. A growing commitment to racial justice meant advocating for students of color, supporting the need for a more diverse teaching staff, and collaborating with the civil rights organizations that were fighting for these goals. In 2006, the BTU joined with Black community and civil rights organizations— including BEAM—to critically evaluate the previous twelve years of education reform in the state, citing the urban and minority dropout crisis, race-based achievement gaps, and inequity among suburban and urban schools as critical areas showing the failure of "reform."[29] In 2013, the BTU protested "performance evaluations" that disproportionately targeted Black and Hispanic teachers.[30] In 2016 the Boston School District addressed the personnel issue once again, mandating a teaching staff that reflected the city's now majority-minority student body. Yet a 2018 report sponsored by the BTU and a coalition of civil rights organizations showed that while the student body was now 86 percent Black, Latino, and Asian, the teacher corps had barely diversified in the previous decade, and in fact the portion of Black teachers had declined from 24 percent to 20 percent.[31] Black students comprised 35 percent of the student body. Meanwhile Latino students were 42 percent of the student body, with only 10.1 percent Latino teachers.

A big difference, though, was that the BTU was now *joining* the civil rights organizations calling for diversity, rather than reacting defensively against the concept. In 2017 Jessica Tang, the first person of color and the first LGBTQ activist, as well as the first woman in decades to serve as BTU president, ran on the "BTU for All" slate that represented both the long evolution of the union from its stances of the 1970s and a new insurgency. Tang came up through the ranks as a BTU reformer, leading the "BTU Votes" initiative in 2012 to increase member participation by allowing mail-in ballots. She ran for union Vice President in a contested 2013 election and worked with the United Caucuses of Rank and File Educators. Endorsed by Mel King and other community activists, Tang brought a strong background working for racial, social, and economic justice, and was an outspoken advocate for social justice unionism and union democracy. "Our work as unionists extends beyond the classroom to include advocacy for economic and racial justice within our communities," the BTU for All platform read.[32]

Black Worker Struggles on Many Fronts into the Neoliberal Era

Twenty-first-century Black worker activism has continued to center on the issue of access to work, especially in those sectors of the city's blue-collar economy that survived the manufacturing collapse like construction and the public sector. In a few notable cases, racially progressive unions fought for racial equality inside and outside their organizations. Black workers and their organizations experimented with a wide range of old and new tactics. Although more unions came to embrace the goal of diversity in the twenty-first century, the intertwined forces that segregated and marginalized Boston's Black population, privatized the public sector, and emphasized "development" based on the city's knowledge economy conspired to keep a disproportionate segment of the Black working class unemployed or marginally employed.

Case studies of racially progressive unions at the Colonial Provision meatpacking plant in Boston's Haymarket, at Boston City Hospital, and at the General Electric plant in Lynn reveal several common threads. These unions had strong leftist identities among the leadership that included a vision for deep structural change and an active commitment to racial equality. They were committed to union democracy and long-term member education and involvement. And they emphasized relationships with progressive community organizations and a commitment to social change in the interest of the larger working class, rather than the business-union approach aimed primarily at benefitting their own members. All of these cases also revealed the structural limitations to what a union could accomplish, as Colonial Provision closed in 1986, Boston City Hospital was privatized in 1996, and General Electric shrank its labor force from almost ten thousand to just over one thousand by 2018.[33]

Boston's construction unions, in contrast, had long been politically connected bastions of Irish-dominated parochialism. They allied with politicians and city agencies promoting "development" projects that frequently either bypassed or undermined communities of color, and they controlled entry into the industry through union apprentice programs. Building trades unions have traditionally been more interested in excluding competition rather than organizing new members, since their power came from offering their members privileged access to jobs. "Grandfather" or "father-son" clauses kept newcomers and especially people of color out of union apprenticeship programs.

Some of the major Black worker mobilizations from the 1970s on focused on gaining access to these positions. Black workers in Boston pushed for affirmative action hiring quotas for people of color through organizations like the Third World Jobs Clearing House and United Community Construction Workers. Visionary leaders including Mel King and Chuck Turner formed the Boston Jobs Coalition, which responded to white flight by linking affirmative action goals with the issue of urban residency, calling for guaranteed hiring minimums for Boston residents along with minimums for workers of color. Over the objections of the now-suburban-dominated unions (whose center of gravity moved as working-class whites moved out of the city), the slogan "Boston Jobs for Boston People" won the day as the city imposed quotas that stood up to several union- and industry-led court challenges.

Over time the position of Boston's building trades evolved, and both the unions and the city—from 2014 to 2021 led by former building trades president Marty Walsh—have promoted initiatives to bring both women and youth of color into trade apprenticeship programs. Still, even inside Boston the industry generally failed to meet its mandated goals. Furthermore, the industry has become increasingly bifurcated in the new century. In more heavily unionized regions and sectors (like downtown development), even nonunion firms tend to offer decent wages and working conditions. But in nonunionized regions and sectors (like residential housing), conditions are much worse, and the workforce is likely to be subcontracted, immigrant, and Hispanic.[34]

The public sector offered another arena in which Black workers struggled for union jobs against white unionist recalcitrance. Black workers and their organizations fought for residency requirements, for affirmative action, and against discriminatory civil service exams. When Black applicants succeeded in being hired, they formed organizations and caucuses within their unions to defend their rights in the workplace. In addition to the case of teachers discussed above, some of the major struggles have taken place among police and firefighters. White-dominated unions in these sectors had been fighting affirmative action since the 1970s. Just as federal intervention was required to integrate Boston's schools, a federal consent decree in 1973 ordered the city's fire department to integrate by hiring one minority candidate for every new white hire. The police and firefighters unions fought all the way to the Supreme Court to challenge a 1981 layoff order that challenged union seniority rights by requiring that layoffs respect affirmative action goals.[35]

The affirmative action equal hiring requirement did, over time, increase minority presence in the fire department. When the 1973 consent decree was revoked in 2003, the union celebrated. Firefighters Local 718 president lauded the court decision, saying that henceforth hiring would be "according to the score . . . It doesn't matter what race, color, creed or religion, it should just be the highest score. That's what the union has always felt. That's the fair way. There should be competition one-on-one. If you beat me, you deserve [the job]."[36] Such language, of course, ignored the structural factors that had led to whites' privileged access to positions on the force to begin with. Hiring patterns reverted: between 2003 and 2010, new hires were over 90 percent white. Meanwhile, a *Boston Globe* investigation that year found that the department was still highly segregated, with the busiest and most prestigious units with the greatest opportunity for advancement being over 85 percent white, while the least desirable units were over 50 percent nonwhite. Furthermore, 69 of the department's 72 high-ranking officers were white.[37] Boston's police department operated under a similar court-ordered consent decree until 2004. People of color comprised 40 percent of the force in that year; by 2010 this had fallen to one-third, where it remained in 2018. In 2017, 80 percent of the 56 recruits accepted to the police academy's most recent class were white.[38]

In 2018 Black worker organizations like the Massachusetts Association of Minority Law Enforcement Officers (MAMLEO) and the Boston

Society of Vulcans protested that the residency requirement—which should have benefitted candidates of color who then comprised over half of the city's population—was being circumvented through a loophole that granted a "residence preference" to veterans even if they did not live in the city. The veterans' preference tends to create recruits who mirror the racial makeup of the state, which is close to 80 percent white, rather than the city, where whites are less than half the population. In 2013 the *Globe* reported that veterans—who were automatically bumped to the top of civil service eligibility lists—comprised 25 percent of police officers hired by the city in the previous five years. A 2014 class consisted "almost entirely" of veterans—and only 11 out of 63 were people of color.[39]

The Tangle of Exclusion in the Twenty-First Century

Llana Barber argues that Boston recovered in particular ways from the crisis of deindustrialization, suburbanization, and disinvestment. Seeking to attract a new tax base by luring wealthy residents along with medical, financial, and knowledge industries, the city invested public resources in gentrifying while concentrating poverty in "crisis neighborhoods" of Roxbury, Mattapan, and parts of Dorchester. Public investment came to follow a trickle-down theory, betting on development that would attract wealthy residents or job- and revenue-creating corporations, but which had the effect of further marginalizing and concentrating Black neighborhoods and poverty.[40]

Boston's Seaport District is emblematic of the city's development strategies, dubbed by the *Boston Globe* in 2017 as "A Brand New Boston, Even Whiter than the Old." Billions of dollars in public funds underwrote the servicing and construction of a vibrant new seaside neighborhood, in which the city's Black population was excluded from every phase from designing and building to living and working. "What happened in the Seaport is not just the failure to add a richly diverse neighborhood to downtown. It is also an example of how the city's black residents and businesses missed out on the considerable wealth created by the building boom," the *Globe* team concluded.[41]

The tangle of exclusion made up of housing, jobs, schools, income, and wealth continues to shape the class status of Black Bostonians. New Deal labor and housing reforms widened the racial class gap by providing benefits to workers and home buyers while discriminatory laws and practices excluded Blacks from the new jobs, neighborhoods, and loans.

Reforms of the 1960s and 70s prohibited discrimination and opened both job and housing opportunities, just as the neoliberal era brought union-busting, runaway plants, shrinking of the public sector, and deregulation of mortgage markets.[42] The carceral state increasingly came to manage dispossessed populations of color.

Black working-class organizations continued to fight for access to work and economic justice more broadly. The organizations tend to be deeply neighborhood-based and focus on the links that comprise the tangle of exclusion. The Dudley Street Neighborhood Initiative was formed in 1984 with the mission of reclaiming "a neighborhood that had been ravaged by disinvestment, arson fires, and dumping." The organization's 1993 Declaration of Community Rights listed community development, health care, environment, education, affordable housing, child care, public transportation, and other demands, as well as affirming that "we have the right to share in the *jobs* and prosperity created by economic development initiatives in metro-Boston generally, and in the neighborhood specifically." Rights *on* the job necessarily come after the right *to* a job, and the right to a job was understood as enmeshed in broad infrastructural needs. The organization's activities in the second decade of the new century focused overwhelmingly on housing—opposing eviction, foreclosure, and gentrification, and supporting tenants' rights and affordable housing—and on access to decent jobs.[43]

When Chuck Turner was elected to the Boston City Council in 1999, he brought the issue of Black unemployment to the mainstream of city politics. In addition to the public sector residency issue around which he had organized for two decades, Turner spearheaded a "ban the box" initiative that the city approved in 2005, to reduce hiring discrimination by eliminating the box on job application forms requiring applicants to disclose whether they had a criminal record. The city would only contract with businesses adhering to fair policies, including not using a criminal record as an automatic bar to employment. The Boston Workers Alliance, formed in Roxbury in 2005, led the fight for Criminal Offender Record Information (CORI) reform at the state level, which in 2010 made Massachusetts the second state in the country to "ban the box." The BWA worked with the city to strengthen its code in 2014. Like so many of Boston's Black working-class organizations, the BWA understood the problem of joblessness as societal and structural. As the Alliance put it in a statement, "Our members work to improve their job situations by developing the necessary skills and resources to find work. At the same time, it is clear that job training and business resumes are useless if no one is hiring. We recognize that unless we demand a societal change to have fair work for all, members of our community will be forced to compete, like crabs in a barrel, for fewer and lower-paying jobs. When we unite, we are fighting for more than a paycheck. We are fighting for jobs for our youth and stable work that we can raise our families on."[44]

Other organizations continue to emphasize the structural nature of Boston's Black community's ongoing marginalization. The Black Economic Justice Institute was formed in 2012 to support the Boston Jobs Residency Requirement and to fight for Good Jobs Standards and against gentrification in Roxbury. The BEJI collaborates closely with the UJIMA Initiative, which explains that "the challenges facing our communities—gentrification, poverty, homelessness, lack of food access, unemployment, and lack of health care—are all interconnected."[45] Its Blue Hill Corridor Planning Commission cited "Economic Development, Jobs, Education, Housing, Health, and Public Safety" and most especially, community empowerment and control, as critical to the redevelopment of the area. The Boston Jobs Residency requirement has continued to be a key strategy for workers of color fighting for access to jobs on the basis of solidarity, rather than competition, with Boston's white working class and its organizations. The ordinance was updated in 2017, raising the percentages for hours worked by Boston residents to 51 percent, by workers of color to 40 percent, and by women to 12 percent. BJC treasurer Melonie Griffith reiterated that "a benefit of this ordinance, often overlooked, is that it links the principle of affirmative action for workers of color and women to the principle that all residents of Boston, regardless of race, have a right to a fair share of construction work going on in Boston. We need more policies bringing benefits to all workers in this City while strengthening worker solidarity."[46]

Alongside the struggle for access, the autonomist tradition has also persisted among Black organizations into the twenty-first century. One DSNI initiative succeeded in turning a sixty-acre parcel, known as the Dudley Triangle, into a community land trust. The Trust emphasized the development of affordable housing and community-controlled neighborhood institutions, but also the development of a locally controlled economy.[47] The Boston Workers Alliance promoted worker-owned cooperatives including a wide network of urban gardening and a composting business called Cooperative Energy Recycling and Organics (CERO), in conjunction with the DSNI. "From a community land trust that preserves land for growing, to kitchens and retailers who buy and sell locally grown food, to a new waste management co-op that will return compost to the land, a crop of new businesses and nonprofits are building an integrated food economy. It's about local people keeping the wealth of their land and labor in the community," journalist Penn Loh reported in 2014.[48] The combination of racial exclusion and deteriorating options for the working class has increased the attraction of these alternative and automomist projects, even as the fight for access continues. Boston's unions continue to stand at a crossroads as they navigate their commitments to their members, to the political status quo, and to the very unfinished struggle for racial justice in the city.

PART II

Boston's Workers and Unions Confront the Twenty-First Century

CHAPTER 4

It's Not in the Water

Surviving the Neoliberal Onslaught in Lynn, Massachusetts

An interview with Jeff Crosby by Aviva Chomsky (April 26, 2018)

The AFL-CIO and many individual unions have struggled to shift from business unionism, a focus on representing only their members' economic interests, to social movement unionism, which seeks to represent the working class more broadly. IUE-CWA Local 201 in Lynn, an aging industrial city of some hundred thousand just north of Boston, offers a remarkable example of a union that has been engaged in this process through decades of nourishing deep ties to the larger community. This local represents workers at General Electric's Lynn facility, one of the largest and longest-lived manufacturing plants in the Boston area, and several other smaller employers. Established in 1892, the GE plant has employed generations of Lynn workers, peaking at twenty thousand workers during World War II, when it produced turbo superchargers for Allied aircraft. Since the 1980s, Local 201 has, like manufacturing unions nationwide, faced dramatic job and membership loss as well as corporate pressure to relinquish the historic union benefits it had won.

But the local has worked to sustain itself, through its prominent role in the North Shore Labor Council and as an important force in Lynn politics and working-class organizing. Like many of New England's industrial cities, Lynn has a history of working-class radicalism. Unlike many others, though, Lynn remained a manufacturing center throughout the twentieth century. Union activism was sustained by new generations of workers who explicitly connected their struggles in the plant with progressive politics in the city and beyond. Here, long-time president of the union and the North Shore Labor Council Jeff Crosby, now retired, talks about the vicissitudes and successes of the labor movement in Lynn.

AVIVA CHOMSKY. How would you describe the state of the labor movement in Lynn?

JEFF CROSBY. Local 201 survived the neoliberal onslaught since the 1970s as a vibrant influence in Lynn. The local has engaged in a thoughtful, aggressive strategy that built on one hundred and fifty years of trade unionism in the area and the social movements of the 1960s and 1970s. The union defended the livelihoods of its members through consistent internal and external organizing, and an economic and political strategy that maintained the union as an independent voice for its members, through victories and defeats.

I punched in on the second shift at the Lynn River Works on February 20, 1979, following the President's Day holiday. Margaret Thatcher, of "There Is No Alternative" to capitalism fame, was elected on May 3. Ronald Reagan was elected in November. I was privileged to work at GE for thirty-three years as a grinder and a local union officer during a period of epic defeat for the working class, and not just in the US. What we had thought was normal—the conceit that our children could assume or at least aspire to do better than we did—turned out be an illusion, and the period of post–World War II working class gains was just a blip in our two-hundred-year history.

Overall the labor movement in Lynn is still getting its brains beat in. The late twentieth century brought GE job loss through transfers to other countries and the US South. It put extreme pressure on unionized GE workers to make concessions on collectively bargained agreements at the local and national level. Each IUE local at GE was and is pressured to make any deal possible to survive, regardless of the hard-won national contract GE workers had built since 1933.

We had 8,700 union members when I punched in in February of 1979. There are now about 1,200 GE workers, and others that we organized into the local. They don't have a pension anymore. I got a pension. New hires only have a 401K. Many now start at about $10 an hour below the full rate, and it takes them ten years to get to the full rate. [Note: since this interview the union has successfully reduced the pay progression to seven years.] Union density in the GE chain has dropped consistently since 1946. Nationwide. So we've gone from 100 percent to probably—I'd take a wild guess and say 10 or 12 percent now. Our contracts are bargained nationally. So that's kind of the context, for GE workers in particular. The school custodians' union has been cut in half, it's all been outsourced, to nonunion, low-wage folks. There are half as many custodians as there used to be. That used to be a good job. So what's happening to the working class materially in Lynn, we're not even talking about housing, or any of that, just job-specific stuff, has been pretty devastating. So when we talk about a successful story we need to understand that we're standing on rubble. We're fighting from the ashes of the labor movement, and there is tremendous suffering out there. So the political appreciation that somebody who reads this might have, that "Oh, this is a cool labor movement, they're doing such cool stuff"—OK. But we are hurting. We're getting bloodied and beaten. And that really weighs on you.

Yet 201 survived, and to a surprising degree, prevailed. What I think can legitimately be called a success is the political character of the movement in Lynn. The labor movement, and the broader movement, has a politically progressive nature to it, and there have been alliances built with some depth and some sustainability between the unions and the other sections of community organizations, people of color, etc.

The labor movement in Lynn has, consistently and over time, determinedly reached out to other parts of working-class people to try to build a different political vehicle. I would say we've been successful in that, in trying to create a social movement and a form of political power that's different from what exists in a lot of places. Or than what existed twenty-five years ago when we started working on this.

AC. You've talked about Local 201's reputation and being asked whether there was something in the water in Lynn that created labor radicals. So, is there something in the water?

JC. It's not the water. I would say the elements that helped shape the consciousness and politics of the labor movement in Lynn are at least three things. One is the history of a kind of labor republicanism, which is not like a Marxist trend, although there was always some of that, and there were anarchists and stuff, going way back, socialists of different stripes, but this kind of radical, anti-establishment, anti-corporate "we stand for what this country really could be, which is not run by the rich and powerful. It should be run by us—the regular working people." So that history actually is still present. And it's rooted in Lynn's nineteenth-century shoe industry and the migration of shoe workers into GE.

If you look at surrounding towns, they had some of that similar history, the mills in Salem, the shoe manufacturing in Beverly, the leather workers in Peabody. But nothing replaced it. They just deindustrialized, and the progressive labor, that historical radicalism, kind of dried up. In Lynn it went into GE. You know, you scratch a GE worker and you find a shoe worker. When I punched in it seemed like there were a lot of people who used to be shoe workers, or their family was shoe workers, and that had an impact. And I still think it exists, even today, although now it's much farther away from them.

The second thing is that Lynn was always the crossroads of a lot of social movements. So if you go back in the Civil War period, you had immigrant groups, you had women's rights groups, it was a center of abolitionism, so I think those historically have left a footprint, you know, this pretty dense kind of community organizing with different kind of folks that were indigenous to the community.

And the other thing more recently is the conjuncture of the '60s generation, someone like me. I was a 68er, a '60s radical kid, dropped out of school. You're unemployed, you get to a certain stage in your life where it would be nice to have a job. My arrest record was longer than my work record, so I needed to settle into something, and a place like GE, where you can make a living and be in the labor movement, was a good place for me to end up. But then also there were just folks who worked in the plants, there were Vietnam vets, radicalized by the war, and then there were bikers, who were kind of anti-establishment guys, who were anti-company. Some people had community organizing backgrounds. So all those people kind of came together in 201, inherited the kind of footprints of traditions that I mentioned, ideologically and politically, and they congealed to push forward and take over the local eventually, and kind of push it in a progressive direction, and become a dominant force in the leadership for a long time.

201 has been the dominant group of the labor movement in Lynn since the '30s, since they organized. The biggest union. It's a family town, it's a family plant, so you have people in the plant who are fifth generation in the same factory. I sometimes say, it's one of the longest historical locations of large-scale manufacturing in one place anywhere in the country! So it has that kind of history, and just large numbers. During the wars [Second World War, Vietnam], at different times it's

been up to thirteen thousand to twenty thousand, and then you didn't have the kind of transportation that you have now. People tended to live in Lynn. A lot of the retirees have stayed in Lynn. So it's a powerful force, just in terms of size and historical roots.

The other thing is that this was a UE shop. Elements of our democratic structures were rooted in the UE.[1] But I think the kind of radicalism in the GE workers goes way back before the UE. So the UE came and went, but the sort of labor traditions in Lynn preceded them and survived them. Some left historians say it's the UE, that's what did everything, because they were left-wing, but I don't think that's accurate, although it definitely was an element. So those were all sort of things that were the background that took us to where we got.

But then after a while you saw union density going down and down, and every contract's harder. There's lots of efforts we made to organize, to go across the chain and link up with other locals. Four or five years I spent trying to organize nonunion plants, all over New England, with almost no support from the International. We actually had groups of workers in nonunion plants, in Maine, in New Hampshire, small groups, six, seven people, that we worked with in the '90s. And the International finally dropped the whole thing; it wasn't turning out dues payers any time soon. I really think that organizing those plants was the right thing to do, and had we sustained it, I think we'd be in a really different position. Because we knew that sooner or later they're going to go after the nonunion plants. Because they were making what we were making, you know? And had roughly the same contract. And now, they've really gone after the nonunion plants. And they're not like us, I mean, they have no response.

So basically, we saw that happening, we saw density dropping, we saw numbers shrinking, work moving out, work transferred to everywhere from Maine to North Carolina, to Hungary, to South Korea, to China. So that created a very broad base for anti-free trade work and anti-NAFTA work. So we made a huge campaign around that. And we also tied that into our local bargaining, about trying to keep work from going overseas.

There's different ways you can do it. You know, you can rail against the foreigners who are "taking our jobs." We were really careful about that, as best we could be. We would use Jesse Jackson's quote, which was: "The Chinese aren't taking your jobs, GE's taking your jobs to China." We'd publicize things, like that the US Chamber of Commerce, led by GE, was fighting any effort to build independent unions in China.

Just one last story on how globalization radicalized our members. On January 2 or 3, 1994, after NAFTA was implemented on January 1, there was a revolt by the Zapatistas. One of the guys, a white guy on our legislative committee, brought in a newspaper to me. He was all excited. And he shows me a picture of these guys with guns and masks, taking over the city building. And he goes, "Wow, look at this, Jeff! These guys *really* hate NAFTA." And it created a basis for people to think of themselves in relationship to people they never would have thought about otherwise, but who actually had some similar interests perhaps.

AC. The AFL-CIO also started to move away from Cold War ideologies and toward a more progressive international solidarity in the 1990s and 2000s, right?

JC. Especially with Colombia. The Colombia stuff started also I think in the late '90s. I went on a Witness for Peace trip in 2002. When I came back people were interested, and I did like thirty speaking things. Also the AFL took up Colombia quite a bit. And they brought people here who were under death threat, and they built some solidarity, and came out against the Colombia Free Trade Agreement. By now we had done a lot of work around free trade stuff so people kind of got it, the idea that this was bad for them. And there was some resistance, people said to me sometimes, "You care about those Colombians more than you do about us." But we also kind of created space where that kind of stuff was at least acceptable, and it was at least OK that the union did that kind of work.

One of the things that we were totally clear on was that these other things were in our interest directly. They weren't like side education campaigns. These were things that if you had any brains at all, a manufacturing worker in the US has to be thinking about, for your own survival. We also knew this was different and counter to the kind of thinking that most of the labor movement had been involved in for many decades. So we had to be really good at what we did in our day-to-day work, you know, we had to really be good at representation, and grievances, and health and safety. And that was always our foundation.

In the early '80s, there were left-wing groups in the plant who tried to say, "We should take up Central America," and all this stuff, and I think to most people it just sounded like outsiders trying to tell them what they should do. So we were pretty careful about always trying to integrate it, and to do our foundational work really well. And to make people understand what was really happening, what neoliberalism was.

We did a lot of education on that. The CWA, once we merged with them in 2000, had a lot of educational stuff. That in these really difficult circumstances, if we had a strategy, we could find space to try to make advances and defend ourselves. Even though the circumstances were pretty unforgiving, and in some ways unbeatable. There is only so much you can do when you have massive economic tides and political tides against you.

The CWA had something called the CWA triangle which is kind of their organizing model. Collective bargaining and representation is the foundation. And then one side is organizing the unorganized. And the other side is political action. They call it a triangle because if you take any one side out, the whole thing collapses. But the foundation is the bargaining and representation. That's always on the bottom.

AC. Can you say something about the relationship of 201 to the larger labor movement, and the North Shore Labor Council? And how this connects to the Lynn labor movement's special character?

JC. The political character of the movement is broader than us, than 201, but it's felt most clearly in 201. You know, it's manufacturing. Some of the stuff that's happening now, with the teachers, for example, which is really progressive, is more of a national phenomenon, with the destruction of the public sector, and charter schools. It's more driven by that than by "my dad was a GE worker." But you get the impact, that it affected the rest of the movement.

The only people that have been the head of the North Shore Labor Council are from Local 201, or the teachers' union. The way I got to be head of the Labor Council was I got elected president of the union, Local 201, in 1991. A bunch of people from the executive board of the Council came to me after I'd been in office for three or four months, and they said, "Well, you need to be the head of the Labor Council." And I said, "I'm not even in the Labor Council!" There wasn't much really going on with it. They did the traditional things, they would endorse candidates, but that was about it. The good thing was there was nobody to tell us what not to do. So, we could do anything we wanted. It was a completely open field.

The labor movement is very sectoral in this country, because it's based on pragmatism, and no overriding theory, and a sort of Gompers view of unionism. No overriding vision. So it's always a struggle as to how do we bring in different sectors. In the Labor Council, you really need to have affiliated unions who can bring their strength into it, which is different from having an individual who maybe contributes his or her efforts but has no real connection to their union. So we do both. If you find someone that wants to help, God bless them, you know? Some of the people I brought in, they weren't even union members, we worked with them in the Rainbow Coalition, and they just wanted to do something. At the meeting last night, a guy came to me and said, "I got two people interested in coming down. One's a retired teacher, and the other one, I'm not sure if she's union or not, but I said, 'We do a bunch of stuff' and they'd like to come to meetings." But you also really need to work at keeping your institutional base and ties, so we work really hard at bringing in different sectors. Like, what can we do for the building trades, for example?

The building trades are a very different kind of animal. They exist to get work. On the outside people think of them as being fat, dumb, and happy, and making all this good money, but you're also laid off four months of every year. Every day you go to work, you're putting yourself closer to getting laid off at the end of the job. They know they've got to fight and scrape for every job. They maybe have a narrow sense of what that means, but they certainly know how to fight. So for us, it became: "How do you reach out to the building trades? What do they want? They want work! So how do we help them do that?" So the lower Washington St. project was a way for us to help get some union work and build our ties. And then within that, you're like, "OK, which of these folks have a vision? How do we find partners?"

There are sectors of them who are most threatened by immigrant workers, like the painters, the carpenters, the laborers. In our case, a lot of interesting work has been with the painters. Their national president is an African American guy, and the previous president was pretty progressive. They do a lot of work with worker centers and organizing, they hire a multiracial staff, so within that you find some people you can build a little bit of a deeper strategic relationship with.

SEIU, you would think, their base is mostly more people of color, and poorer workers, in building services, or even in health care. But we've never been able to get them to pay much attention to Lynn in a consistent way. They come in and do stuff around elections, and are pretty effective. But they're giant locals, and they've got statewide and national strategies. It's much harder to get their attention on something like building independent political power in Lynn because they have other things on their plate.

So, the painters are better partners for us right now than SEIU, which you wouldn't expect, necessarily. You consistently try to be responsive as a labor council to each of your affiliates as best you can. And figure out what can we do that's of use to them. Because everyone's fighting for their lives.

AC. How do you build participation in your labor council?

JC. The culture of our Labor Council is really, really different from, and almost sort of deliberately a counterculture to the labor movement as a whole. It's based on giving lots of people a chance to do stuff and supporting them. It attempts to be much more welcoming to women, so there's a women's committee, which is an autonomous space, and that's where we're most tied in with immigrant groups, through the women's committee.

We've had professional translation at our meetings when needed. We helped start the worker center, although it's totally autonomous from us, which is something the Federation was pushing at one point. And it's typically about half women, which is unusual in the labor movement, for a labor council. And we put everything we had into scraping up enough money to hire a staff person, so there's one full-time organizer. There are only two labor councils in New England that have full-time staff. As a CLC with their own staff, that we pay for, there's only us and Boston. So that's a big deal. That multiplies our capacity. Their job is to get people involved. And we've gotten fabulous organizers, one after another. All women. I tried to look for a guy to hire—I couldn't find any!

People are very clear on the culture. We had a meeting for new Executive Board members and we gave them a little bit of our history, and why our council is the way it is, at my house, for dinner the other day. And people went on and on about that. "I like this council. People are welcome. People are warm. People care." So when you create that kind of culture, which was intentional, you draw more people like them. And sometimes people who don't feel they really have any space in their own local to do anything! So the culture has something to do with our success. And we work hard, with some success, and some failures. It's a very white council. We don't have a lot of involvement from the locals with the most members of color. We're trying to find ways to deal with that also. But through alliances and through our external work, we've developed a fairly high amount of respect and relationships with other groups.

AC. What about community organizations?

JC. The first community organization we developed really strategic links with was Essex County Community Organization (ECCO), a congregation-based community organization, about twenty-five years ago. We were trying to deepen our ties with our membership, so we did repeated campaigns, what we called one-on-one efforts. The core internal organizing was the foundation of everything. So we'd do these one-on-one campaigns where we'd try to talk to every single member, on a contract coming up, or whatever. We did one like that, a survey of our members around what their biggest needs are. We did it with our legislative committee, which we made kind of a progressive pole in the union, to get the activists who really wanted to do this kind of work in one place where we could talk about stuff. I think we got nine hundred surveys returned, mostly done in one-on-one conversations. What we found was that the number one issue was jobs. Even though *they* had a decent job, they were afraid of losing it. And if you wanted to really scare the shit out of somebody, you'd say, "Where are your kids going to work?" Everybody knew that we were going down the tubes, and most people were pretty pessimistic, and the propaganda was like, "Manufacturing is dying, everything is going overseas; if you're still making stuff you're like a dinosaur, your days are numbered." So no one in their right mind would even want their kids to go into it.

At the same time, ECCO was getting organized in Lynn, particularly with St. Stephens Church, which has always been an activist church in Lynn—it's an Episcopal church, multiracial, always had progressive leadership. They were doing a similar kind of thing, and they came up with "jobs" also. We got into conversations with them, and what we found was that I'd go to the Zion Baptist Church and one of our really strong stewards was there, in the choir. And St. Stephens—one of our trustees was active in that parish. And First Lutheran, one of the guys came to us, one of our militant guys, he said, "They're way more tougher than you guys! You know, ECCO really gives the politicians a bunch of shit! You guys are a bunch of wimps!" So we'd go to the churches and we'd find links between our activists and their activists, often the same people.

So we formed a jobs team with them, and eventually came up with the E-team. The E-team is a machinist training program. I think we've done twenty-two classes, over twenty-three years. It's a partnership between 201, the Labor Council, and ECCO. The idea was, let's find something that we can train people for, where they can actually make a living. Our standard was: a living wage, a career path, and some kind of benefits. We settled on machining because they were closing all the machinist training programs. Right when we founded this, they closed Peabody High School's machine shop. And we knew the demand was going to continue, even though the fad was that if you're not doing computers, you're out. We knew that wasn't the case, and we figured a lot of machinists were my age, so in fifteen years they were going to be disappearing from the workforce. New England, the North Shore, has a long history of machine shops. There has been machinist skill here for a long, long time—generations. And we felt that's a strength to build on.

There was some controversy to that project. I remember one guy saying, "I don't understand why the preachers are going to be able to tell us what to do!" That was a leftist! We were going to train our members in the class, people who didn't have machining skills and were in dead-end jobs, because they were eliminating more and more of the unskilled and semi-skilled positions. That's one of the ways we sold it to the membership. But now, the low-seniority machinists, who were already on the jobs, are like, "Wait a minute! The union's going to train somebody with seventeen years, they'll then upgrade onto my job, and the next layoff comes, and I'm gone! And the union's doing this to me!" Because everybody assumes there's another layoff coming. I mean it was just grim.

That never happened. Nobody lost their job because some senior person got upgraded over them. But it was just a really hard time, because everyone was scared, everyone's thinking about losing their jobs. So we had to deal with that kind of resistance. Our argument was, "We're getting weaker, we're getting smaller; we need friends and allies, these are our neighbors." The other thing that happened is that some of the people's kids started getting into the E-team and then into GE. So when our members' kids got in there, they became diehards. Over time people really saw the value. Now there's probably three hundred E-team grads who are in the plant. And we made it that 201 people had preference, so up to a third of those seats in the class—something like thirty people a year—would be reserved for 201 people. Because we did the work, along with ECCO, to create the program. So that became a real plus. And now we have a base in the plant of the E-team people, some of whom are really core activists in the union now. Because they kind of felt they owed the union before they ever got in. Like the trades, you know. That's how you get your job.

And then it kind of becomes "OK, it's acceptable," so we work with community groups. A lot of our members' churches were in ECCO. There have been three ministers at St. Stephens since then, and those things get built and rebuilt over time. But that's kind of how it started. And then we did some electoral work, with Neighbor to Neighbor. Maria Carrasco had been active with Neighbor to Neighbor, and we supported her for the School Committee, and helped her with our school unions. The school employees, the custodians' union played a big role in helping her. She was the first Latina elected to the School Committee. I was influenced by writing on the concept of working people's assemblies. We took this out of Fletcher and Gapasin's book [*Solidarity Divided*], and a few other people, Sam Gindin. This was a conscious political proposition, by people like myself. I mean, union density is like, what are we at now, 6 percent of the private sector? So when people say, "Why do you do this?" I say, "6 percent." You know? Where are you going to go? 6 percent of the private sector. So people could understand that to have any power, and defend our interests, in the plant or anywhere else, we needed allies. And why shouldn't we go with our friends and neighbors, who are working-class people, and should be our allies, but they're not in unions?

We always said, "We're an alliance between clergy who care about their members, their parishioners, more than one day a week, and union leaders who care about their members more than 8 hours a day." So we all realized that our people live in this world, they have all these issues every day that you can't fix with a union contract, that you can't fix with a prayer on Sunday. So what are we going to do?

That's what some people now call "whole-worker organizing." Our concern with our members was always more than just the contract. If they don't have a housing problem, their kids do. We'd say, "Are your kids still at home?" and they'd say, "Yeah," and we'd say, "How old are they?" and they'd say, "twenty-eight, thirty-two." Everybody's family was still with them. Half, a third of the people. Because kids couldn't get a job, couldn't find a place to live. With that kind of approach, it's a lot easier to get people to think beyond just on-the-job issues. Because everybody's out in the world trying to get by. And the issues, all the issues of social reproduction, the decline of the public good, have very concrete impacts on members' lives. Over time, and it took time, it took repeated work—people overcame. They saw some successes in it. They saw the E-team help people, and help their own families, and the crisis gets worse and worse.

I think the problem you have is that you have to show some victories in something that matters. And the balance of power is so skewed in this country that victories are hard to come by, especially if you're in a declining industry. Sometimes you're sitting in a conference, and someone says, "What's the answer? More strikes!" Yeah, right. We have 6 percent density at GE. Our structural power is not what it used to be. They're really mobile. It's not like Richmond, California, where they have an oil refinery with a bazillion dollars' worth of pipes underground. They're not going to move that. But they'll move GE. They already have. So those are tougher issues that don't give you simplistic answers, and they don't give you a very clear route to a victory to show your people you're getting somewhere. GE unions have made some pretty significant concessions to try to stay alive. But now people coming in are making less money, not with a pension, and they're like, "What's the union doing for me?" And we have to defend ourselves short term and give them a fairly long-term answer also.

AC. What would you say are some of the main issues facing the working class in Lynn, and how the union and the Labor Council have been involved in a working-class agenda for the city?

JC. It's different now, when the new immigrants came in. They didn't know anyone that works at GE. They didn't know what the gear plant is. You have to use a whole different language when you're talking about development, even.

I think it was 2011 that we started the New Lynn Coalition. We said we need a permanent voice for working class people, that's union and non-union, multiracial, multi-sector, citizens and undocumented. We knew from the beginning we'd have people who were renters, people who were homeowners, people who own a couple houses and rent to people. So our vision was, we've done all this, we've done some joint electoral work. We need to get more involved in local politics. Not because that's where the solutions were, but because that's somewhere we can actually influence. We talked about a bunch of issues from the beginning. About two and a half years ago we started what we call a visioning process, or Phase One of our work to change the city. So we met with each organization and had a discussion about "What does Lynn look like? What do you want Lynn to look like?" We started with groups like Neighbor to Neighbor, the Labor Council, and Local 201. 1199 is affiliated but actually, except for one individual, that doesn't really play a big role. At the time, Haitian Elders—although they've now changed their name and they're not in it anymore—Mass Senior Action, Lynn United for Change, Lynn Health Care Task Force, ECCO, Matahari, maybe eight groups. And so we sat down with each of those groups and did this visioning thing.

It was really interesting, because, for example, environmental stuff came up a lot. It didn't come up from the old Lynners, it came up from like the Dominicans and Guatemalans, or poorer folks, who felt it in their neighborhoods, and also who had seen what had happened in their home countries. When big companies came in and wrecked everything. Polluted everything. So that was a really good process, and then in January of 2017 we ratified our five points: affordable housing, job training, multiracial anti-discriminatory hiring in the city, sanctuary city, and ending wage theft. Then we took those into the municipal elections. We kind of forced wage theft and housing into the discussion pretty successfully. And we were able to move directly into the successful campaign for an anti-wage theft ordinance that the Lynn Worker Center had started. The Labor Council took it up in a big way. Wage theft was the first big campaign we took up as an entire group, besides an anti-foreclosure ordinance led by Lynn United for Change a couple of years before. Partly we picked this because we thought it would be the easiest one. Affordable housing is going to be a lot tougher, with a lot more resistance. Now, Phase Two is to take that to a much broader group. It's probably going to take us another year or two, but the idea is to build another circle, and we'll find either people we want to bring into New Lynn, or if that's not appropriate for them, remain as allies. So we're trying to continually build more power. Because we think even though we won wage theft, it gets steeper when we're talking about housing or sanctuary.

Keep in mind, if you do this at a regular Local 201 union meeting, you might have thirty people there. Out of maybe fifteen hundred members. Then it goes in the union paper and has some impact, but it's only a minority. But the labor council's different. The labor council is really wedded to this. We had forty-four people at our meeting last night. That's getting to be sort of normal. That's bigger than they used to be. Those people, they've been there for month after month, and they're the activists from their locals—they're really committed. Teachers, more and more, are really committed. But in most cases you're talking about a pretty small slice of actual membership that knows anything about this stuff or is really involved.

AC. In terms of the unions, you mean?

JC. In terms of the unions. Community groups are a lot different. But even there, half the members don't know what we're up to in New Lynn because they're involved in their own campaigns. But they're much different organizations. If you come to Lynn United for Change, it's because you care about housing. If you come to Local 201 it's because you got a job at GE! You could be a fascist, you know, but you just got a paycheck from GE so you're in the union. So they're really different that way.

When we founded New Lynn, there were a couple of criteria. First of all, we said for an organization to join—this was based on our experience and just politics—you had to have a membership base that was working-class people. As opposed to either middle-class policy people or pure advocacy groups. So the service provider nonprofits are our allies, and some of them will support us as actively as they can. But we wanted actual groups with a working-class base. And people had to agree to our four points, which were: to build our own research capacity; political action, especially increasing working-class voter participation; economic development that will work for *all* of the people of Lynn; and political education and culture—trying to raise political consciousness and bring people together across the boundaries of race, neighborhood, etc.

The important thing about the founding of New Lynn is that it was from the beginning meant to be permanent, and to deal with all issues affecting working-class people. Really, really different, and much more difficult, than a coalition to pass a bill or something. So you have to constantly be going deeper and deeper, and constantly getting feedback from each group about what the tensions are, and who's been disrespected, and who hasn't been funded, and if it's all white people running it. It's a constant effort to be kind of self-aware, and try to make space to talk about stuff like that. And grow.

As well as strategy! Like, "What are we doing? What's going on?" Right now, we don't really know what to do about housing. We've been talking about that for a long time. We've gone from linkage, to community benefit agreements, to inclusionary zoning. We now kind of feel like inclusionary zoning is a good thing to do, but everybody who's done it feels like it's a Band-Aid. So what do you do? The market is going to transform housing. It's like standing there when your jobs are moving to Mexico, what do you do? So those kind of things require constant, just constant effort. If you let down your guard for a minute, then fractures appear that make it difficult to sustain the kind of permanent working-class pole that we're trying to build in the city. There's not a lot of places that are doing that, but it is what we aspire to. We've had some success. And you know, your success is only as good as the last fight. Defeat is always around the corner.

The neoliberal model has taken over the world by the throat. So what are we going to do in Lynn? We're operating within limitations. We recognize that. We're trying to do political education so that more and more people understand. Obviously to have a significant impact on the conditions of our lives, we're going to have to work with people in other places. We can't change the world in Lynn! We need state-wide independent political organization, because a lot of the key policy issues are fought out at the state level. But we're going to change what we can, and then go from there. And we're excited about it. It's new challenges, new things, and we're optimistic. We understand what's going on in the world; this is a long change. I know in my own union, the Communication Workers Union, the leadership is explaining to people that there are no short-term solutions. There aren't any. It's not the next election, that won't do it. We need to be involved in that. But we need long-term power-building for working-class people that involves both union and nonunion workers, community-based organizations based on common interests, and mutual respect that's permanent. And that's the kind of power we're trying to build in Lynn.

CHAPTER 5

If We Don't Get It, Shut it Down!

University Cafeteria-Worker Organizing, the Information Economy, and Boston's Inequality Problem

Carlos Aramayo

We deserve better, and we're going to do anything and everything to get it.[1]

—*Thomas Gross, Northeastern cafeteria worker*

One of the first things passengers hear when arriving at Boston Logan Airport is a recording of mayor Marty Walsh welcoming them to the city. The mayor proudly proclaims Boston as the "Hub of the Universe"—a riff on a moniker first used by Oliver Wendell Holmes more than a century ago—and then goes on to highlight the city's accomplishments in medicine, education, and technology. This embrace of the information economy by Boston's political leader mirrors the region's economic and cultural priorities during the last thirty years.

During this time, the city's political, economic, and cultural leaders have aggressively rebranded Boston. Boston's future prosperity, these leaders argued, depended on linking the private sector with world-class public research institutions. They believed that the city, wracked by tribal, hate-filled, neighborhood politics, needed to turn outward. Boston had to embrace the world and transform itself from a cold, racist, sports-obsessed, parochial island into an international capital of the information age.

In many ways, this digital reimagining of the region has been a success. Boston, along with neighboring cities Cambridge and Somerville, has undertaken public initiatives to reshape the physical and economic reality of the region. In Boston, the entire Seaport district, a badly blighted deindustrialized neighborhood, has been radically transformed. Anchored by a publically-funded convention center and the Institute of Contemporary Arts, as well as the Vertex headquarters and soon-to-be-opened GE Headquarters, this area's economic growth has been fueled by the new economy.[2] In Cambridge, the state and city have incentivized technology and pharmaceutical companies like Google and AmGen to open facilities in Kendall Square, adjacent to the Massachusetts Institute of Technology.[3] The windfall from this boom has not, however, been shared equally.

As the medical, technological, and educational industries have grown, service industry jobs have been created to cook, clean, and wait on the innovation economy's creative minds. According to the City of Boston, the service and hospitality industries are the second fastest growing sectors of the city's economy after health care.[4] However, while tech visionaries, research scientists, and administrative professionals flourish in this new economy, service-sector workers have not reaped the digital revolution's spoils. Instead, they have struggled to survive as the city has become increasingly unaffordable.

Hospitality jobs do not, however, *have* to be low-income jobs. Over the past several decades, Boston's hospitality and service industry workers have fought to change the nature of, and compensation for, this kind of work. Workers have unionized, negotiated, lobbied, and struck to transform these jobs from part-time, low-income jobs to family-sustaining full-time employment. In particular, cafeteria food service workers have organized in remarkable numbers with UNITE HERE Local 26.[5]

This chapter explores how the innovation economy is exacerbating income inequality in Boston and also serving to stimulate service-worker organizing on college and university campuses in the city. By examining how rising housing, health-care, and transportation costs disproportionately affect low-income Black and brown workers, it shows how rising unaffordability has created the material conditions for grassroots organizing. The article then examines several cafeteria-worker campaigns to explain why and how over one thousand cafeteria-workers have unionized in the past five years; looking particularly at how growing workplace organization and militancy help solve Boston's growing income inequality. By focusing on how workers created cultures of solidarity across ethnic, gender, and racial boundaries, this article sheds light on the quotidian, behind-the-scenes struggles of workplace organizing. What motivates workers to take militant action in the face of significant risk to their livelihoods? How do workers organize themselves to overcome the challenges of solidarity? And how do workers build bold campaigns that win?

Housing, Transportation, and Health Care: An Unaffordable City

The unaffordability of Boston in many ways starts with housing. After stagnating during the 2007-2009 Great Recession, housing prices in Boston have risen steadily. Citywide, the median home price increased 47 percent, from $359,000 to $530,000 between 2011 and 2016.[6] This increase in housing costs has been accelerated by luxury development in the urban core and real estate speculation in gentrifying neighborhoods. In practical terms, sky-rocketing housing costs have made purchasing a home unaffordable for most workers in the low-income service sector. At the end of 2017 the *Boston Business Journal* estimated that a home buyer would have to earn $97,465 a year to afford a median-priced home in Boston, assuming they could amass a 20 percent down payment.[7] Given that the median wage in Boston is slightly over $56,000 a year and that most employees in the service and hospitality industries earn less—on the high end, a full-time unionized housekeeper makes $44,616 annually   purchasing a home is impossible for service sector workers.[8]

To make matters worse, gentrification and real estate speculation have disproportionally affected working-class communities of color. While housing prices have risen in every neighborhood of the city, the largest increases have been seen in the city's Black and brown neighborhoods. In East Boston, the center of the city's Latino community, condo development has caused median home prices to balloon by a staggering 152 percent between 2011 and 2016. Likewise, in Roxbury, the city's traditionally African American neighborhood, the median housing price increased 107 percent between 2011 and 2016.[9] According to *Imagine Boston 2030*, 27 percent of the city's Black residents are living in poverty, with housing cost burdens (rents, mortgage debt, etc.) being a significant cause of financial stress. The city estimates that up to 21 percent of Boston households, most of them in traditionally Black neighborhoods, are "severely cost-burdened," meaning they spend more than 50 percent of their income on housing.[10] Extraordinary housing costs and their disproportionate effect on the Black working class are a major contributor to a startling statistic first published in *Imagine Boston 2030*: the median net worth of a Black family in Boston is only $8.[11]

This real estate boom is not only making home ownership impossible for low-wage service sector workers, it is also causing the rental market to explode. Rental costs averaged $2,038 a month, the third highest in the country.[12] Black and brown workers in the service industry have been forced into a precarious economic situation by the rising cost of housing. They are faced with increasingly difficult and disruptive choices as they try to make ends meet in an unaffordable housing market. With wages increasing at an anemic rate, they must decide whether to leave the urban core, seek alternative living arrangements with family, or find second and third jobs to make mortgage or rent payments. Rising housing costs and a crumbling transportation infrastructure have pushed lower income workers out of the urban core and added new stresses on working people's time and income. Housing and transportation costs, driven up by the wealth of the new information economy, impoverish the people of color who cook the meals and clean offices at the universities and hospitals that are leading Boston's digital renaissance.

The Health-Care Crisis in Boston

The health-care industry is a major driver of Boston's twenty-first century economy. Teaching hospitals like Massachusetts General Hospital, Brigham and Women's Hospital, and Tufts Medical Center dominate whole neighborhoods of the city and bring research and development dollars to the area's economy. World-class medicine has not, however, meant affordable health care. To the contrary, studies have shown that teaching hospitals drive up the cost of health care in Massachusetts through consolidating providers in closed networks. All of the research hospitals in Boston are flagship institutions for big health-care groups; for example, Partners HealthCare, the largest provider network in Massachusetts, is the owner of Massachusetts General Hospital. According to the state's Health Policy Commission, this type of provider consolidation increases health-care costs without improving patient outcomes. In particular, the commission points out, provider consolidation leads to patients receiving routine treatment at high-cost research and teaching hospitals instead of at lower-cost community hospitals or clinics.[13]

Rising health-care prices, like housing costs, disproportionally affect low-wage workers. Health insurance premium costs in Massachusetts are among the highest in the nation, with commercial spending on health care being 6–9 percent higher than the national average. Practically, this means that the average total premiums for family coverage in employer-based plans for the bottom quartile of wage earners was $16,300 in 2015, with employees bearing 34 percent of this cost, or $5,500. According to the Massachusetts Health Policy Commission, total health-care spending—including premium share and other out-of-pocket costs—adds up to 30 percent of household income for a family of three earning $60,000 a year. "These costs," the report concludes, "disproportionately impact low-to-middle income residents and result in persistent health-care affordability concerns for individuals, families, employers, and government in Massachusetts."[14] In Boston, where a mortgage or lease often eats up half of working family's income, health-care costs can quickly amount to another third. With less than 20 percent of their income remaining for all other expenses, workers in the service and hospitality sectors live on the edge of poverty, facing difficult choices about how to provide for themselves and their families.

Housing, transportation, and health care are unaffordable for workers in the service and hospitality industries who have faced wage stagnation during the past decade. While this trend has not gone unnoticed by elected officials, the best solutions to this problem are the ones being forged by service workers themselves. Through organizing, activism, and militant action, low-income workers are forcing institutions that profit from the new economy to share some of their information-age windfall.

Organizing the New Economy

Low-income workers have not sat idly by as Boston's booming new economy has created an affordability crisis. They have advocated for themselves and their families using a diversity of organizational strategies and political tactics. By lobbying, petitioning, rallying, picketing, and even striking, workers have influenced public policy and popular debate on increasing inequality. Seizing on the problems facing low-income workers, campaigns like the SEIU Fight for $15 and the Raise Up Massachusetts coalition have organized to increase the state's minimum wage.[15] These campaigns have combined political activism, smart messaging, and small but loud worker walkouts, to comprehensively pressure the state legislature to increase the minimum wage to $11.00 in 2017.[16] Community Labor United's (CLU) campaign to end wage theft, while not yet resulting in a legislative fix, has greatly raised public awareness about the vulnerability of low-income immigrant workers to wage and hour violations.[17] In this vein, attorneys like Shannon Lis-Riordan have prosecuted a number of high-profile cases of wage theft in Boston's restaurant industry, many of them resulting in large payouts to workers.[18] These types of campaigns against wage theft and worker misclassification as independent contractors have been amplified by vigorous activism from worker centers like Centro Presente, Restaurant Opportunities Center, and the Brazilian Worker Center. Finally, the Massachusetts Nurses Association (MNA), has become a leading advocate for health-care access and affordability. In 2016, it spearheaded a successful ballot initiative to make Massachusetts the first state to require employers to provide paid sick days.[19]

UNITE HERE Local 26, the union of hotel, cafeteria, and restaurant workers, has taken a different approach to the problem of income inequality. While all of the successful campaigns mentioned above have mobilized low-income workers in the service and hospitality industries to advocate for statewide regulatory changes (increased minimum wage, paid sick days) or judicial remedy (payment for stolen wages), Local 26 has demanded that institutions profiting from the new economy contribute directly to solving the problem of income inequality in Boston. Through grassroots mobilization of service and hospitality workers in the city's universities, convention centers, hotels, and Boston Logan Airport, Local 26 has built a militant worker-led Union that is growing and winning life-changing concessions from new-economy employers.[20]

The Wave of Organization, 2012–2014: How Can We Fight for Money If We Don't Have Respect?

Over one thousand workers on nine Boston-area campuses joined UNITE HERE Local 26 between 2012 and 2014, part of a nationwide campaign that touched fifty campuses and organized thirty-six hundred new members. UNITE HERE's organizing strategy aimed at building support among students, faculty, alumni, and the public for low-wage workers at visible and wealthy institutions.[21] In Boston, the largest group of workers organized at Northeastern University, where four hundred cooks, cashiers, and servers who worked for Chartwells, the university's contracted food service provider, voted overwhelmingly to unionize in

April of 2012. Such campaigns, while worker-led, were not spontaneous. Instead, they were meticulously planned and carefully executed, with each campaign tailored to each University campus.

The consensus on unionization was forged in countless secret conversations between workers and union leaders. Because intimidation and misinformation are the most successful management tactics to divide workers, secrecy played a critical role in these campaigns, with workers building whisper networks on each campus prior to taking their demands public. This was done in a three-step process. First, in consultation with union organizers, the workers seeking to organize identified workplace leaders who were agitated and trustworthy. Then, rank-and-file workers from already unionized shops (and later students) surveyed identified leaders about workplace conditions, but *not* about union preference. This was usually done under the guise of a research study or a canvass on community workplace standards. These survey conversations helped make a final determination if the identified worker was agitated, trustworthy, and interested in changing their working conditions. Finally, assuming everything checked out, a worker-organizer introduced the new contact to the campaign. By following this sometimes-Byzantine approach, workers seeking to organize succeeded in keeping their campaigns secret while they built a consensus about unionization away from the eyes and ears of anti-union managers. The building of a secret network also enabled the workers to control the timeline of the campaign: they decided when to announce their union drive publically, only doing so when they felt strong enough to weather management's opposition to the union.

Hundreds of workers were organized in this way, and, over the course of these campaigns, an interesting consensus emerged. Cafeteria workers were nearly unanimously dissatisfied with their economic conditions—most workers earned under $11 an hour and had no access to affordable company-provided health care—but these problems did not top their list of reasons for wanting change at work. Instead, disrespect, sexual harassment, and racism were consistently named as leading reasons to unionize. Black and brown workers felt invisible and dehumanized by management and by university administrators. As Angela Bello, a Colombian immigrant and one of the rank-and-file organizers at Northeastern put it, "I've stayed in the job because I need that stupid job. I've felt like a worm. They made me feel like a little worm inside a plant. . . . When people are scared and people are working in fear, that's when I push myself to say that's not right. This is America...at least give us what we deserve: respect."[22] Workers reported being humiliated at work and constantly threatened with the loss of their jobs if they spoke up or even called in sick. Another Northeastern worker, José Taibot, a Honduran immigrant and grill cook, reported being held at work despite having intense chest pains. His manager refused to believe he was ill and threatened to fire him if he left his workstation. He had to complete his work before scrambling to the hospital, where emergency room doctors determined he was having a heart attack. "The managers [were going to] let me die here," Taibot said, "They never apologized—they attacked my life. . . . That's why when I found out that the union wanted to organize, I was the first one to stand up and get in line."[23] During the organizing campaigns in these cafeterias, the union became a vehicle for expressing rage and opposition to this regime of racist harassment and disrespect. As Bello summed it up after the workers at Northeastern won their union election, "I wanted this union to end the mistreatment and injustice we all face while working here. It has been a long fight and we faced pressure from our bosses not to unionize, but we came together and demanded fairness. All we want is to be treated with respect."[24]

After a critical mass of worker-leaders decided to commit to unionization in secret, large organizing committee meetings were held to plan the campaign. All of the members of the committee showed their commitment to the campaign by taking their photos for a public petition announcing their intent to organize. These committee members then took responsibility for building consensus in favor of unionization among their coworkers, pledging to sign them up on union cards during an organizational blitz lasting several days. In addition, these worker-leaders reached out to student groups to seek support for their campaign. Rather than alienating the students with surprise picket lines or inflammatory rhetoric, committee members organized students to support their cause before confronting management with their demands. By telling their stories of disrespect, harassment, and racism at the hands of the management, workers on multiple university campuses built alliances with a diversity of student groups. These alliances succeeded not only because workers told compelling stories of mistreatment and disrespect, but also because of the unique role they played with students. As Ren Kenney, a student at Simmons during its unionization campaign explained, "When I first got to Simmons, the cafeteria workers treated me with kindness, like family. They take care of us. So when the workers started organizing, I had their back the way they had mine. That's what community is about."[25]

Student-worker alliances proved essential in pressuring management to recognize the union and negotiate first contracts. By organizing students—the clients of institutions of higher education—to support worker demands for respect and representation, pro-union workers isolated cafeteria management and the university administration. This blunted management's ability to run a classic anti-union campaign based on fear and intimidation. It also made it difficult for management to refuse to bargain in good faith once the workers had won union representation. Workers incorporated campus leaders into their organizing committees and gave them agency to determine how to effectively use student power to win the campaign. Students then directly confronted their University administrations, demanding institutional leaders address the disturbing disrespect reported by workers and recognize and negotiate with the union. As the Northeastern chapter of Students Against Sweatshops reported:

> Students took their organizing to a new level by doing public delegations to some of the most abusive managers in the campus dining areas and officially forming Huskies Organizing with Labor, a coalition of 46 Northeastern student groups standing side by side workers as they continued their fight. By March, students and workers upped the pressure even more and hosted one of the largest worker speak-outs on campuses this year, with nearly a dozen workers telling stories of years of enduring Chartwells' abuses to a crowd of over 500 students and faculty.[26]

Facing student unrest, University administrators scrambled to control the situation and began to pressure cafeteria managers to allow workers to decide on unionization in an atmosphere free from intimidation. Weeks later, workers had won their union.

The success of student-worker alliances shows the heterogeneous nature of the new economy. Students attending higher education institutions in Boston, many of whom study STEM subjects, bristle when confronted by the inequality the new economy has perpetuated. While these students benefit from the influx of information-economy resources, they do not support university labor policies that impoverish and disrespect Black and brown service industry workers on their campuses. Instead, whether out of guilt or political conviction, students at every institution where cafeteria workers have sought unionization have demanded university administrations and food service contractors treat workers with respect and pay a living wage. This points to a vulnerability in the labor logic of the new economy: while the market encourages displacement, income inequality, and the exclusion of low-income people of color; many of the people working in the information economy actively oppose these effects when directly confronted by them.

Strike's On: The Fight for Sustainable Lives in the New Economy

The union contracts won by the members of UNITE HERE Local 26 on Boston's university campuses changed the lives of thousands of workers. These contracts and the public fights that won them helped address years of disrespect in the kitchens of the region's university cafeterias. Workers won job security, immigration status protections, enforceable anti-harassment policies, disciplinary grievance procedures, and hiring and scheduling transparency language in their contracts. They also won economic improvements: an average worker at Northeastern, for example, received an almost $4 raise over the course of first five-year contract workers signed in 2012.[27] In addition, workers got access to a union health plan that reduced some co-payments and deductibles. These contracts did not, however, make a job at the university's cafeteria economically sustainable in Boston's increasingly unaffordable booming economy. By the end of the first contract at Northeastern, workers had a voice and were treated with more respect by the management; they had not yet transformed cafeteria work into a family-sustaining job.

Beginning in 2015, university food service workers in Boston began to discuss how to combat rising inequality. While these workers had won modest economic improvements in their contracts, these gains lagged significantly behind the rising cost of living. As housing, health-care, and transportation costs rose with the influx of information-economy wealth, workers felt left behind. On university campuses, the seasonal nature of cafeteria work (and ever-shortening academic semesters), exacerbated this problem. Low-income workers struggled to make ends meet with full-time jobs which only lasted eight or nine months of the year, with most having to rely on unemployment for additional income. The seasonality of these jobs, combined with the uncertainty of scheduling, often made finding a second job difficult or impossible, with many employers not interested in workers who, at best, were available intermittently over a few months each year. This situation was worse at universities like Harvard that directly employed (rather than subcontracted) their workers. Because the state of Massachusetts categorizes these workers as educational employees of a nonprofit, tax-exempt institution, these employees do not qualify for unemployment benefits. As a result of low wages and contingent, seasonal work, most university cafeteria workers made less than the City of Boston's recommended family-sustaining income of $35,000 per year. The workers who served the students at these information-age institutions continued to live in poverty, many relying on state or federal assistance to afford housing or health care. Boston's universities faced an income inequality crisis.

Workers saw this problem as an industry-wide predicament. They also saw that universities—with their ever-rising tuition, greatly expanded operating budgets, and huge endowments—were financially capable of solving this crisis. Beginning at Harvard University, worker-leaders and UNITE HERE Local 26 staff organizers developed an organizational strategy to build consensus on the economic problems facing cafeteria workers and the tactics necessary to win major concessions from the region's higher education industry. Rank-and-file union leaders discussed income inequality, the increasing unaffordability of the Boston region, the economics of higher education and the new economy, and, most importantly, what needed to be done to improve the wages, benefits, and working conditions of cafeteria workers. "In the earliest stages of the campaign, we met with as many people as possible," said Mike Kramer, the food service director for UNITE HERE Local 26. "That was the first step—conversations with hundreds of people. People were very clear about the problems they were facing and some had ideas about ways to take the problems on, but they were scattered and unsystematic ideas. We tried to cohere this into a set of demands that were both clear and bold."[28] To do this, these leaders resolved to build large organizing committees on all of the area's campuses. Once built, these committees formulated these bold demands on each campus by surveying hundreds of workers across the city. These surveys not only established a consensus on economic demands, but also engaged workers on what it might take to accomplish a radical improvement in wages and benefits. Bluntly put, the survey asked, "Will you be willing to strike without pay to win your new contract?"

The first contract to be renegotiated was at Harvard University.[29] Unlike their counterparts across the city, cafeteria workers at Harvard had been members of Local 26 for decades. Despite having a mature contract and relatively high wages, these workers still felt the squeeze of the cost of living in the Boston area. In addition, these workers faced an administration seeking to increase their health-care costs and committed to only modest wage increases. To make the situation worse, the University had greatly reduced the length of academic semester, leaving workers without jobs for more than four months of the year. This meant that a majority of the cafeteria workers at Harvard, the wealthiest educational institution in the world, earned less than $35,000 a year. In addition, the University was determined to shift the cost burden of health care onto the workers. Having successfully, and controversially, pushed health benefit cost increases onto the faculty and the unionized clerical staff in the previous year, the university administration believed that dining hall workers would also concede to these changes. Harvard's administration badly miscalculated the situation in their dining halls. Cafeteria workers—squeezed by the booming new economy and the University's cost-cutting, bottom-line decision making—were not ignorant of the economics of higher education. They had developed an analysis of the institution's business model and built an organization capable of making real, popular demands of Harvard. More importantly, these were clear demands that fueled the organizing: not a penny more on health care and a minimum guaranteed income of $35,000 a year. These cooks, cashiers, and cleaners were ready for a fight.

This fight culminated in a twenty-two-day strike that disrupted campus life and deeply embarrassed the Harvard administration. The simplicity of the worker's demands quickly translated to broad public support. Students walked out, rallied, sang, and even danced with the workers, alumni opened their pocketbooks to support the strike fund, and radical marching bands attending the annual HONK! festival made the strikers their *cause célèbre*.[30] Within days, the strike was national news, with national media outlets clamoring to tell the story of the University's refusal to meet the worker's simple demands.[31] The broad appeal of the strike was best (and most comically) summarized by blogger Hamilton Nolan writing in *Deadspin*. In an article entitled, "Idiots Who Run Harvard Let their Low-Wage Workers Go on Strike," Nolan wrote, "Harvard University has an endowment of $35 billion and employs 47 Nobel laureates."

> But they weren't rich or smart enough to pay their dining hall workers enough money to stop them from going on strike this morning. Harvard's academic resources must not extend into the realm of PR. If they did, someone could have told the school that no matter what

happens, they will lose this PR battle, for the following reason: They are Harvard, and they have $35 billion, and the workers who serve food to fucking Harvard kids for a living (contemplate the reality of this job) just walked out because you refuse to give them what they are asking for, which, according to their union, is "affordable health care and sustainable incomes of at least $35,000 a year," and the ability to work for the whole year.[32]

The strike was won in three weeks, with the workers achieving all of their demands and the campus cheering their victory.

The Harvard strike succeeded because workers took large-scale militant action to win simple, well-articulated, and broadly poplar demands. By organizing the rank and file, worker-leaders and union organizers built a broad consensus that was easy to explain to students, professors, and alumni. As a result, a campus alliance formed which supported the worker's demands and isolated the administration. Without the support of major campus stakeholders, the administration was left with no choice but to capitulate to the union's demands.

This model of broad-based organizational consensus building to form simple, bold demands, followed by campus alliance-building and militant direct action, was reproduced in 2017 at Northeastern University. Here, many cafeteria workers—despite having won respect, dignity, and job security in their first union contract—lived in poverty. The average annual income for a dining hall employee was less than $22,000 a year, with many workers forced to rely on state assistance for health care and housing. Some workers even reported regularly using food stamps to feed their family, according to surveys done by worker-leaders and union organizers.[33] As Shante McCorvey, a food service worker on the campus, put it: "With what Northeastern pays me, I can't afford to pay for the academic programs my 11-year old daughter needs, or for her to have her own bedroom apart from her two younger siblings. . . . We live in low-income housing and every day is a struggle."[34] Economic insecurity, particularly in the face of rising housing and health-care costs, was felt by workers across the campus. As they organized for their new contract they decided to take inspiration from the workers at Harvard that had just won their strike. Understanding that Northeastern was an expanding institution that embraced the new economy and promoted its growing academic stature, cafeteria workers made a simple proposition: they deserved to earn the same wages and benefits as workers at Harvard. In fall 2017, they went public with familiar demands: affordable health care and a guaranteed minimum income of $35,000 a year.

Like at Harvard, workers organized a campus-wide coalition to support their campaign. Dozens of student organizations backed cafeteria workers' demands, with hundreds of students occupying the campus center during the release of a near-unanimous petition announcing a potential strike. With campus sentiment strongly favoring the worker's demands, the table was set for a replay of the chaos that had engulfed Harvard's campus the year before.[35] There was, however, no strike. Instead, at the eleventh hour, the University's food service subcontractor, Chartwells, agreed to all of the union's demands.

The university administration and Chartwells did not explain why they capitulated, but many workers and union organizers speculated that it was in part because Northeastern's leaders realized they were on the verge of being publicly humiliated as Harvard had been in 2016. The potential power of a public campaign was already on display in the days before a settlement was reached. With an open-ended strike seemingly inevitable, worker-leaders, students, and union organizers began urging the planners of major on-campus events to make commitments to respect picket lines. One of the events that workers and organizers targeted was the Clinton Global Initiative University conference, a signature event for former president Bill Clinton's foundation. The Northeastern administration, keen to promote the institution as a leader in the new economy, saw this event as a boon to the University's growing reputation. As Northeastern President Joseph E. Aoun succinctly put it: "Northeastern is a global community of innovators and change-makers… It is the ideal institution to welcome representatives from around the world committed to social entrepreneurship and improving the human condition."[36] The convergence of the Clinton Global Initiative and a potential strike of cafeteria workers created a perfect storm. With one thousand young "global innovators" descending on the campus to discuss the world's social and environmental challenges, cafeteria workers saw an opportunity to highlight the haves and have-nots of the new information economy. Using social and earned media, workers issued a public challenge to Bill and Chelsea Clinton: Would they cross the picket line of striking Black and brown workers or move their event elsewhere? In the end, this question was not answered. University administrators and Chartwells managers did not want to see a repeat of the embarrassing strike that rocked Harvard a year previously on their campus.

* * *

University cafeteria workers in the Boston area have offered an example for how working people in the service industry can combat income inequality. Through workplace organizing, these cafeteria workers have been able to articulate clear, simple, and aspirational demands that have broad popular support on their campuses. They have done this through the unglamorous and tedious work of consensus-building. By having thousands of conversations with rank-and-file members, student leaders, and union leadership, dining hall workers have built super-majority organizations that organically develop aggressive demands aimed at solving both the quotidian and social economic challenges faced by service sector workers. The process of winning real representation at work has enabled these workers to directly address issues of racism, harassment, and discrimination. Freed from some of the daily indignities of the workplace, cafeteria workers continued to organize and build consensus around economic and social issues. This continued focus on organization and insistence on the transformative potential of worker militancy led to the strike campaigns at Harvard and Northeastern. More importantly, this focus enabled workers to win real financial and social victories. It is now accepted in Boston that cafeteria workers must earn a minimum of $35,000 a year and have affordable health benefits.

These victories also show the potential value of cross-generational and cross-class alliances in the new economy. In Boston, the higher education industry has placed itself at the center of technological and medical innovation, with research and development dollars flooding university campuses and affiliated start-up companies. Young people—students, professionals, and tech entrepreneurs—have flocked to the city to participate in this digital renaissance. While this influx of wealth has exacerbated the city's affordability crisis, the outpouring of support for organizing workers on university campuses has shown that many young people participating in the information economy do not want to be complicit in economic inequality. Instead, when workers took militant action for clear, aspirational demands, students and other young people joined the picket lines, rallies, and speak-outs. The willingness of millennials to participate alongside service workers demanding a fair share of the booming innovation economy demonstrates that broad alliances can be built to combat the worsening inequalities of the new economy.[37]

It remains to be seen if this combination of worker militancy and broad multigenerational cross-class alliances can be reproduced in other parts of the growing service industry. Workers in Silicon Valley—another increasingly unaffordable center of the innovation economy—have already borrowed a page from cafeteria workers in higher education. At dozens of tech companies, cafeteria workers have begun significant organizing campaigns using this same mix of organizational acumen and coalition-building. These campaigns have already won concessions from companies like Facebook, Intel, and Yahoo by emphasizing the contradictions between the Bay Area's often liberal social values and its unaffordability for working people.[38] In 2018, Marriott hotel workers in seven cities (including Boston and San Francisco) went on strike demanding major economic improvements in their contracts. Facing a ballooning cost of living in these major hubs of the new economy, workers neatly summarized their demands with the slogan "One Job Should Be Enough." Outside of UNITE HERE's organizational jurisdiction, there are hundreds of thousands of service industry workers who are living in poverty. Will other unions and worker centers engage these workers in the long and difficult process of building grassroots, majority-militant organizations capable of making aspirational demands?

This question is even more urgent in light of the Covid-19 pandemic. The economic fallout from this crisis has fallen heavily on the service sector, with public health restrictions causing mass layoffs in the industrial food service and hotel industries. In Boston, over 75 percent of Local 26's members are out of work as of September 2020, with bleak prospects of returning to work before the development and distribution of a vaccine. This unprecedented downturn puts the hard-fought gains of the past decade of organizing and striking in the hospitality industry in danger. Employers, keen to cut labor costs in a recession, will be tempted to take aim at the wages and benefits of unionized employees. In order to keep these gains, and to ensure a recovery that benefits working people, union members will have to build on their history of grassroots workplace organizing and militant mobilization. The pandemic need not dampen hospitality workers' aspirations, but in order to keep moving forward, they will have to get back in the streets. An economically just recovery is possible, but not without real demands from working people.

CHAPTER 6

Non-tenure-track Faculty

On the Vanguard of a Renaissance in the Boston Labor Movement?

Amy Todd

In December 2015, adjunct and part-time faculty at Brandeis University voted by a 5–4 margin to unionize, joining other faculty in the Boston metropolitan area organized by the Higher Education Chapter of the Service Employees International Union (SEIU) Local 509. The Boston campaign was a continuation of SEIU's Faculty Forward movement, launched in Washington, DC, in 2014, which seeks to organize non-tenure-track faculty regionally, across campuses in metropolitan areas including Washington DC, Boston, and Chicago.

The unionization of higher education faculty nationwide is a response to deteriorating working conditions in public and private colleges and universities. Traditionally, we associate higher education with a set of values related to the pursuit of knowledge for the public good, values often articulated in the mission statements of institutions. Over the past several decades, however, these have been gradually replaced with a new set of values related to generating revenue and cutting costs. This transition, commonly referred to as the rise of the "neoliberal university," is understood within the context of diminishing government support for educational institutions and students. While the reduction in state and federal support has had the most direct and obvious effect on public colleges and universities, private colleges and universities like Brandeis are also affected, since they rely heavily on public research grants, tax benefits, and public loans and grants for their students. As a result, it is now clear that the neoliberalization of higher education and its consequences on faculty extend to very selective and expensive private institutions. Much to the surprise of students, parents, and the faculty themselves, even at "elite" institutions in Greater Boston, many faculty members lack basic job security, a living wage, and benefits.[1]

Using Brandeis as a case study, this chapter provides an analytical framework for understanding the unionization of non-tenure-track faculty. At the time I joined the union organizing committee on campus, I had been an adjunct faculty member in graduate professional studies for ten years and, before that, a graduate student in the anthropology department at Brandeis. Following our successful unionization campaign, I remained involved in contract negotiation as well as efforts to build an active rank-and-file membership until the courses I taught were "retired" and I was no longer employed by the university. As a non-tenure-track faculty member at UMass Boston, I remain an active member of the Massachusetts Teachers Association, which represents faculty and staff in public schools (K–12) and public institutions of higher education in Massachusetts. I also continue to attend meetings and actions involving faculty organizers from public and private colleges and universities in Greater Boston and beyond. These experiences provide a broader perspective on labor in Greater Boston.

In 2015, Brandeis was only the most recent example of the successful unionization of non-tenure-track faculty at a private institution of higher education in Greater Boston. Adjuncts at Emerson College organized under the American Association of University Professors in 2001, and five other Greater Boston institutions (Boston University, Northeastern, Tufts, Lesley, and Bentley) had already been organized as part of the SEIU Faculty Forward campaign.[2] At most public colleges and universities in Massachusetts, non-tenure-track faculty, along with tenure-track and tenured faculty, K–12 educators, and staff are unionized in chapters of the Massachusetts Teachers Association. The unionization of graduate student workers at both public and private universities in Greater Boston has also been on the rise. The campaign at Brandeis, however, focused only on the unionization of non-tenure-track faculty.[3]

Among the private colleges and universities organized by the SEIU in Greater Boston, there is significant diversity in school size and in the proportion of classes taught by non-tenure-track faculty. With just five thousand students, Brandeis is a small player in comparison to

Northeastern University (twenty thousand) or Boston University (thirty-two thousand). Founded in 1948 by members of the American Jewish community, Brandeis publicly proclaims a commitment to social justice, a fact that the organizing team incorporated into our campaign. Despite its small size and newcomer status, Brandeis is one of the country's most selective and expensive colleges, costing $73,120 per year for tuition, fees, and room and board in 2020. While these and other factors contribute to a Brandeis-specific context for organizing, many of the themes to be discussed below are shared with other campuses.[4]

Neoliberalism and the Myth of an "Economics of Scarcity" in Higher Education

The so-called "adjunct" (a term to be explored in greater depth below) is a relatively recent addition to the post–World War II labor story that Green and Donahue tell in *Boston's Workers*. Writing before the adjunct crisis emerged in higher education, Green and Donahue focused on the manufacturing sector, where "vast changes," including relocation of production away from urban centers and automation resulted in an "economics of scarcity" that profoundly weakened industrial labor. Green and Donahue note that the service sector in Boston did not experience these changes, and thus service workers' unions remained relatively strong, especially in the civil services, where unions such as SEIU have built strength. In the 1970s, Green and Donahue observed a general lack of union power "in the city's large universities, insurance companies, publishing houses, and hospitals."[5]

Interestingly, the "economics of scarcity" in industry described by Green and Donahue does not apply to higher education faculty. Though higher education has experienced its own "vast changes" that have weakened labor, unlike in industry, there has so far been no major relocation of "production" (teaching and scholarship) from urban centers, to other parts of the country or the world where labor is weak. And while higher education is undergoing technological changes, including the introduction of classes taught entirely online, predictions that Massive Open Online Courses (MOOCs) and automated grading would one day displace faculty have not (yet) come to fruition.[6]

In fact, contrary to the supply and demand narrative reproduced in many well-intentioned articles about the "adjunct crisis," higher education has experienced substantial *growth* since World War II, beginning with the GI Bill, which was instrumental in opening higher education to working class students and increasing the percentage of Americans with college degrees. And while the number of doctorates (potential faculty) awarded in the United States is on the rise, the Bureau of Labor Statistics 2017 *Occupational Outlook Handbook*, reports:

> Over the past five decades, college and university employment—both in terms of absolute numbers and as a percentage of total employment—has increased significantly. . . . In 2008, about 1.7 million of the people employed on campus were postsecondary teachers (that is, college professors and instructors). Their number is projected to increase to over 1.9 million—an increase of over 15 percent—from 2008 to 2018. Over the same period, employment in all occupations is projected to increase about 10 percent.

Notably, however, the Bureau of Labor Statistics also predicts that "in all fields, there is expected to be a limited number of full-time non-tenure and full-time tenure positions. Many colleges and universities are hiring more part-time positions."[7] This has certainly been the case at Boston-area colleges and universities, including Brandeis.

The replacement of tenure-track positions with non-tenure-track positions has occurred across the nation as universities adopt managerial strategies that prioritize reducing labor costs.[8] Adjunct and part-time faculty are generally paid far less than their tenure-stream colleagues and are often ineligible for employer-sponsored health insurance, retirement, and other benefits. Hiring adjuncts also allows administrators to fine-tune their budgets by canceling classes or simply not renewing appointments. The fact that faculty may be dismissed for any reason (or no reason at all) undermines academic freedom and, ultimately, faculty power. This, in turn, undermines the ability of tenure-stream faculty to resist the structural transformation of faculty labor.

Greater Boston remains a desirable place for education due to the presence of Harvard, MIT, and other high-status institutions as well as the technology and medical industries with which academia is closely associated. According to a 2018 Bureau of Labor Statistics report on Boston-area employment, the education-health-care sector is the number one employer in the "Boston–Cambridge–Nashua, Mass.–N.H. Metropolitan New England City and Town Area."[9] Colleges and universities in the Boston area have been expanding in terms of the real estate they occupy, student enrollment, and course and program offerings. What were relatively small institutions with specialized niches have grown in size and scope. Private colleges and universities have increased their summer and evening offerings and many private colleges, including Brandeis, Boston University, and Northeastern, have developed advanced degree programs for "mid-career professionals" in subjects such as management, bioinformatics, and, not surprisingly, higher education administration. Increasingly, these additional programs are offered entirely online and are taught by adjunct faculty.[10] Although the overall trend has been toward growth, a recent flurry of closures of very small liberal arts colleges in the Greater Boston area, some of which have been absorbed by larger universities, points to a potential shift in the market moving forward, a consequence of the decline in students graduating from Massachusetts high schools.

An economics of scarcity model might predict that the growth of an industry would lead to increasing power among workers. This, however, has certainly not happened in higher education. On the contrary, growth has occurred in tandem with the *degradation* of postsecondary teaching positions in many respects, including faculty governance, job security, working conditions, service load, and compensation. An example that went viral in social media was Southern Illinois University's solicitation of adjunct faculty into what they euphemistically called "zero-time" (meaning uncompensated) positions to assume such responsibilities as teaching, serving on thesis committees, and applying for grants.[11] This is just an extreme illustration of the seemingly counterintuitive fact that the growth of an industry may actually be correlated with the *degradation* of work in that industry.

Yet, despite evidence to the contrary, the myth persists that the adjunct crisis is the result of "perilous market conditions" creating an oversupply of teaching labor. While more applicants may be competing for tenure track openings than in the past, there is no evidence that the adjunct crisis can be resolved on the supply end. As Blaine Greteman notes, even if we were able to "adjust the size and structure of our graduate programs to improve the placement of our students in decent, satisfying jobs, inside or outside academe," this would not resolve the adjunct crisis.[12] The suggestion that adjuncts simply "withdraw their labor" and find jobs outside of academia also misses a critical point: the degradation of postsecondary teaching positions stems not from a lack of demand for classes *or* a glut of potential educators but from a qualitative and quantitative structural reconfiguration of faculty labor in response to budgetary priorities on the part of management.[13]

Following the postwar growth of higher education, institutions of higher learning entered what is often called a "neoliberal phase" caused by shrinking public investment in both public and private universities. This phase, which began in the 1970s, saw the outsourcing of essential campus functions, such as food services and custodial work, to private companies. At universities with graduate programs, graduate students have been increasingly used as a source of cheap and disposable labor in the guise of academic apprenticeship. Rising tuition, aggressive marketing campaigns, and increasing reliance on partnerships with for-profit corporations to generate revenue are also part of the neoliberal university.

Increasingly, faculty find themselves working as wage laborers rather than salaried professionals, a shift Zabel refers to as "proletarianization."[14] These faculty have little or no job security, a phenomenon labeled "contingency" and "precarity." In the past few years, with the growth of such companies as Uber and Airbnb, it has become clear that the "adjunctification" of faculty is just one example of a much larger phenomenon that is more generally referred to as the "freelance" or "gig" economy.[15] Terms such as "adjunctification" are now being applied to workers in other sectors, while "gigification" is now being applied to faculty in higher education. Given the overall decline of working conditions in the neoliberal university, the rise of faculty unions is hardly surprising.

The Unionization Campaign at Brandeis

Over the past three decades, Brandeis has been quietly increasing the proportion of teaching, research, and service work done by non-tenure-track faculty. The existence of a wide array of non-tenure-track titles suggests that this process was done piecemeal by departments and programs faced with staffing shortages but no "tenure lines" to fill them. In fact, one of the first tasks of the SEIU staff organizers and the emerging faculty organizing committee was to identify and decipher faculty titles. We examined the webpages of departments and programs and compiled a list of likely non-tenure-track faculty with titles ranging from the familiar (adjunct lecturer, visiting assistant professor, instructor) to the less familiar (visiting poet-in-residence, post-doctoral associate, senior scientist, and senior research associate). In the end, nineteen titles or categories were included in the bargaining unit: adjuncts; assistant adjunct professors; associate adjunct professors; adjunct associate professors; adjunct lecturers; adjunct professors; adjunct associate professors of the practice; instructors; senior instructors; lecturers; senior lecturers; part-time fellows; in-residence writers, poet, and artists; research professors; associate research professors; assistant research professors; professors, assistant professors, and associate professors outside the tenure structure; professors and associate professors of the practice who are not on multi-year contracts; and graduate students who teach courses beyond their stipend and are compensated on a per-course basis.

The campaign to build a union revealed a set of challenges, some of them anticipated, and other less so. The most predictable challenges stemmed from the lack of job security and the transient nature of adjunct work in general. Additional challenges arose from our efforts to organize faculty who teach exclusively online and therefore could not be contacted through the ordinary channels (outside of classrooms or during office hours). But faculty organizers were most surprised by challenges related to status differences among non-tenure-track faculty members. These challenges, each of which will be discussed below, are by no means unique to Brandeis; they are found in varying degrees on both private and public campuses in the Greater Boston area and beyond.

While the following discussion emphasizes the role of faculty members in the unionization campaign, it is important to recognize the essential role SEIU staff organizers played. Though they were not necessarily experienced in higher education organizing or the peculiarities of the Brandeis campus, they developed appropriate organizing strategies in collaboration with faculty, motivated us to press forward in the face of various setbacks, and did a substantial amount of actual outreach on campus. The faculty on the organizing committee often commented on the fact that without SEIU staff organizers, the campaign would not have succeeded.

Fear of Reprisal

Not surprisingly, many non-tenure-track faculty members were reluctant to visibly support, let alone participate in, the unionization drive. Even when they recognized the value of unions and believed unionizing would ultimately lead to protections against retaliation, they assessed their personal risks as too high to become involved in the campaign. One faculty member quietly told me in person that she was going to vote for the union but absolutely could not in any way be seen as pro-union by administration. Retaliation from her supervisor was, in this faculty member's opinion, certain and absolute. The job, though part-time and by many measures not well-compensated, was essential to her family's financial well-being. Despite her support for the campaign, she would not participate in any email correspondence about it, conduct outreach to other faculty members, or attend any meetings. Organizers reported many other faculty who supported the union but wished to remain invisible.

Most of the faculty who joined the organizing team (which included approximately ten active members) were exceptional in their willingness to assume risk and speak out publicly in support of the union. Throughout the process, we spoke to reporters from the two campus newspapers, the *Brandeis Hoot* and the *Brandeis Justice,* as well as the the *Boston Globe,* which has covered adjunct and graduate student unionization campaigns throughout Greater Boston.[16] We voiced our support for the union at a campus-wide speak-out on the plaza organized by the Brandeis Labor Coalition, a student group, and we engaged in direct one-on-one outreach to potential members. We also attended faculty dinners and orientations in order to publicize the campaign. For example, at the annual faculty dinner for the division of graduate professional studies (discussed below), three faculty members, including me, wore buttons supporting the union. During the standard round-robin introduction, each of us in turn publicly voiced our support for the union and encouraged the other faculty to sign union cards. Outside the dinner, we had set up a table with information on SEIU Faculty Forward, answered questions about the unionization campaign, and encouraged faculty to sign union cards on the spot, which several did.

Some of the most active members of the organizing committee, it should be noted, were relatively protected from retaliation. One had just signed a five-year contract with the university, which she felt would take her to retirement age. Others had nothing, or very little, to lose: One long-term faculty member had already been told that her contract, after ten years, was not going to be renewed, a decision she believed was related to her new boss' political views. Another faculty member, who was finishing up his doctorate, was on a one-year, non-renewable visiting assistant professorship.[17] In addition, he was teaching in the anthropology department, which had a pro-union culture and unanimous support from tenure-track faculty. Other members of the organizing team were Brandeis graduate students who anticipated moving on to other universities in the near future. And still others had seen their real wages decline and their working conditions deteriorate to the point where they were willing to risk losing their jobs altogether. Unfortunately, this meant that the organizing team began to dissolve shortly after winning our union. Nevertheless, the organizing committee did include long-term non-tenure-track faculty who were truly dependent on their positions at Brandeis to support themselves and their families. Understandably, some were reluctant to be highly visible in the campaign.

In addition to modeling courage, we planned a series of actions designed to build and publicize community allies. Tenure-stream faculty signed a petition supporting the campaign. Other unions on campus, including the food workers of UNITE HERE Local 26, also publicly supported the campaign. The student-run Brandeis Labor Coalition became a champion of the cause, organizing speak-outs and tabling to spread the word that many of their beloved teachers lacked decent pay, working conditions, and job security. The editorial boards of both campus newspapers endorsed the unionization campaign, as did the Brandeis Democrats. The Waltham City Council issued a resolution supporting fair wages and benefits for adjunct faculty at Brandeis and its Waltham neighbor, Bentley University, supporting the right of Waltham's adjuncts to form a union, and calling for a free and fair election process.[18] We also won support from parents of current students, alumni, and local faith leaders.

Perhaps the most successful aspect of the campaign emerged from the work of a small but very committed faculty-run communications committee whose members creatively used the university's own mission statement to build community support. They created the slogan "What Would Louis Do?" to draw attention to the fact that Justice Louis Brandeis, for whom the university is named, was a friend of labor. A Brandeis Faculty Forward Facebook page created and administered exclusively by faculty was populated with news items about injustices to non-tenure-track faculty, other university unionization campaigns, and calls for solidarity with non-tenure-track faculty and other workers in Greater Boston and beyond. These were interspersed with motivational posts and updates from our own campaign.

Organizing a Distributed Workforce: Challenges Presented by the Growth of Distance Learning

The second major challenge to organizing faculty at Brandeis is one that will certainly intensify in the future: the growth of online education. As Gottfried and Zabel observe, contingent faculty in general "are atomized.

With temporary jobs on a single campus or part-time positions on multiple ones, they have little chance of developing the workplace bonds that sustain concerted action."[19] On the surface, it would appear that this is even truer of online faculty. In fact, at other Boston area universities previously organized by SEIU, organizers decided not to tackle the challenge of organizing online faculty, leaving online programs out of the bargaining unit. As a faculty member who taught in an exclusively online program, graduate professional studies, I was committed to having GPS faculty included in the campaign and, eventually, in the bargaining unit. One of my roles was to modify traditional on-campus outreach tactics like classroom visits, tabling, and speak-outs to reach online faculty as far away as Toronto, San Francisco, and Dublin. As it turns out, the same technological tools that allow for a distributed faculty workforce can be used to bring them together. Outreach was accomplished fairly effectively through an eclectic strategy that employed LinkedIn, Facebook, Skype, text messaging, and live conferencing. In fact, I have observed an increase in use of these kinds of tools for bringing together even traditional faculty, who typically work from home on non-teaching days, during breaks between semesters, or while on sabbaticals.

It was also necessary to address the specific labor concerns of online faculty. For example, shortly before our campaign began, GPS began issuing contracts that granted the university the right to use the content of an online course in full or in part for any purpose. Many faculty expressed alarm at the fact that they might invest considerable time into developing an online course (which, to comply with GPS standards, had to include original faculty-authored material) only to have it turned over to another instructor. This move on the part of administration appears to have primed GPS faculty for unionization, making them some of the most active members of the organizing team. This was surprising even to me, given that GPS faculty rarely come to campus, are in many cases employed full-time outside of academia, and include a significant number with a managerial background. Though we were able to overcome some of these challenges, they persisted as we moved into contract negotiation and implementation.

During contract negotiation we faced a number of anti-union tactics that sought to divide distance-learning faculty from their on-campus colleagues. These included a set of justifications for paying distance-learning faculty less than on-campus faculty. Administrators tried to argue that online teaching is *easier* than on-campus teaching, a claim the faculty systematically countered with details of the work entailed in building and delivering an online course. Administration then claimed that online faculty should be paid less because, unlike on-campus faculty, they are not forced to live in the metro Boston area, where the cost of living is high. This argument should be filed away in the heads of all faculty organizers, as it clearly raises the specter of outsourcing to parts of the country, and even the world, where overall cost of living and, presumably, wages are lower. Contract implementation has been equally challenging for GPS faculty. As of the writing of this essay, we continue to fight to retain intellectual property rights and job security.

Growth of online education may remain one of the biggest challenges to organizing higher education faculty. SEIU's focus on higher education *regions* will need to grapple with the fact that a local university may well employ faculty living on the other coast or in other countries, as is the case with Brandeis.

Organizing the Credentialed Class

There are major differences between higher education teaching and other service-sector work with respect to the costs of entering the occupation, what Green and Donahue refer to as "capital-entry requirements." In an indirect manner, these costs pose significant barriers to organizing. Regardless of their class background, most faculty have post-graduate degrees, and many have PhDs. Depending on the discipline and terminal degree, capital-entry requirements, even for a temporary adjunct faculty position, involve years of education as well as research, writing, and teaching that is poorly compensated, if at all. The median number of years to finish a PhD in the humanities was 6.9 during the period 2003–2012.[20] In addition, all faculty, including those off the tenure track, engage in continuous professional development, conducting research, attending conferences, and doing creative work. For most non-tenure-track faculty, not only is professional development uncompensated, but it often involves unreimbursed expenses. Though probably not typically seen as "capital-entry requirements" by the faculty themselves, insofar as these and other activities factor into hiring decisions, they function as such.

At Brandeis University and other Boston-area colleges and universities, many non-tenure-track faculty closely identify themselves and their colleagues with their academic credentials, from degrees to professional association memberships to publications and creative work. This professional identification appears to contribute to a failure to identify as "labor." As Zabel observed of adjuncts generally:

> The majority of college and university teachers are members of the working class, since they are compelled by financial need to sell their labor. Unfortunately, most—including the misnamed "adjuncts"—do not see themselves this way, nor are they regarded as workers by society as a whole. . . . The ideology of professionalism, and the widespread tendency to identify workers with the industrial working class are stubborn impediments to class consciousness.[21]
>
> While faculty may express sympathy and appreciation for workers who hold positions with lower capital-entry requirements than themselves, such as clerical, custodial, and food-services staff, they do not see themselves as equals at work in the sense of sharing a common interest in creating a healthy and just working environment. Even if they are lower income, non-tenure-track faculty possess "symbolic capital" that puts them in association with other people who hold jobs with high capital-entry requirements (i.e. "professionals"). Building solidarity across deeply internalized divisions proves extremely challenging in both faculty unionization campaigns and campaigns to engage faculty rank and file in union activities and actions affecting other service sector workers.

While the inability to "connect" with non-academic workers on campus was frustrating, it was not surprising. Nor was it immediately or obviously relevant to our unionization campaign, though as I will argue in the conclusion, in fact, it has a very deep relevance which needs to be addressed. What *was* surprising was the degree to which *more secure* non-tenure-track faculty identified with their *tenured* colleagues while distancing themselves, in rhetoric and action, from "the adjuncts." In other words, as will be discussed below, the hierarchy that has emerged *among* non-tenure-track faculty seriously hinders organizing.

We often hear that academia has become a "two-tier system" with adjuncts and other non-tenure-track faculty on the bottom and tenure track and tenured faculty on the top. Recognizing the existence of two tiers—and the fact that those below are not on a pathway to the top— was an important stage in the development of labor consciousness among adjunct faculty. But the situation at Brandeis and many other Boston-area institutions suggests that something more complex, and more detrimental to union work (not to mention to the tenure system), is occurring. This is hinted at in prior analyses of adjunct organizing. In *Reclaiming the Ivory Tower*, Joe Berry divided the approximately seventy-five job titles he identified for higher education faculty not into tenure-stream and non-tenure stream faculty but into "regular" and "contingent."[22]

While in some ways this is a more useful division, by preserving the two-tier model we fail to recognize a major threat to organizing faculty. At Brandeis, as in academia in general, the proliferation of academic titles over the past thirty years reflects the emergence of a third tier below tenure-stream faculty but above adjuncts. This third tier, though not explicitly recognized by Berry, is evident in his identification of "salaried," "core," and "continuing" faculty, titles which imply, but do not guarantee, reasonable assurance of work in the future.[23]

The use of words like "above" and "below" indicates a hierarchy in terms of compensation and job security, but not a chain of command. Among non-tenure-track faculty, the higher-ups do not typically direct the work activities of the lower-downs, nor do they take responsibility for them. However, microaggressions, such as treating colleagues as invisible or dismissing their contributions to teaching, research and service, create a *de facto* pecking order which adds to the pain of those who are already experiencing poor compensation and job insecurity. Furthermore, insofar as the culture of academia is attached to a notion of meritocracy, faculty at the bottom may internalize the view that their position is a reflection of personal inadequacy.[24] Even if they recognize the structural violence inherent in a neoliberal university, regular interaction with their more-fortunate colleagues on the tenure track is demoralizing. Of course, these same circumstances, once shared and processed with others, can be the source of empowerment, as we saw at Brandeis.

The existence of three tiers (two categories of non-tenure-track faculty plus the tenure-stream faculty) also creates an opportunity for administrators to weaken unionization campaigns through classic divide-and-conquer tactics. At Brandeis, approximately six weeks before the union election, the Faculty Senate (comprised of tenure-stream faculty and "contract faculty" non-tenure-track faculty on multiyear contracts with benefits) distributed a two-and-a-half-page "Union Process Information Brief" to faculty based on "informational discussions" with Brandeis University Executive Administration and Legal Counsel. Though the stated intent was to provide "factual information" about the unionization process while taking a "hands off" approach, much of the document had an alarmist tone that appeared to be specifically targeted at the contract faculty who occupy the middle tier between tenure-track faculty and adjuncts. A section entitled "Responses to Recently Asked Questions" stated that it was "difficult to anticipate" the "potential net costs" to contract faculty. The document also left open the possibility that "benefits or sabbatical eligibility could go down under a union contract," stating "There is no ability to speculate about this question. The Brandeis Administration does not represent the SEIU in that question. That is part of the collective bargaining process." Perhaps the most anti-union sentiment expressed in the document was advice for faculty who did not wish to interact with union organizers: "If you ever feel that you are in a situation that you feel someone is inhibiting your ability to be on this campus and work you need to call public safety." Overall, the union was presented not as a group of mobilized faculty but as an all-powerful third party that had the potential to make things unpleasant for, if not endanger, faculty, particularly those in the middle tier, who already enjoyed relatively decent pay, job security, and benefits.

As noted, the Faculty Senate at Brandeis includes tenured faculty, pre-tenured faculty, and non-tenure-track contract faculty. Tenure-stream faculty had been involved in the unionization campaign only as allies. At this point, however, contract faculty *were* part of the unionization campaign and potential bargaining unit members. In fact, two members of the organizing committee were contract faculty. The Union Process Information Brief, though nominally created and distributed by the Faculty Senate, contained sophisticated language typical of anti-union communications issued by university administrators during faculty and graduate student unionization campaigns. Specifically, the language appears to have been carefully crafted to lead contract faculty members to believe that contract negotiation might result in the loss of their existing benefits. Presenting contract negotiation as one-sided, with the union calling the shots and administration's hands tied, also had the potential to tap into a generalized fear expressed by a few faculty members that a union might demand such high wages and costly benefits that the administration would be forced to lay off faculty or even shut down programs. But none of the SEIU contracts that had already been negotiated at Greater Boston universities led to layoffs or cuts in salary or benefits. Administration could easily have reassured faculty of their commitment to protecting existing benefits, a commitment the union itself had already made, but instead chose to leave the question ominously open. Overall, while it is not possible to say exactly to what extent administration authored portions of the Union Process Information Brief, it clearly served as a union-busting tool.

At about the same time as its release, a letter to the editor from a full-time, non-tenure-track, contract faculty member was published in the *Brandeis Hoot*. This faculty member asserted that Brandeis was unique in its positive treatment of non-tenure faculty. "I am proud to be part of a university committed to social justice which has done and is doing what is right, with or without a union," she concluded. A reply to her letter from a tenured professor challenged each of her assertions, including that of Brandeis's uniqueness: "In contrast to what is written above, I don't believe that the University is committed to social justice, and certainly not any more than most any university is—'social justice' just happens to be the centerpiece of the University's branding mechanism."[25]

Not surprisingly, a few days later, a group of contract faculty requested a meeting with faculty organizers and SEIU staff. Though many had signed petitions in favor of unionization and some had even signed union pledge cards, a small but vocal number of contract faculty expressed strong opposition to joining the union themselves. Some objected to joining a union at all, viewing themselves as professionals, not laborers. Others said they might have considered joining a teachers' union, such as the National Education Association or the American Association of University Professors, but they felt that joining a union of service workers was inappropriate. Some who had signed union pledge cards claimed they had not understood that if the faculty voted to unionize, they themselves would become part of the bargaining unit. Some said that paying union dues would be "subsidizing the adjuncts." But the most common concern, not surprisingly, given the Union Process Information Brief, was that unionizing with adjuncts would threaten their privileged status at Brandeis. As one faculty member put it, she had spent years working to achieve a long-term contract, participation in faculty governance, decent pay, and a sabbatical. She did not need to pay union dues for these things and did not think it was fair that others might acquire them through collective bargaining.

Not all contract faculty agreed with these objections. In fact, one of the most outspoken members of the organizing committee at that meeting was the contract faculty member who, after ten years of service, had not had her contract renewed. This faculty member reminded her peers that they too were vulnerable to being let go without just cause if, for example, a new department head had different academic or political priorities than his or her predecessor, or a student complained about the content being covered in class. A contract faculty member might be subject to discrimination or harassment or might be displaced by the friend of a tenured faculty member in need of work. Without the protection of a union, any non-tenure-track faculty member whose multiyear contract is not renewed has little or no recourse.

Despite the power of these arguments, it became clear to the organizing committee that the inclusion of full-time contract faculty would jeopardize the election. In the end, they were excluded from the bargaining unit and they remain nonunionized. Since the growth of a "three-tier system" is likely part of a national trend in higher education, understanding and responding to resistance to unionization from those who "enjoy passing" as tenured is important.[26]

Conclusion

The story of unionization of higher education faculty is remarkable for several reasons. First, the rise of unions at universities runs counter to the overall trend over the past fifty years, during which the percentage of workers in unions has shrunk.[27] Second, it is remarkable that the recent growth of unions in higher education is happening at private colleges and universities, where overall rates of unionization have been lower than in the public sector. It is also occurring in a segment of the population that once belonged firmly to the professional or credentialed class, potentially bringing together groups that would not otherwise work together in solidarity. Finally, non-tenure-track faculty have the potential to reach a large audience, including our students, the media (adjuncts include many prolific writers), and one another, as adjuncts often teach in multiple universities. Adjuncts thus have the capacity to shape public opinion in the debate about unions.

Each of these remarkable aspects of unionization, however, is associated with serious challenges. Though adjuncts are poised to shape public debate over unions, they do not easily connect with non-academic workers on or off campus, a problem that is likely to increase in the future since, as unionization rates shrink overall, fewer faculty are likely to have come from a union background, and to have personal experience taking collective action. In addition, as higher education becomes less accessible to working-class students, future faculty are even less likely to include members with first-hand experiences with unions. A lack of understanding of unions among non-tenure-track faculty was acutely visible in the questions and concerns raised by the contract faculty at Brandeis. The three-tier problem may therefore represent a significant threat to unionization of non-tenure-track faculty.

It must also be acknowledged that winning a union is not even half the battle. Contract negotiation and implementation, as well as maintaining a vibrant rank and file, continues to challenge faculty organizers at each of the Boston area campuses organized under the SEIU. At Brandeis, the fragility of the original organizing team was particularly unfortunate. Of the original members, one very committed member did not have her contract renewed, two graduate students and a visiting assistant professor found positions elsewhere, one long-term faculty member in graduate professional studies quit when he was excluded from participating in a program he had been instrumental in developing, and this author, after ten years of employment, had the three classes I taught "retired," leaving me with the option of reapplying for a position from scratch or considering myself passively laid off. Other formerly active members of the organizing team drifted away as family and other commitments demanded their attention.

Having enumerated many challenges of organizing non-tenure-track faculty, I would like to end this essay on a positive note. Besides winning a union, this campaign has led to the forging of interpersonal relationships on and between campuses that did not previously exist. As Gottfried and Zabel note, "If collective bonds are to come into being, they must be forged, at least initially, not in the process of work, but in the course of struggle."[28] What was once a social void, consisting of numerous non-tenure-track faculty working in isolation, enduring financial and other indignities alone, is morphing into a vocal, empowered, and even joyous community. Non-tenure-track faculty members in Greater Boston are bridging divides across academic disciplines and across universities, congregating in backyards, bars, and coffee shops, taking over university and online spaces, and marching in solidarity with other campus workers and workers beyond the university. If non-tenure-track faculty are indeed going to serve as a vanguard in the renaissance of the labor movement, nourishing this nascent community must be a high priority.

CHAPTER 7

Raise Up Massachusetts

Experiment in a New, Universal Labor Movement

Harris Gruman

The Trump election, while an alarming lurch to the right in itself, is the culmination of two long-term, intertwined trends in American, and to a large extent global, politics. As the increasingly embattled union movement continues to lose effective bargaining power for workers, the postwar trend of shared prosperity has given way to skyrocketing wealth for a small elite and income inequality. The Trump regime simply poses the existential question to the labor movement and our democracy in the most urgent terms.

Raise Up Massachusetts, a labor-community-faith coalition of over sixty organizations, has a twofold mission with a critical edge: to raise up Massachusetts as an alternative to right-wing national politics, but first to raise up Massachusetts to actually *be* an alternative in reality. That is, our state's dirty secret, that the Commonwealth of Massachusetts is both a bastion of liberal values *and* a case study in growing inequality, reveals the depths of the crisis of American liberalism, a crisis that cost Democrats the Congress, and now the Presidency.[1]

The *Boston Globe* regularly asks: If Massachusetts were a nation, how rich would it be? They have found it to be the fourth-richest nation per capita in the world, after Norway, Qatar, and Switzerland.[2] At the same time, Massachusetts has one of the most extreme levels of income inequality in the US. The map of relative inequality has great political significance: in election season we obsessively scan those blue and red color-coded state maps, and have come to expect a pattern, years-old now, of a blue west coast and northeast, with blue islands in the southwest and northern Midwest. But the color-coded map below—in which the darker the state, the worse its income inequality—bears no consistent resemblance to that pattern. Instead, deep-blue California contends with deep-red Texas in inequality; ultra-liberal Massachusetts competes with survivalist Wyoming. Is this the world Trump voters were intuitively sensing while we scoured data on 538.com?

Figure 7.1: Map of US income inequality

For the past forty years, Massachusetts, leading the national trend, has had an extremely unbalanced economy, one in which 85 percent of all income and wealth gains go to the top 1 percent. It was not always that way. The postwar social contract of union jobs and high marginal tax rates (see the columns under "1947-1973" below) favored shared prosperity.[3] The national decline of unions has severed the previous link between productivity growth and rising wages. The new levels of profit have, in turn, fueled a forty-year political assault on progressive taxation and a growing attack on social insurance (e.g., health care, retirement, unemployment).

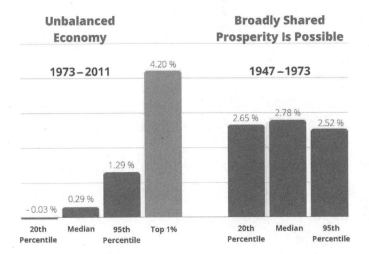

Figure 7.2: Massachusetts economy: from shared prosperity to extreme inequality

Union Membership Percent of All US Workers 1948 to 2010

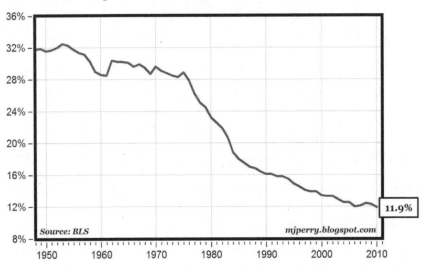

Figure 7.3: Decline of percentage of workers in unions 1948 to 2010

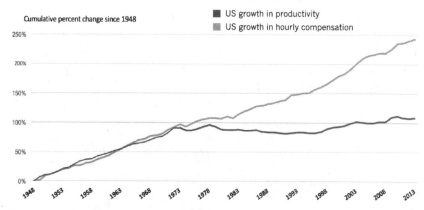

Figure 7.4: Productivity goes up while wages stay flat.

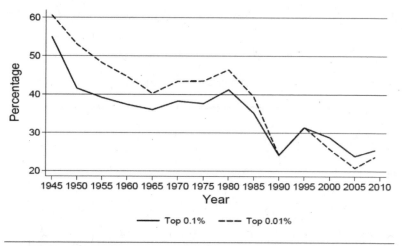

Source: CRS calculations using Internal Revenue Service (IRS) Statistics of Income (SOI) information.

Figure 7.5: Decline of effective tax rates on the wealthy

In 2013–2014, Raise Up Massachusetts waged an all-out campaign to reverse that trend, winning an increase in the minimum wage from $8 per hour to $11 per hour in the legislature, and paid sick days for all workers at the ballot. This labor-community coalition sees itself as nothing less than a new type of union for the one million lowest-income workers in the state, filling the void left by declining enrollment in traditional unions. Our victories represented a three-year contract with 10 percent raises each year and a new sick-time benefit—a great contract by any union standard these days. In 2017, when this contract was fully phased-in, Raise Up fought to renew the contract by placing a $15 minimum wage and a universal paid family and medical leave program on the ballot. That pressure led in 2018 to victory on both after an aggressive legislative campaign, greatly improving "the contract" for low- to moderate-wage workers here. Now Raise Up is challenging the state's one-hundred-year history of regressive taxation. How was this accomplished? Is this a model for a new universal labor movement, one that mobilizes civil society across sectors? If so, how will it be sustainable, organizationally and financially?

The Raise Up Model

Raise Up is the latest in a series of economic justice coalitions focused statewide in Massachusetts. From 1998 until 2006, the Working Family Agenda (WFA) forged an alliance between labor and working-class community advocates and progressive and so-called "lunch-bucket" legislators around a fairly long list of winnable economic justice bills and budget priorities. While many of the victories were small, they did materially help the most vulnerable, with initiatives like reducing welfare work requirements for single mothers and students and piloting an emergency rental voucher program. But the WFA also won some sweeping reforms, often in coordination with a short-term, single-issue coalition. The most significant of these were 1999's temporary $100 million increase in child-care funding, two increases in the minimum wage, in 1999 and again in 2005, a $1 billion progressive tax package centered around closing the capital gains loophole in 2002, and the Massachusetts health-care reform of 2006, often misnamed "Romney Care" to earn credit for "bipartisan" cooperation. Despite some impressive work in coalition democracy (the WFA met in the State House in a quasi-parliamentary atmosphere with open debate and voting), the grab-bag of issues and the always-simmering tension between legislators and activists gave the coalition an overly loose and fluctuating level of commitment. As a result, the next coalition, the Campaign for our Communities, or CfoC (2007–2013), still made up of labor and community advocates but no longer directly including elected officials, went to the opposite extreme of focusing on the one overriding unity issue of the WFA years: growing the state resource pie through "fair and adequate revenue." This coalition, however, found itself running up against the inertia in the Democratic-dominated legislature even as income and wealth inequality were rapidly worsening. Its main victories were either vitiated by trade-offs (instituting combined reporting to limit corporate tax avoidance was coupled with an overall reduction in the business tax rate) or purely defensive (defeating ballot initiatives in 2008 to repeal the income tax and, in 2010, to cut the sales tax by half).

After the decisive defeat of a coalition-backed progressive tax bill in the spring of 2013, key coalition members, including labor groups like the AFL-CIO and SEIU, and community organizations like the Coalition for Social Justice, Progressive MA, and the Massachusetts Communities Action Network, a statewide interfaith consortium, reviewed the lessons from the WFA and CfoC experiences. One lesson from the two coalitions was to avoid both a laundry list of priorities *and* a single win-or-lose focus (revenue). This meant a limited set of no more than three priorities, each with broadly significant outcomes and a path to victory. On the leverage side, we recalled the only time we proactively used the ballot-initiative process to win something big against legislative inertia and powerful interests. In 2005, the health-care reform bill was only taken up in earnest by the State House after WFA groups and legislators coalesced with the Affordable Care Today issue coalition to qualify a progressive version of reform for the following year's ballot. From that point on, winning sweeping affordable health-care became a question of when, not if. Therefore, the core of what would become Raise Up Massachusetts committed itself to a proactive ballot initiative strategy.

In the summer of 2013 two popular wage and benefit reforms, increasing the minimum wage and earned sick time, became the heart of the unity campaign. The minimum wage, though repeatedly raised by the earlier coalitions, had always been allowed to degrade with inflation to low national levels, and the earned sick time legislation had been stymied by the legislature for ten years. Signature-gathering to qualify both for the ballot re-energized the coalition, broadened it, and mobilized member organizations' activists on an unprecedented scale. On the labor side, SEIU's capacity to collect tens of thousands of signatures at the neighborhood level (elaborated further below) was augmented by the AFL-CIO's collections at Labor Council and affiliate meetings, along with street-level work by union activists from AFT and UAW. Community organizations with strong volunteer bases, like the Coalition for Social Justice, Progressive MA, Neighbor to Neighbor, and Jobs with Justice, hit supermarkets, athletic fields, transit hubs, and town dumps. And the state's largest interfaith consortium, Massachusetts

Communities Action Network, collected an amazing 72,000 signatures from their congregations and communities. By late fall of that year, Raise Up had collected over 265,000 signatures, far more than the 65,000 needed to certify each question, and the most collected by all grassroots efforts (that is, without outside, paid signature gatherers) in the state's history. Significantly, that total was collected one-third by unions, one-third by community organizations, and one-third by faith groups.

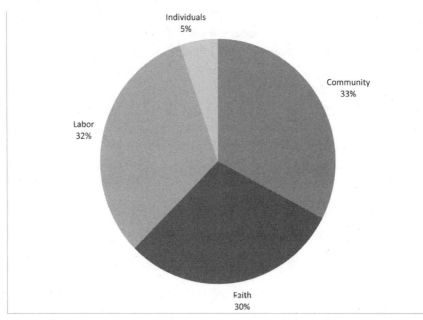

Figure 7.6: Signature collections by type of organization

With both questions certified for the November 2014 ballot, Raise Up rallied its now activated labor, community, and faith volunteer base around pressing our agenda in the legislature, first by fending off an attempt to trade the higher minimum wage for a weakened unemployment insurance system, then winning passage of an $11 per hour minimum wage (50 cents higher than that proposed in the ballot question, in exchange for a smaller increase in the tipped-worker minimum wage than was proposed). The earned-sick-time ballot provision went on to win handily, by 59 to 41 percent.

With these two sweeping victories—establishing what was then the highest statewide minimum wage and what remains one of the most comprehensive paid-sick-time policies in the nation—Raise Up had in fact negotiated a statewide contract for the million lowest-wage workers in the state, or one-third of the workforce. In December 2014, with a three-year phase-in of our victories in progress, Raise Up began defining the next contract fight for 2017. Unlike the previous coalitions, which moved from issue to issue, Raise Up would more closely emulate union work. This means conceiving of the low-wage workforce (and sometimes, as in the case of paid family and medical leave, the working class as a whole) as engaged in an ongoing struggle for a fair stake in society, making steady progress in improving wages and benefits. For example, once a group of low-wage workers like janitors, home-care workers, or child-care providers is unionized within SEIU, over a series of contract fights they move well beyond minimum wage without benefits to living wages with health and retirement security. In only ten years, SEIU 32BJ's Boston-area janitorial contract, covering seventy-five hundred workers, now earns members $20 per hour with full family health coverage. Applying that union model, Raise Up aims to build on the gains of each campaign while marching toward shared prosperity and an economy that works for everyone.

The power of this "new labor movement" emanates from pooling the three organizational bases of the working class: unions, community organizations, and faith groups. By organizing working people where they work through their union, where they live through their community organization, and where they worship through their congregation, we significantly broaden and deepen their connection to the movement. Even those unorganized at work are quite often active in their neighborhood or place of worship, and many working people belong to more than one of these kinds of communities. In Lynn, Massachusetts, a Raise Up activist collecting signatures announced: "I'm a member of 1199SEIU at Union Hospital, I'm a member of Neighbor to Neighbor in my ward, and I attend St. Stephen's Church, which is part of the interfaith alliance." Though a Dominican immigrant recently earning under $15 per hour, he is as fluent in progressive US politics as any *Nation* reader. The depth of self-identity with the labor movement has always been a key to its strength and sustainability, and the unity of union, neighborhood, and congregation greatly expands and reinforces that self-identity.

Combining these three sites of organizing, as well as the diverse range of organizations within each, requires a system of shared work based on accountability. Raise Up has used open-source computer systems, including online voter files, documents, and reporting systems to pioneer a truly collaborative approach to big campaigns. Activists report signature or canvass results via web forms that update results by organization, geography, and individual in real time. Besides making management of such campaigns easier, it also stimulates over-achievement by coalition partners through a spirit of friendly competition and transparent accountability. Below is a sample portion of an online google doc showing progress by organization toward their goal in numerical and percentage terms (the names of groups have been hidden here for confidentiality):

Table 7.1			
Goal	Reported	%-to-Goal	Organization
500	501	100%	Community
3,500	4,861	139%	Labor
5,000	4,959	99%	Labor
500	189	38%	Community
1,000	684	68%	Community
2,000	452	23%	Labor
2,000	1,037	52%	Community
300	489	163%	Community
17,500	19,797	113%	Community
600	737	123%	Community
500	404	81%	Community
2,000	1,365	68%	Labor
4,000	4,505	113%	Faith
700	816	117%	Labor
5,000	6,020	120%	Labor
300	217	72%	Community
2,000	471	24%	Community
2,700	2,709	100%	Community
15,000	22,129	148%	Faith
200	142	71%	Community
2,000	1,902	95%	Faith
5,000	3,705	74%	Labor
1,000	1,152	115%	Community
1,000	705	71%	Community
20,000	28,678	143%	Labor
5,000	1,443	29%	Community
12,001	9,331	78%	Community
500	347	69%	Community
2,500	1,452	58%	Community

500	232	46%	Community
15,000	15,599	104%	Labor
2,500	2,173	87%	Labor
10,000	5,435	54%	Labor
1,500	1,563	104%	Labor
2,500	503	20%	Labor
1,000	892	89%	Labor
1,000	669	67%	Faith
2,000	1,589	79%	Community

In this way, Raise Up is using smart technology to enhance traditional shoe-leather political organizing and create a unified campaign out of diverse and independent groupings.

Decision-making within the coalition is structured in a way reminiscent of the Working Family Agenda. The Grassroots Coalition, made up of all active partner organizations (each with one vote), forms the coalition's legislature, choosing priority issues/campaigns, deciding key components of each policy initiative and whether to accept or reject compromises offered by state government. The Steering Committee is the coalition's executive branch, running day-to-day operations like staffing, budgeting, fundraising, and IT, and formulating and executing campaign strategy. It is comprised of the fifteen or so organizations that either make the greatest commitments of funding and activists (for example, the Massachusetts Teachers Association and the American Federation of Teachers, the Boston-area SEIU locals, MA Communities Action Network, Coalition for Social Justice, Progressive MA, and Jobs with Justice) or represent a large sectoral interest (like the AFL-CIO, the C-3 Voter Table of urban community groups, and the progressive Alliance for Business Leadership).

The current campaign was chosen and refined in a multistage process. First, forty or so major initiatives were presented to the Grassroots Coalition and evaluated in terms of breadth, significance, and viability. Then coalition partners voted for their top three priorities. Results were presented and analyzed to properly assess support across similar initiatives. The three top issues were approved as priority campaigns by a vote of the coalition. Next, the Steering Committee oversaw an extensive battery of research on public opinion about the three priorities to suggest refinements of Raise Up's specific demands for each. For example, this research informed the decision that progressive tax reform that met our economic analysis and mission—that is, reforms that taxed the biggest winners in our economy, the same ones currently taxed at the lowest effective levels—would also be pegged only to investments in public education and colleges and transportation infrastructure. As our pollster noted after conducting focus groups with working-class voters: "The face of economic security in Massachusetts today is a reliable way to get to work and a college education without lifelong costs." These specifics were also put to a vote of the whole coalition before drafting policy language. The resulting three-part campaign to win a millionaire's tax, a $15 minimum wage, and a paid family and medical leave policy reactivated the breadth and balance of the New Deal approach to shared prosperity. No wonder Raise Up is drawing the attention and ire of organized corporate and investor interests, as evidenced by a 2017 *Boston Business Journal* cover story, which declared: "Raise Up Massachusetts. It's doubtful that any three words inspire more dread and frustration among the state's major business advocacy groups than that trio."[4]

Raise Up Grassroots Coalition debates policy for the 2018 ballot

One of the most interesting developments of this intensification of the struggle over the economic direction of our state is an invigorated state legislative response. The Joint Committee of Labor and Workforce

Development has even taken the unprecedented step of calling for tripartite negotiations between Raise Up, the business lobby, and the legislature to craft a mutually acceptable paid family and medical leave program before the measure reaches the ballot. Victories driven by the threat of ballot initiative on statewide cross-sectoral demands by Raise Up are forcing new levels of economic negotiation in state politics.

Deepening the Model

The success of the Raise Up model depends on having a rich context of reinforcing approaches and institutions within the labor movement and at the local and regional levels. Before Raise Up came together, labor had been building strong community labor connections through affiliate membership programs like the AFL-CIO's Working America and strong local coalition tables like Community Labor United and Lynn United for Change, discussed by Jeff Crosby in this volume. I will highlight two that I am particularly familiar with from my work at SEIU Massachusetts: SEIU Community Action and the Fast Food Committee.

While canvassing their members in the low-income neighborhoods of Massachusetts' cities, SEIU locals representing home and health-care workers (Local 1199), child-care providers (Local 509), janitors (Local 32BJ), and municipal employees (Local 888) found they had members in nearly every building, and that their members' neighbors shared similar economic issues and political values. The SEIU State Council decided to start canvassing everyone in those precincts, signing them up as affiliate "SEIU Community Action" (SCA) members and engaging them in our issue and election work, sometimes even taking up issues motivated by these nonunion members, such as affordable housing and quality schools. The dual goal was to create a sense of membership that superseded the distinction between organized and unorganized working-class neighbors, while intensifying the political strength of working people at the electorally-meaningful level of voting jurisdiction (e.g., precinct, ward, or city). Over the six years of this program, we have signed up eighteen thousand SCA members, nearly 20 percent the size of our traditional union membership in the state, and even organized two new union bargaining units out of these affiliate members. A particularly telling example of the success of this approach was its application in 2012, the year labor progressive Elizabeth Warren won her Senate seat.

In the first half of the year, SCA focused on defending Medicaid from the Wisconsin Republican Paul Ryan's congressional drive to cut its funding through federal block grants. In our low-income communities we could unite families (most of whom are insured by MassHealth, the state Medicaid Agency), seniors (who need long-term care through Medicaid), and workers (10 percent of whom in our targeted cities actually work for the Medicaid program). Canvasses, rallies, call-ins, and postcard drives lifted up Medicaid as essential to our community and as a litmus test for federal elected officials and candidates. SCA teamed up with other low-income political organizations from the coalition to cover the hundred and twenty-five lowest-income precincts in the state for voter education, registration, and mobilization. Materials were jointly branded in each neighborhood as SEIU Community Action, Working America, Neighbor to Neighbor, Coalition for Social Justice, etc., and were delivered face-to-face at voters' doors by an army of over a hundred political organizers from the collaborating organizations. On Election Day in November 2012, statewide turnout topped the 2008 Obama surge vote by 2.5 percent, defying all predictions. Further analysis found that our low-income cities were 7 percent over the 2008 surge, and our target one hundred twenty-five precincts were 14 percent over the surge vote, revealing how a statewide uptick that carried Elizabeth Warren out of recount territory had come barreling out of the lowest-income neighborhoods of the state.

Another nontraditional form of labor-movement recruitment has been fast food organizing around the Fight for $15, which is a national SEIU initiative with a local strength in the Boston area. Despite the uncertainty of ever winning a traditional union for these workers, the SEIU fast food committees have brought a diverse and militant worker group into the heart of the union, one which helps drive the demands for a broad movement of economic, racial, and immigrant justice. Raise Up's focus on the minimum wage and sick time were based on the overlap of these nonunion worker members of SEIU in coalition with their neighbors in other community and faith groups. The other national affiliate worker program, Faculty Forward, focuses on low-wage workers with the highest educational credentials, adjunct and non-tenure-track professors, but in the Boston area, SEIU has brought most of these workers into traditional NLRB-recognized bargaining units.

Finally, regionalizing the Raise Up coalition at the level of key areas of the state is crucial to its ability to build activist power as broadly and deeply as possible. Several counties have strong local Raise Up tables, usually anchored in one of the state's larger cities, like Worcester, Lynn, Springfield, and Fall River. These tables, mirroring to the extent possible the makeup of the statewide coalition, help intensify the work of collecting signatures and the in-district lobbying of legislators, and they are crucial for ballot-initiative field campaigns. These intermediate levels of organizing—affiliate member programs and regional tables—have helped Raise Up open the labor movement to universal participation of both organized and unorganized workers and their families. They are also a connective tissue that enriches the more transactional relations between organizations at a statewide level.

Some Key Challenges: Lessons and Opportunities

The most important challenge for Raise Up and for a renewed labor movement in general is ensuring that it is grounded in the working class, at least to the extent that the traditional labor movement has been, while doing so more inclusively than in the past in regard to race, gender, and occupation. Since income is such a key measure of class and work status in our society, and funding is a major force in political power, I will begin with the challenge of financing the movement, which is only a part of the broader issue of democratic participation.

Unions are almost the only vehicle expressing the financial power of working people, funded as they are by the dues, fees, and voluntary contributions of their members. Other active and potential political players are funded in the main by the 1 percent: that is, nearly all candidates for federal and statewide office (and many for more local offices), as well as most 501(c)(3) and (c)(4) organizations of the right or the left. Raise Up's most staunchly progressive and effective community partners receive a majority of their funding from what I call "the left wing of the 1 percent." Even an exceptionally grassroots-funded campaign like that of Bernie Sanders relies much more than unions do on middle-class and upper-middle-class donors. The decline of union density is simply excluding more and more working people from financial participation in politics altogether, a situation that will further exacerbate the disconnect between political debate and working-class concerns.

Union financing, especially of political action, is viewed in a highly distorted way, most unfortunately on the left. Wealthy funders speak about union money as if it came from sources more unsavory than their own inherited wealth or capital gains. Community organizations treat it as less legitimate than their donations from foundations and rich "angels." The press harps on Raise Up's campaigns as "union-funded" as if that were more suspect than a self-funding billionaire candidate. So I ask them: where does the union's money come from? One hundred percent from our members. And for SEIU, that means mostly from low-wage workers like child-care and home-care providers, hospital orderlies, and building cleaners. Raise Up's ballot questions are not funded by "Big Labor"; they are funded by low-wage workers and teachers.

The membership's role in deciding how their money is used is a particularly acute question in relation to political spending. To the extent that dues are used for representation and servicing in the workplace and the negotiation of contracts, their allocation is fairly uncontroversial, but how members' contributions to their locals' political committees or their locals' contributions to state and national bodies are used can be an obscure process. Massachusetts SEIU, however, has made a successful effort in its Locals and State Council to make one key area of its use of political funds as transparent and participatory as possible: the endorsing of candidates. Our local unions run member-driven processes in municipal and district races before endorsements are considered by the elected leadership, and for gubernatorial and US Senate races, the State Council runs statewide forums attended by over five hundred members who score the candidates. Further, joint endorsement forums in our SCA cities include the full participation of both nonunion SCA and Fight for $15 members.

Massachusetts SEIU 2014 gubernatorial candidates forum

Less participatory are decisions about coalition spending like Raise Up Massachusetts, though these certainly are expected to conform to the decisions of the elected leadership and national conventions. For that reason, members often raise questions about why their funds are being used to support nonunion workers, whether in fast food, SEIU Community chapters, or the low-wage workforce in general via Raise Up victories. Interestingly, when these issues are explained at the highest level of strategic thinking, members are not merely persuaded but energized by the answers, suggesting the value of engaging member participation in these nontraditional labor initiatives to the greatest extent possible.

A broader financing base in the working class for all potential partners could improve the democratic grounding of labor-community coalitions. Instead of debates about unions' exclusivity vs. community groups' dependence on wealthy philanthropy, we would share a focus on motivating and organizing the most diverse conception of working people into a powerful, self-funding coalition. Progress in the direction of working-class funding for all politically active coalition members would help resolve precisely those questions of representation and decision-making power that are currently obscured by radically incommensurable organizational structures. Apples-to-oranges comparisons make it difficult to assess who actually represents whom in the coalition decision-making process. That a small organization, funded by a few wealthy donors, should have the same, or even a similar say over coalition resources as a union of thousands, funded entirely by its working-class members, is absurdly undemocratic. Yet the question remains: how can or should these other voices be heard within the coalition?

Furthermore, a shared stake in a resource base from grassroots members would enhance all partners' feelings of strategic responsibility in their use. Working people can only successfully challenge the united money-power of big business and wealthy investors by balancing social transformation with viability. To win statewide campaigns, especially on the ballot, means choosing winnable campaigns based on public opinion research (what does the broad working public want?) and power/opposition analysis (who will oppose us; what are their resources?) before pitting people-power against the money power. Raise Up has found that rebuilding shared prosperity requires a highly strategic sequence of demands, not unlike the process of ongoing collective bargaining. The goal must be "the left wing of the possible," and determining what that is requires both research expertise and vigorous coalition debate. Who has the most weight in the decision-making should include a realistic analysis of the actual base, funding, and leadership of the participating organizations. Increasing the voluntarism of union membership and financing, on the one hand, and broadening the funding and decision-making base of 501(c) organizations, on the other, would help build a shared standard of legitimacy.

Shaping a Labor Movement for the Twenty-First Century

It's too early to tell what experiments like Raise Up could do to revive the power of a movement for working people, but the evolving strategies of Raise Up Massachusetts and similar ongoing coalitions for shared prosperity around the country suggest some intriguing developments in relation to labor history. In brief, Raise Up is bridging an unlikely pair of traditions: the Scandinavian model of structural reform and jurisdiction-wide negotiations with the pre-Wagner Act era of voluntaristic, often more community-based than union-based, working-class organization and action. Many of Raise Up's aims and accomplishments evoke, if at a very nascent level, the methods of northern European social democracy and labor. The statewide focus, the blend of negotiating, legislation, and election work, and the goal of structural cross-industry reform belong to this model and its successes.

Raise Up's slogan of "building an economy that works for all of us" expresses a similar intent, one that the Massachusetts Budget and Policy Center and other trusted economic advisors have helped monitor and evaluate. Unlike the shop-by-shop negotiating of traditional Anglo-American unionism, the aspirations and demands of this model focus on the big-picture limitations to and possibilities of rebalancing an unfair society.

At the same time as Raise Up seeks this broad impact, the coalition partners' membership is mainly organized on a voluntary and community-based level, more like a Depression-era Council of the Unemployed or Alinsky coalition than the AFL-CIO of the 1950s. In the current situation, the corporate right is dismantling the protected labor regimes of the National Labor Relations Act, and even attacking the later compromises of Taft-Hartley that limited the reach and militancy of unions while allowing them to strengthen existing fiefdoms. Regrounding the labor movement in more open worker associations could make a virtue of necessity. The spontaneity and élan of pre-NLRA worker movements would be a welcome boost to morale and participation. The viability of a more voluntaristic model is borne out in recent decades by the experience of countries with very different labor movements than those of northern Europe, ones like Brazil, France, or Italy, for example. In any case, a labor movement that is inclusive of working people regardless of race, gender, or occupational classification, and even beyond workplace altogether, is a welcome counterweight to tendencies to technocracy, statism, and corporatism inherent in the New Deal and northern European Social Democracy. It also leavens the "big government" appearance of a union movement increasingly limited to the arenas of public employment and political transactionalism without needing to eschew those realities.

Whatever the lessons and inspirations of the past, however, the most important labor history will be whether coalitions like Raise Up can build a labor movement for the future. A working people's movement that moves beyond traditional work and even the workplace is long overdue as an adequate response to the decline of jobs in an ever-increasingly automated economy. Moishe Postone has rightly pointed out that the theoretical basis for such a universal movement already existed in the mature work of Karl Marx, who, he argues, saw the worker ("the proletariat") less as *the* agent of historical change and more as just one type of the "social individual," a person conscious of social structures and committed to the free development of all individuals. A transformative labor movement, then, is made up of such social individuals, whether organized as workers, community members, or identity-oriented or morally inspired activists. Postone notes that this insight has grown only more urgent in the face of computerization, robotics, artificial intelligence, and other forces that are rendering more and more of the 99 percent redundant in a capitalist system.[5] A movement that broadens its base and its demands—that is, not just for a greater share of the "product" but for more work/life balance in general through victories like universal paid family and medical leave— is one that is beginning to grapple with these profound insights and trends. As long as these considerations motivate immediate engagement and bargaining with the state and corporate interests, progress is possible. Just as money will find its way to politics, working people must as well.

CHAPTER 8

Coalition Building in the Age of Trump?

Lessons from the Solidarity School

Eric Larson

"Crisis" is hardly a new word for the US labor movement. Though new forms of labor organizations have emerged, unions themselves have repeatedly issued emergency calls since the 1970s, as the radical economic restructuring of the neoliberal era began. But the rise of Trumpism has undoubtedly ushered in a new kind of crisis. Its racist energy is oriented at crushing unions while co-opting the white working class, as Donald Trump's romantic visions of Rust Belt workers and repeated calls to make the Republican Party a "workers' party" attest.[1] Trumpism has legitimized forms of white supremacy that the post-Civil Rights era of "colorblind racism" had generally pushed out of public discourse. New England is hardly exempt from these dynamics, as leaders of majority-white unions in this area have reported the rise of Trumpism in their organizations.[2]

What is labor education doing in a moment such as this? What should it do? I concluded in a recent article—published amidst the rise of Black working-class protest in the Black Lives Matter movement—that Black feminist theories about "bridge-building" could help shape labor education's response to an important tension within the US working class. While white and Black workers are mostly united about the positive role of unions, they are highly divided about the fairness of the criminal justice system.[3] More than simply one "wedge" issue amongst others, the criminal justice system has played an essential role in dividing Blacks from whites in a post-Civil Rights era allegedly dedicated to promoting a colorblind society. Policies of mass incarceration, partly through the War on Drugs, created what Michelle Alexander has called a "New Jim Crow" system, even as Black freedom movements attempted to create truly equal societies. In an era of colorblind racism that stigmatized explicit and public forms of racism, criminality served as a potent code language, or racial "dog whistle," for anti-Black political messaging.[4] "Felony" has become the new "n-word," as one Black minister recounted, and the "criminal" has become the figure that society has "permission to hate."[5] Trumpism has re-mobilized this colorblind code language, particularly through its law-and-order rhetoric and platitudes about police benevolence, even as Trump himself has infused public discussion with forthright racism.

This essay situates one specific labor education effort, the Rhode Island Solidarity School, within these racialized political dynamics, and it examines how bridge-building models have shaped, and could shape, labor education's contributions to coalition-building in the Trump era. It considers the case of the Solidarity School, a biennial, bilingual (Spanish/English) workers' seminar founded in 2011, in a present moment that necessitates a kind of transformative labor education, one attuned in particular to confronting the toxic masculinity and racialized scapegoating of Trumpism. Using interviews with key participants, Solidarity School documents, and my own experiences as coordinator and co-founder, this chapter discusses the history and accomplishments of the school as well as the conflicts, obstacles, and internal tensions it has faced. The fundamental goal of the Solidarity School has been to create a solidarity-based social fabric—a bridge-building political culture—upon which local coalitions could strengthen themselves. The essay suggests that the Rhode Island Solidarity School's efforts to foster long-term relationship building and a kind of coalitional sensibility amongst participants has taken on particular importance in the current political climate.

Coalition-Building Across Difference

Progressive sectors of the US labor movement and labor education have frequently referred to the labor movement as one in crisis. The historic victory of the New Voices leadership slate in the 1995 AFL-CIO election marked the ascension of union leaders who pledged to fundamentally change the Cold War bureaucratism and conservatism of the federation. Yet nearly twenty-five years after that victory, unions have not changed enough to stem the tidal wave of attacks on organized and unorganized workers. Much of the New Voices program ultimately left basic structures in place.[6] Commentators who have advocated for different kinds of social movement unionism or worker-center-led organizing advocate fundamentally changing unionism.[7] Efforts as wide-ranging as the revival of the Industrial Workers of the World in the 2000s to the powerful efforts of workers' centers have experimented with implementing these profound kinds of changes. Other scholars have discussed forms of leadership that challenge charisma-based (male) leadership in unions and social movements. Using the example of Ella Baker in the Civil Rights movement, for instance, Barbara Ransby has discussed the importance of grassroots forms of leadership based on collaborative work.[8]

Scholars and activists have also advocated new forms of coalition-building to confront the crisis. For unions in particular, losses over the last several decades have made it increasingly difficult to win *without* non-union allies. At the 2013 AFL-CIO convention, the federation's leaders acknowledged this dynamic and recognized that in the contemporary era, "[c]ommunity is the new density." Some of the new writing on union-community alliances has focused on balancing power differentials inside labor-oriented coalitions, since unions' paid staff, resources, and sheer numbers of members have allowed them to dominate coalitions with other kinds of community organizations.[9] Amanda Tattershall, for instance, advocates "partner" coalitions, in which all members are equal members; Amy B. Dean and David B. Reynolds argue for "deep" coalitions across regional economies.[10] Since its early years in the late 1980s, Jobs with Justice has argued for the importance of "permanent coalitions" between unions and other organizations, rather than ad hoc alliances around short-term political objectives. Such long-standing local coalitions allow for deeper levels of trust and reciprocity, its founders have argued, and allow them to be ready to contest the next crisis that local working classes will inevitably face. Jobs with Justice sees solidarity as a quality to build from the bottom up as well as between organizational leaderships.[11]

One of the key focus areas of the Solidarity School has been to nourish a grassroots, solidarity-based social fabric upon which local organizations can build deep and lasting coalitions. Indeed, in addition to the importance of the new kinds of coalition *structures*, the political *cultures* of coalitions and movements also matter.[12] Even the early Jobs with Justice coalitions suffered from the co-opting influences of the white populism and nationalism of the 1980s, which in many ways was a preview of today's Trumpism.[13] Without extensive forms of antiracism education, labor intellectuals Bill Fletcher and Fernando Gapasin have argued, unions and coalitions are bound to stumble across explosive "racial trip wires," prevalent in contexts of both colorblind racism and the more explicit white supremacy validated by Trumpism.[14]

Other theorists and activists have discussed how, and if, cross-racial coalitions can work, or if the efforts of Black organizations are destined to be appropriated, silenced, or otherwise marginalized in coalitions with powerful white-led groups.[15] Women of color feminist theorists offer additional insights about race and the inner dynamics of multiracial coalition work. Audre Lorde has written extensively about the importance of bridge-building and coalitions in societies structured by racial, class, gender, and sexual hierarchies, yet she and others also discuss how such efforts can reinforce the same power structures they claim to contest.[16] Much like the Black Lives Matter organizers they inspired, these theorists recognize that workers (and all people) don't define themselves based on only one of their social positions. To create "labor-community" coalitions, it's necessary, then, to question the usefulness of conceiving "labor" and "community" as fundamentally different in the first place. It's necessary to recognize that workers are simultaneously people who work *and* people who inhabit communities. Their sense of social class is lived through categories like race, gender, and sexuality, rather than isolated from them. This kind of formulation is different from models of bridge-building that focus mainly on how to bring together constituencies understood as essentially different (for instance, labor interests versus civil rights or women's interests).[17]

If it's important to build bridges, who does it and how is it done? Since those at the bottom of the socio-economic ladder have historically been excluded from union organizing efforts, bridge-building work informed by feminists of color focuses on "lifting the floor" to benefit all workers, rather than growing the economy and hoping a "rising tide" will "trickle down" for everyone.[18] In addition to challenging the dominant vision of the working class as reactionary, white, and male, these theories also examine how subordinated groups, like women of color, are often expected to take on the politically fraught labor of bridging differences.

"Those who profit from our oppression," Lorde wrote, make it "the responsibility of the oppressed to teach the oppressors their mistakes . . . Black and Third World people are expected to educate white people as to our humanity. Women are expected to educate men," Lorde explained.[19] To foster a bridge-building political culture within and around coalitions, then, it is critical for labor educators to create spaces where the emotional and political labor of bridging differences is shared, rather than a burden shouldered by a few. After all, as Cherríe Moraga has written, "a bridge gets walked over."[20]

The Solidarity School: History and Political Context

The first discussions about creating the Rhode Island Solidarity School began in 2010, with ideas of coalition-building paramount to its objectives. The political context resembled 2018 in a variety of ways. The rise of the Tea Party in the wake of the Great Recession and the election of Barack Obama had legitimized racism, nativism, and anti-unionism in ways that were increasingly dangerous to local working-class social justice organizations. Anti-immigrant policies and policing, particularly State Bill 1070 in Arizona and the racial profiling policies of Sheriff Joe Arpaio in Maricopa County, were some of the most visible invigorations of the racialized targeting of immigrant workers of color.

The Tea Party, along with the Right in general, had also gained momentum in attacking labor unions. Republican governor Scott Walker's attempt to dismantle Wisconsin public sector unionism with the Wisconsin Budget Repair Bill of 2011 generated massive protests and the occupation of the Wisconsin state capitol. The movement of unionists and their supporters attracted nationwide support, and unions and academics have shown how these anti-union efforts were not isolated responses to budget issues (as Walker claimed) but rather part of a national stealth campaign by far-Right funders.[21] Indeed, the attacks on immigrants and public sector unions had led to a crisis in coalition-based organizing in Providence, a city that suffers from gentrification, segregation, and excessive corporate power not unlike Boston and other US cities. Local racial justice organizers at Direct Action for Rights and Equality (DARE), based in the historically Black South Side, noted the difficulties and contradictions of mobilizing their members to support unionized public sector workers (mainly teachers and civil servants), who themselves were under attack. After all, had public employees like school teachers—most of whom were white and suburban—supported their students' neighborhoods? Likewise, local immigrants' rights organizers discussed the difficulties of alliances with unions. In a local Jobs with Justice meeting, the executive director of DARE suggested the need for a "Jobs with Justice university" for members (not staff) of local unions and community organizations to learn about putting these dynamics in broader contexts of structural forces. The Rhode Island Solidarity School formed in 2011 in response to this call to explore the possibilities and difficulties of solidarity. It billed itself as a program to discuss how "injustices intersect."[22] Today, it continues to explore topics like racism, immigration, income inequality and capitalism, patriarchy and heterosexism, and policing and imprisonment in both local and global contexts.

While other working-class organizers have formed solidarity schools elsewhere in recent years, ours drew its name partly from the work of Kim Wilson at the University of Massachusetts Dartmouth Labor Center and the Women's Institute for Leadership and Development, which ran a seminar called the Solidarity School with Massachussets Jobs with Justice in the late 1990s and early 2000s.[23] Our Solidarity School, which has been run biennially, tends to be composed of fifteen to twenty area residents. I have coordinated the school since the beginning, and the staff of the local Jobs with Justice has also taken on recruitment, curriculum development, and planning work. Since 2012 the school has an advisory committee that also helps plan curricula and recruit participants. The majority of the participants in the school are union members or members of community/immigrant organizations. Classes tend to be around 60 percent Black and brown (mostly Latinx) and 40 percent white. They have averaged 60 percent men and 40 percent women. The majority usually are non-union workers; unionized workers tend to compose around 40 percent of the classes. Union members have come from AFSCME, the Teamsters, the United Auto Workers, the Carpenters, UNITE HERE, and SEIU Healthcare. The racial justice organization Direct Action for Rights and Equality has been perhaps the most consistent source of participants. Immigrant workers tied to the Olneyville Neighborhood Association and English for Action, and immigrant activists and youth from the Providence Street Youth Movement (PRYSM), have also been regular participants.

Recruitment: Depth Rather than Breadth

The solidarity school's focus on depth, not breadth has been tied to strategic, ideological, and logistical factors. It was partly shaped by a belief in popular education that bases itself on a deeply participatory learning process that disrupts the hierarchies that distinguish teacher from student. Inspired by Brazilian theorist Paolo Freire and others, popular education is about emancipatory learning, generating new forms of collective identification through discussion, and tying education to social action. As Freire has argued, the focus should be on how collaborative, dialogue-based learning can be the base of creating an "education that enlarges and amplifies the horizon of critical understanding of the people, to create an education devoted to freedom."[24] The deep level of engagement required through popular education methods is easier in small groups.

While the Solidarity School's organizers—myself, the advisory committee, and Jobs with Justice activists—value all kinds of participation, the "level" of participants has been an occasional site of tension for the Solidarity School. During a discussion about recruiting participants to the school in a meeting with local organizational representatives in 2015, the executive director of a local immigrant worker center stated that it was unclear who the Solidarity School was intended for. Would the materials or discussions be too advanced for workers who enter their office because they were victims of wage theft, yet have no experience with organized politics or political education? "If you say 'organizing' to one of our members," she said, "they'll think you're talking about cleaning the house, not community organizing." Basic concepts would need to be explained. Is the Solidarity School, she asked, hoping to recruit people like them? Or long-time staffers? Or people who have joined, but are mostly new, to such organizations? These questions have spurred us to ask ourselves: Is it useful to mix people with different levels of experience (for instance, union staff with members with little experience in organized political work)? Or is it better to narrow a group to hone and define materials and discussions?

The school has never fully answered the question about the level of experience of participants, and the sessions have mostly yielded mixed results. This is partly because the school leaves part of its recruitment to local organizational leaders in a way that can build a sense of organizational co-ownership of the school. Instead of recruiting openly through public announcements, through formal applications, or by selecting members of organizations itself, the school requests that organizational leaders select their own members. This approach has been specifically advocated by some Jobs with Justice directors, whose local coalition is composed of many of these organizations. It has been a way to respect local leaderships.[25]

But that's not the only form of recruitment. A group of early graduates of the school and the coordinators formed a Solidarity School advisory committee after the second Solidarity School in 2012. The committee has helped supplement organizational recruits with workers from a range of different spheres, including formerly incarcerated and unemployed workers, nonunionized immigrant domestic workers, white service sector workers, and young workers in high school. Without the relative diversity of the advisory committee, it would have been difficult to recruit workers with such a range of experiences and backgrounds. The original advisory committee consisted of a white woman who was a former union carpenter and current service worker, a second-generation Dominican American carpenter and member of a racial justice organization, a Latina immigrant factory worker, and myself, a white male academic.

An Experience, Not an Organization: Challenging the Nonprofit Industrial Complex

Another recruitment strategy, however, reflects the school's general approach to be an experience, not an organization. Mindful of critiques of the institutionalization of movements into the "nonprofit industrial complex," the Solidarity School founders, including the author, originally intended the school to prefigure its participatory solidarity goals in its very structure. While foundation funders increasingly impose short-term planning on movement organizations through requiring them to measure impact with concrete deliverables and numbers, our school focuses more on long-term relationship building.[26] It wasn't intended to be a hierarchical structure with a director, paid staff, and a fixed division of labor. It wasn't intended to be a charity or structured like a social service agency, either. In terms of recruiting, then, it asks its graduates to agree to recruit someone new for the next school. While the school offers childcare, transportation, and food, it encourages participants to take on some of that labor by occasionally sharing food with the group or giving rides to each other.

The school has continued to function on a budget of around $1,000 for each six-session school, partly due to its aspiration to be independent and unbureaucratic, partly due to lack of paid staff and the limits of donated labor in doing fundraising work, and partly due to significant in-kind donations. The school relies on community ties to identify and locate a host of guest facilitators who donate their labor and expertise. The first Solidarity School, in particular, was funded by a Community Partnership grant from a national academic association, and it also benefitted from ties to supportive faculty and students at Brown University. After the grant, it has relied on grassroots fundraising by asking participating organizations to contribute or by running fundraiser parties. While the Solidarity School has shifted away from the university sector in general, it has grown closer to Rhode Island Jobs with Justice, whose staff has donated crucial resources of time, effort, and space.

Yet its efforts to resist nonprofitization and dependence on external funders has also generated informal kinds of power that can reproduce the power relations of dominant society. Feminist Jo Freeman argued in the 1970s that informality in activist organizations can obscure the very real ways that charisma and social and cultural capital can create a "tyranny of structurelessness."[27] In these cases, hierarchy and power exists even when no explicit structure legitimizes it. Especially in the beginning, the school would not have been possible without the extensive hours donated from the author, as well as his (Ivy League) university connections.

Solidarity across Difference

Shortly after the creation of the school's advisory committee, the group created a mission statement that helped define the school's objectives and distinguish them from the political education programs of other local organizations.[28] The Solidarity School, the mission statement detailed, was dedicated to developing political sensibilities that would facilitate coalition work. The statement affirmed that, "The mission of the Rhode Island Solidarity School is to develop community members' capacities as bridge builders within and between unions, organizations, and communities. . . . The school brings together diverse groups to explore the barriers to solidarity and what has happened when people have overcome them." For the first time, the school embraced the language of bridge-building to conceptualize its ideas about difference and building connections. We have approached this task in a variety of ways. In our first session in 2015, I led a conversation about bridges as a metaphor for solidarity. But it fell flat, and I later realized it was too abstract. Popular education, indeed, is based on building shared knowledge through participants' concrete experiences and realities. In contrast, in our first session in 2017, we created four groups—two of union members, and two of nonunion workers. We asked the union members to make lists of what they thought was good and bad about their union; we asked the nonunion participants to make lists of what they thought was good and bad about their community, as they defined it. The subsequent discussion, led by Rhode Island Jobs with Justice director Mike Araujo, revealed how the groups shared many of the same values about what they would like to see—such as courage, togetherness, inclusion, and mutual aid—just as they shared many of the same ideas about what impedes those goals.

In addition to providing space for participants to find what they have in common, the school seeks to develop bridge-building capacities by directly addressing how workers live *different* realities due to their skin color, gender, and other factors. We led an opening exercise in 2015 in which workers formed a "living bar graph." Participants moved the tables and chairs to the side and attempted to form the bars of a graph that displayed median wealth according to race and gender. Black women's median wealth was represented by one person, and Black men's by a few more. Participants quickly realized it was impossible to create a graph to the correct scale; the bars for white men and white women would have extended far past the confines of our spacious meeting room.

Undoubtedly, the worker-participants themselves have offered the most profound lessons about difference, especially in terms of racism and police power. After hearing one union member refer to undocumented people as "illegal immigrants," another participant opened a conversation about the derogatory nature of the "i-word." The union member later thanked her, and several months later he told me it was a profound learning experience. During one of the early sessions of the 2017 school, facilitators let the group decide if it wanted to hold our session as planned or attend a city council hearing about the Community Safety Act, a bill sponsored by working-class organizations of color. The bill, which aimed to limit police profiling and abuse, faced fierce opposition from the Providence Fraternal Order of Police, among other constituencies. The organizations needed the council members to see a chamber full of supporters. After a discussion, the group decided to go, despite the considerable logistical difficulties the change would entail (such as rides, food plan, etc.). The connections the members had built with each other humanized a debate that, for most of the white participants, likely seemed distant or even threatening. In addition, the presence of Black union members recounting how their families had been victimized by police demonstrated just how misleading any fixed separation between "labor" and "community" issues can be.

Regardless of what facilitators have designed for sessions, one of the main comments from evaluations since 2011 is the benefit of being in the same room with different kinds of people. As one youth participant said of the 2017 Solidarity School, the most impressive part of the school was

> seeing people from all walks of life, from high school students, to workers, people from various different communities. Because a lot of people only see one or two types of groups. It's like youth or people from different ethnic groups, but Solidarity School was the first time I actually saw solidarity, people from really different walks of life, different ages, to see how we can make our communities better. And trying to learn. And how to get communities involved in the workforce.[29]

Participants, as well as organizations, keep coming back. Between one-third and one-half of participants have returned a second or even third time, and the year-by-year involvement of local organizations has been crucial to the school's development. One former Rhode Island Jobs with Justice director said that "the Solidarity School was the most intersectional thing I've seen." It significantly contributed to local potentials for coalitions. With the Solidarity School, he said, "we were able to have ambassadors who could straddle those two worlds [of unions and other groups]. It was really important."[30]

Relationship to Current Local Campaigns

Beyond the co-production of knowledge and consciousness, popular education models stress combining thought with action. (Together, Freire identified them as "praxis.") One of the major tensions in the Solidarity School has been its relationship to ongoing working-class struggles, a consideration that has frequently been discussed in terms of how to maintain relationships and momentum after the sessions end. Along with the advisory committee, the Jobs with Justice directors and I have continually concluded that the school lacks a fully designed

outlet for facilitating ongoing activity and relationship-building after the
sessions end.

A variety of influences early on led the school away from directly
engaging with local working-class campaigns. The distance between
our programming and ongoing struggles stemmed in part from concern
about local organizations trying to steer the school into their respective
political camps—that is, to make the school an extension of their
campaign work at the cost of other organizations' struggles. The political
context of the Great Recession—with the rise of the Tea Party, the
attack on immigrants, and so on—put many local organizations on their
heels. In addition, tensions within the local Jobs with Justice about how
its campaign support was divided between member unions was also a
site of conflict. The efforts of the advisory committee, Jobs with Justice
leadership, and myself to directly involve local organizations in the
planning process had mostly led to division, even after the first years. In
some cases, organizations had sought lists of weekly topics the Solidarity
School would cover beforehand in ways that made it seem as though
they would only tell their members about topics that fit in their own
political "silo." When the Solidarity School advisory committee opted
to allow Jobs with Justice coalition organizations to select some of the
themes of the 2015 school in an open vote, the discussion generated more
tension than solidarity. Since then, the Solidarity School only consists
of six to seven total sessions, not every topic can be discussed, and some
organizations and causes have felt left out.

Given the context of 2010 to 2011, it seemed especially important to
me to embrace popular education strategies based on collective discussion,
and also to buffer the Solidarity School from the urgency and inter-
organization tensions of local politics. Early on, the Solidarity School's
identity as a "school," rather than a "training" or a simple extension
of local campaign work, was very important. The discussion between
Myles Horton and Freire about the difference between "education"
and "organizing" helped lead us to see the school as a space for the
co-production of knowledge through dialogue. To best nurture trust-
building, we stressed that participants attend all sessions. The meetings
took place over dinner as a way to foster a collective atmosphere. Early
on, the majority of solidarity school sessions were led by volunteer guest
facilitators, many of whom were local academics. Given this context,
having sessions facilitated by people outside local labor struggles would
allow for discussions of big-picture topics—like immigration, imperialism,

and inequality—in ways that would extend beyond the purview of any single organization's current campaign. Finally, the original academic grant the school received also pushed us to hold sessions at Brown University, rather than in a more working-class setting.

We have made major changes in the last several years to respond to the debate about the Solidarity School's relationship to local campaigns. Though participant evaluations are always overwhelmingly positive, since 2013 at least one evaluation has noted that the school could be improved with more direct connections to local working-class campaigns. The advisory committee and Jobs with Justice coordinators have pushed for similar changes as well. In fact, the school has slowly become much more directly engaged in tying knowledge to action since 2012. In the 2017 school, several of the sessions took place alongside local rallies or meetings, and participants reflected on the proceedings after. We ultimately held two sessions during City Hall hearings about the proposed Community Safety Act, and we had one session at the local May Day rally and celebration. These were coalition-led efforts, facilitated by Rhode Island Jobs with Justice. Ultimately, our original fears about local organizations steering the work were overblown—they were heavily influenced by tensions among a small number of organizations at a particular moment of time.

Conclusion

Union coalitions with nonunion allies are now major parts of labor movement strategies. Yet creating lasting coalitions of equal partners remains a challenge, particularly in the face of Trumpism's efforts to co-opt the white working class, re-energize toxic masculinity, and intensify the stigmatization and criminalization of Black and brown workers. If solidarity is based not only on a lowest-common-denominator similarity (a shared enemy, for example) but a deeper recognition of interdependence and difference, the Solidarity School has sought to forge such interdependence, not only through sharing ideas but through deeper forms of group participation. That participation includes the sense of shared ownership produced through material interdependence (i.e., giving rides, bringing food), popular education-inspired group activities, and sharing the emotional and political experiences of attending rallies and protests together. The coordinators and advisory committee members increasingly strive to participate in sessions as equal participants and learners, and only rarely do they facilitate sessions themselves.

Participant evaluations always attest to the impact of sharing space with different kinds of people. After the May 2017 session, the combination of local building trades unionists who had gained unionized jobs through minority apprenticeship programs and queer youth of color (who knew little about unions) created a particularly engaging, enthusiastic collective discussion. They began to plan holding their own Solidarity School sessions after ours concluded. Other participants have attested to the ways the School has changed their views, particularly of immigration and racism. During the last sessions of each school, students write letters to themselves in which they describe how they will act in solidarity with others in the next six months. We send the letters to them six months later so they can evaluate their engagement with solidarity.

Yet the Solidarity School is also a project that suffers from weaknesses common to community-based unionism and labor education. Its grassroots model (and lack of permanent budget) have made it more difficult to escape "founder's syndrome." I continue to lead much of the work, although the Jobs with Justice director and members of the advisory committee have become integral parts of its functioning. Partly due to comments from our 2015 sessions, the School seeks to have participants lead their own sessions, yet it has not fully developed channels for developing leader-educators, and especially leaders of color, within Solidarity School networks. An advisory committee member attended the United Association of Labor Educators conference in 2015 and in 2018 to co-present on the Solidarity's School's work, and we are developing a network of formerly incarcerated workers with a local immigrant workers' center and Rhode Island Jobs with Justice. But we need more efforts such as these. Ultimately, the Solidarity School has not established a structure and culture as democratic and "leaderful" as it could. Some advisory committee members have argued for deeper engagement with conservative unionists to avoid a "preaching to the choir" dynamic. Jeffrey Santos, a founding advisory committee member, has suggested that the Solidarity School could more deeply discuss union history so unionists understand the historical struggles that produced the union benefits of today. I would like to integrate a segment on the collective resolution of in-group conflict in future years.

Finally, identifying the role of the Solidarity School in relation to local working-class struggles remains an open question. After integrating the school with important local campaigns in 2017, we have an experience to evaluate and build on. As former executive director Jesse Strecker has said, this is always a challenge with political education programs: how do they "translate into action?" These and other questions remain in place as the Rhode Island Solidarity School seeks to engage with transformative models of knowledge and praxis.

CHAPTER 9

Immigrants and Worker Centers in Boston in the Shadow of Trump

Aviva Chomsky

S ince the founding of the AFL in the late nineteenth century, the federation has faced the dilemma of whether to preserve worker gains by fighting to keep immigrant workers out, or whether to broaden its base by welcoming and organizing immigrants. With the tectonic shifts in the US economy and labor market at the end of the twentieth century, which were accompanied by a new wave of immigration, this question became even more urgent. Unions shrank and working conditions and benefits crumbled, while new sectors like fast food, subcontracted cleaning services, and food processing eagerly employed new immigrants, especially those from Asia and Latin America.

Many of these jobs were low paid, precarious, and temporary. Workers might be hard to organize because they lacked legal status, and thus permission to work, in the United States. Many considered their presence in the United States temporary, and cared more about earning quickly to return home, rather than investing in campaigns for better working conditions in the long run. Some spoke little or no English. Many worked in isolated conditions, legally classified as independent contractors rather than employees. Some worked for small businesses owned by members of their own immigrant community, or for family members. Traditional unions tended to assume they'd be impossible to organize. They are frequently excluded from both academic and popular understandings of the category "working class."

Nevertheless, most immigrants are of course workers, and the worker center movement arose in the 1990s to organize them outside of formal union structures. Many come with union organizing or other political experience in their home countries. Many share experiences of marginalization and inequality beyond the workplace, including inadequate housing, underfunded schools, poor public transportation, precarious legal status, and racism. Many have a deep understanding of the global economy, having witnessed maquiladoras, plantations, foreign-owned mines, or exploitative tourism industries in their own countries. Many have very strong social networks through church, sports leagues, and family. If organized labor truly seeks to strengthen social movement unionism, or what Jane McAlevey calls "whole worker organizing," immigrant workers have a lot to offer to the process. And under the Trump Administration, strengthening the links between the immigrant rights and worker rights movements became more essential than ever.

This paper draws on interviews with organizers from three different Boston-area worker centers. The main focus is the Chinese Progressive Association, which founded one of the first Boston worker centers in 1987 in support of workers displaced by a factory closure. Over its thirty years the CPA has pioneered and exemplified many of the different strategies available to marginalized and unorganized workers. I complement the CPA's story with experiences from the Chelsea Collaborative, which started to focus on workers' rights with its new Latino Immigrants Committee in 1998, and the Brazilian Women's Group, which began its workers' project around 2010, in order to explore these organizations' achievements and the challenges they face.

A New Generation of Immigrant Workers in Boston

As Michael Piore argued in 1973, industrial Boston's labor force was continually replenished with migrants, from Europe in the nineteenth century, then from the rural South and Puerto Rico by the middle of the twentieth. These workers filled the lower ranks of the city's workforce, though the nature of their jobs changed over time as manufacturing declined in the city. Today most of Boston's immigrant workers, like most of its workers overall, labor in the service sector. Like native workers, immigrants are bifurcated. Highly educated immigrants have moved into professional positions in finance, health, technology, research, and education, while a much larger population of migrants toils in the hidden interstices of the glittery new economy. They process, package, and serve food; they deliver newspapers; they clean homes, offices, hospitals, and yards; they work for subcontractors in construction; and they care for the disabled and the elderly.

Boston's first significant wave of Latin American immigration came from Puerto Rico in the 1950s and 60s. The Puerto Rican population of Boston leveled off after 1970, counting 37,553 in 2014.[1] Soon Puerto Ricans were joined by tens of thousands of new immigrants, mostly from Latin America and the Caribbean but also from China, Vietnam, and India; the share of Boston's population that was foreign-born hit its all-time low in 1970 and has risen steadily since then.[2] The number of foreign-born residents rose to 151,836 in 2000, and to 177,461 by 2015.[3] In 2014, 27 percent of Boston's population was foreign-born.[4]

The countries sending the most migrants to Boston in 2015 were the Dominican Republic (13 percent), China (10.6 percent), Haiti (7.6 percent), El Salvador (6.3 percent), Vietnam (6.2 percent), Jamaica (4.4 percent), Cape Verde (4.4 percent), Colombia (2.8 percent), India (2.2 percent), and Guatemala (2.2 percent). 29 percent of the foreign-born identify as Hispanic, 24.8 percent as Asian/Pacific Islander, 24 percent as Black, 16.9 percent as white, and 5 percent as "Other Race." Populations of color in Boston, especially Asian and Hispanic, are disproportionately foreign-born, while the white population is overwhelmingly native-born. Only the Black population has relatively equal proportions in the native and foreign-born categories. Twenty-seven percent of the foreign-born in Boston live in poverty, as do 21 percent of the native-born.[5]

In 1995 Andrés Torres examined Latino immigrants in Boston's labor force, discovering a much larger and more diverse population than Michael Piore had found two decades earlier. The number of Hispanics employed in the state of Massachusetts rose from 21,000 in 1970 to 44,982 in 1980 and 83,000 in 1990. In 1995 Boston was home to 58,000 Latinos. Yet Torres lamented what he saw as an "awkward and often uneasy relation between Latinos and labor," observing a "sad irony in this discrepancy in light of the deep tradition of labor struggle in Latino countries of origin, and the overwhelming working-class composition of commonwealth Hispanics." Like the Puerto Ricans that Piore studied twenty years earlier, Boston's Latinos in the early 1990s were concentrated in low-wage positions. Some still worked in the lower ends of the manufacturing sector, but given the overall transformation of Boston's labor market, many also worked in the burgeoning low-wage service sectors, with 69 percent working at these jobs.[6]

Torres confirmed earlier analyses of the divide between Boston's unions and its Black and immigration populations. But he added a new element, which became key in the subsequent formation of worker centers in the city. Green and Donahue had alluded to this issue when they examined some of the organizations formed by workers of color and women in the 1970s, like 9-to-5, the United Community Construction Workers, and the Third World Workers Association, all of which fought for their rights in the workplace and beyond.

As Torres explained,

> For Latinos, the community, not the workplace, is seen as the focal site for organizing activities. Struggles over educational, health, and housing services claim their energies; the battles for political empowerment have greater mobilizing appeal. . . . Straightforward class appeals, emphasizing economic issues alone, will fall short because they ignore the cultural chasm separating the newcomers from the dominant culture of the larger society. To attract the "outsiders," labor has to transform itself, sharing power from top to bottom. More important, it must insert itself into the life of minority communities economically and socially.[7]

Boston's worker centers, like those elsewhere in the country, emerged precisely to fill this niche.

Worker Centers

A decade after Torres exposed the weak links between Boston's unions and the city's low-wage Latino workers, labor scholar Janice Fine offered a similar diagnosis for unions confronting a still more precarious and immigrant-rich labor force nationwide. To meaningfully organize workers only loosely identified with their jobs or their industries, she wrote, unions needed to "broaden beyond job-related identities through the development of ongoing relationships with workers not just at their workplaces but in their communities . . . organizations must be rooted in the community, not just at individual workplaces."[8] Moreover, she noted that the unions most committed to organizing new workers, like SEIU, tended to focus on national strategies and large employers, while many immigrants work for small employers and in the informal sector.[9]

The national context of anti-union legislation, employer manipulation of the NLRB election and bargaining process, and plant closures raise the likelihood of failure and have made unions reluctant to take on "hot shop" or reactive campaigns that inspire so many immigrant worker mobilizations.

Corey Kurtz's 2008 study of Boston's immigrant workers confirmed this reluctance, noting that in the city "even progressive unions such as SEIU and UNITE HERE that organize immigrant workers in particular sectors often refuse to organize smaller workplaces or support rank-and-file resistance to employer exploitation unless it is part of a larger organizing strategy."[10] The city's particular industrial and racial history also exacerbated the divide between the city's labor movement and low-wage immigrant workers and workers of color. What Green and Donahue described in the 1970s was still true decades later. Boston's unions "tend not to challenge the racism that is rampant in Boston's broader labor movement or the role that race plays in facilitating the exploitation of workers of color," wrote Kurtz.[11]

This, then, was the context for the formation of worker centers, organizations made up of and serving low-wage immigrant workers who, due to a combination of racial, cultural, and status difference, and because of their work in underground, small-scale, and subcontracted sectors, have remained peripheral to Boston's unions. Most of Boston's worker centers grew out of pre-existing immigrant/ethnic organizations. "Worker centers, rather than viewing themselves as part of the Boston labor movement, tend to see themselves as a response to its exclusivity," Kurtz explained.[12] Heloisa Galvão of the Brazilian Women's Group elaborated in describing her organization's worker center: "It involves culture too. And language. I think that the cultural component is very important, because they feel comfortable with us, because we are not only Brazilians, we are people that have been through the same situation, and we didn't have documents sometimes, or we were afraid sometimes, or we crossed the border, or we . . . we know what they are going through because we have been there."

Because worker centers are not registered in any kind of central location, and because they vary from small, ephemeral organizations to large and solid ones allied with labor unions or one of several national networks, it's hard to give an exact account of their numbers. Fine found only five nationwide at the movement's tentative beginning in 1992, and 160 in 2007.[13] Kurtz listed five in Boston in 2008: the Chinese Progressive

Association, the Brazilian Immigrant Center (BIC), MassCOSH, the Chelsea Latino Immigrant Community, and Centro Presente.[14]

By 2017, nine different centers belonged to Boston's Immigrant Worker Center Collaborative, founded in 2005, while others (including two of those in Kurtz's study, the BIC and Centro Presente) continue their work outside of the Collaborative. Most, like the Chinese Progressive Association, which formed in 1977 and founded one of the first Boston worker centers in 1987, and the Brazilian Women's Group, which began its workers' project around 2010, are based in specific immigrant communities' organizations. New Bedford's Centro Comunitario de Trabajadores formed in the wake of a devastating immigration raid that arrested hundreds of immigrant workers at the Michael Bianco leather factory in 2007, leaving their children stranded at school or day care. The Chelsea Collaborative formed in 1988 as a city-wide coalition in an overwhelmingly Latino city and began its Latino Immigrants Committee focusing on workers' rights in 1998; the Lynn Worker Center for Economic Justice, formed in 2008, is affiliated with the North Shore Labor Council (the only union-affiliated Center in the IWCC); MassCOSH is part of a nationwide Coalition for Occupational Safety and Health originally created by the new federal OSHA in the 1970s, and is also a member of the national Interfaith Worker Justice coalition.

Stories from the Field

A few case studies from Boston's worker centers in the twenty-first century illustrate the challenges of organizing low-wage immigrant workers in Boston's current economic context. While many scholars argue that unions *must* organize these workers if they wish to recover their power and relevance in today's economy, the obstacles revealed in these cases also help explain why unions have been reluctant or unable to do so. The history and nature of Boston's unions, the nature of today's precarious, low-wage economy, Boston's historic racial divide, and the onslaught of anti-immigrant legislation and sentiment all contribute to a fragile landscape for organizing.

Boston's Chinese Progressive Association exemplifies the interweaving of ethnic, national, and political identities that underlie many worker centers. In some ways, today's multifaceted, immigrant ethnic radicalism is reminiscent of that which inspired US union organizing a century ago. But new immigrant workers and their community activism differ in fundamental ways from today's mainstream unions.[15]

P&L Sportswear and the Birth of a Worker Center

The CPA worker center owed its genesis to massive layoffs in 1985 at the P&L Sportswear Company in East Boston, where hundreds of Chinatown women worked. This campaign, and another at Power One International, illustrate much about immigrant workers' place in the economic restructuring process. The processes also suggest why unions have been largely absent in many worker center campaigns. Both of the campaigns were spurred by workers at factories that were laying off large numbers and preparing to close—typical immigrant employers, but not fertile field for union organizing.[16]

When P&L announced its closure in 1985, recounts CPA executive director Karen Chen,

> These women, they are like god, we're going to lose our jobs, so what are we going to do? So they came to CPA to ask for help. So CPA started trying to organize them, really about trying to get access to unemployment, because at that time, you know, there was no language access for people, so the worker center actually fought for language access. . . . And so basically the garment workers, we have a right to jobs! And so together with some of the activists, some of the more English-speaking younger people, they actually formed a support committee to support the garment workers. And they demanded [state-funded] retraining, so they were able to win funding through a lot of rallying, a lot of organizing, money for training, so we actually started the first bilingual vocational training programs for people with limited English proficiency. So basically the workers met with the city, met with the state, or the people who do the vocational training, and [said] these are the things that we want . . . So after the victory, that was like around 1987, people really felt like we need to have a worker center, where we would primarily focus on workers' rights, and a place for all the workers to come for assistance.

As Chen concluded, "We support the workers where they are at." The emphasis on this campaign was on strengthening legal rights and ensuring workers' access to these rights, rather than necessarily organizing for a long-term voice in the workplace. The target was the state, rather than the employer. The CPA drew on its long history of ethnic community organizing and a commitment to grassroots mobilization. Its pioneering worker center exemplified the organization's orientation toward radical social change.[17]

Power-One

A second major CPA campaign involved Power-One International, a California-based multinational that employed several hundred low-wage and temporary workers at its Allston (Boston) plant manufacturing power conversion equipment. In 2001, Power-One began laying off workers and announced its imminent closing. Chen offered an analysis that placed the situation in global context, and also showed how immigrant workers bring their own concepts of labor rights.

> The electronics manufacturing industry was declining, mainly also because of NAFTA, and all those things, right? And so we started to see a bulk of electronic manufacturing workers being laid off . . . In 2001, one of the major factories in Boston, Power-One, laid off about 400 workers. There's about 300 Chinese, 100 Latinos, and they were moving the factory to Shenzhen, China and Mexico—which is ironic. And the business is not declining, but what they did was a major layoff . . . There were 30 workers who were going to stay to do just samples . . . they were just kind of like the more vulnerable workers, the newer immigrants, some of them were undocumented, I think it's true for both Latinos and Chinese. And then some people were taking piece work, to work at home, but they were not paid for overtime and other things. So meanwhile this company is not losing any profit, they just want to make more profit. Really what the workers wanted was severance pay. Because in China you actually have legal right to severance pay and here you don't. But we started out with that and we find out all these labor violations, initially because the workers organized a work stoppage themselves. And then they're just talking among themselves, like this is crazy, it's all the people who kiss up to the team leaders, the supervisors, who get to stay. So they organized the work stoppage, and then they were threatened by the company. And so they came to CPA and we're like, well, you guys gonna have to continue to take collective action. And then we find all the labor violations, all these things. But we eventually organized the

workers actually to fight to get more funding for vocational training, retraining.

In this case, the CPA sought support from Greater Boston Legal Services to file unfair labor practice charges against the company for its failure to pay minimum wage and overtime, and discrimination against and harassment of workers. [18] In the face of noisy public protest and the legal charges, the company agreed to negotiate with workers and granted concessions on overtime and severance pay. Workers also obtained close to $1 million from the federal government in federal trade adjustment assistance funds, to be used for extended unemployment benefits, English and vocational training, and other services. As two GBLS members who worked on the case concluded, "Legal aid programs must forge deep and lasting community partnerships to make enduring advances in communities of color."[19] Like many worker center campaigns, this one involved specifically labor issues, and made use of labor legislation and enforcement institutions as well as worker mobilization—but did not involve any union.

Beyond the Factory

In the Power-One case, immigrant workers were fighting a large multinational corporation. But immigrant labor issues can become even more complex when workers are employed by members of their own ethnic community or in the precarious, fragmented service economy. The tightness of the ethnic community can be a strength or a weakness in workers' organizing campaigns. In some cases, worker centers challenge norms of ethnic unity in their fight for labor rights. Chen explained:

> We are one of the few groups within the community that actually challenged Chinese-owned restaurants. We've been criticized within the community: Why are you hanging out dirty laundry? And to us it's kind of like, well, labor violations are labor violations . . . I have no problem saying that sometimes our people know how to exploit our own people the most. Meanwhile there's other issues around racism, and all that stuff, which we are also against, but it doesn't mean that we won't fight employers exploiting Chinese workers.
>
> And of course, sometimes it's like, if you look at it, a small employer versus a corporation, they make so much more profit—that may be true. But it doesn't mean that if you open a small restaurant, workers

should be exploited there. We're asking for people's basic labor rights to be respected. So we have done a lot of organizing and outreach in different restaurants, in Chinatown.

Home Health Care: Common Ground with the SEIU?

By the turn of the twenty-first century, more and more of Chinatown's workers had shifted from precarious positions in large manufacturing companies like P&L and Power-One to similarly precarious positions in Boston's burgeoning service and especially health-care economy. Immigrants made up 27 percent of Boston's workforce, but they were 50 percent of those employed in hotels, nursing homes, and restaurants. One fast-growing sector was the home health-care industry—workers who provide in-home care for the elderly, disabled, and those recovering from illness. Most home health jobs do not require medical education or experience. The average wage is $20,000 a year, and one-fourth of home health-care workers live in poverty.[20]

Home health-care employment doubled from one million in 2004 to two million workers nationwide by 2014, and it continued to be one of the nation's fastest-growing sectors, expected to rise to five million workers by 2020. Nine-tenths of these workers were women, and half were people of color. Massachusetts was not immune to the trend: home health-care employment grew in the state from 28,300 jobs in 2000 to 89,300 in 2016. Nationally, about a quarter of home health workers were immigrants in 2017, and in Massachusetts, the rate was 34 percent.[21] "After the garment industry and then the electronic stuff was gone, if you don't want to work in a restaurant, most people go into home care," Chen explained. "So [today] those are the bulk of where the Chinese workers are. I would say that there are thousands of them."

These Personal Care Assistants (PCAs), Chen explained, "are the people who go into elderly's homes to do chores, and that program was meant for MassHealth [the Massachusetts Medicaid program] to save money, instead of putting people into nursing homes, where it could [cost] up to like $60-70,000 a year, per person. So this is kind of like prevention." In Chinatown, the industry tends to hire local workers. "So basically they're bringing people from the same kind of cultural/language background into helping their elderlies with their daily needs. That could include chores, and sometimes help with medicine, if they got injured, bathing them, [help] with their daily needs so that they don't have to go into a nursing facility."

The Century Foundation, a progressive think tank, called the industry an "organizing nightmare."[22] PCAs work individually and rarely come into contact with other workers. Some are contracted by private agencies, while some work directly for their clients, making it exceedingly difficult to identify a bargaining unit. Yet the fragmented nature of the industry means that PCAs are in many ways the new face of the working class. Thus, home health care has become a key sector in which traditional unions and community organizations have sought to collaborate.

In Boston the roots of home health-care organizing lay in the early 1980s, when the United Labor Unions, an independent union affiliated with the national Association of Community Organizations for Reform Now (ACORN) began to organize Boston's African American and immigrant home-care workers. Boston ULU organizers "discovered hundreds of disgruntled and militant African American, Latina, and Caribbean women working below the minimum wage for agencies with contracts from the state. ULU learned where to find these workers, how to follow the money trail, and how to take advantage of the structure of home care—its ties to the welfare state and the bonds between workers and clients generated by the labor process itself." These latter structural issues became very important to the organizing process. The ULU soon affiliated with the SEIU, where it "helped revitalize organizing within that service industry giant."[23] Likewise in New York, California, and Chicago, the SEIU and other unions deepened their experience in a sector so different from the traditional workplace. Organizing the workers meant organizing their clients and fighting in the political sphere for recognition and labor protections.

Internal struggles in the SEIU contributed to setbacks for this initial phase of home health-care organizing. But in the 1990s the SEIU launched a national campaign as part of the AFL-CIO's drive to re-emphasize organizing. Mary Kay Henry, who became SEIU's president in 2010, explained: "It's a sector of the economy that hasn't collapsed in the economic downturn and it can't be offshored." Historian Eileen Boris added, "Homecare workers are the new face of labor."[24] By 2014, SEIU (which split from the AFL-CIO in 2005) claimed over four hundred thousand home health-care workers, a full quarter of the national home health-care workforce. The majority were in California, where these workers comprised 20 percent of the giant's membership.[25]

Part of this new effort was fought in legislatures and the courts. The SEIU argued that since Medicaid ultimately paid home health workers' wages—by reimbursing the agencies that employed them—these workers should be recognized as public employees. California was the first state to agree, in a series of decisions culminating in 2003, and Massachusetts followed suit in 2006. The courts have also debated whether unions can collect fees in lieu of dues from those covered by their contracts who decline to join the union. In contrast to the situation in Massachusetts and California, court rulings in Michigan and Illinois turned home health care into a virtual right-to-work industry.[26]

By 2013, SEIU1199 had organized some thirty thousand Medicaid-reimbursed home health-care workers in Massachusetts, and in 2015 Massachusetts became the first state in the nation to agree to raise their wage to $15 an hour (by 2018).[27] SEIU continued to mobilize thousands of low-wage workers to raise the state minimum wage to $15 for all workers as part of the union's Fight for $15 campaign, a national drive that also sought to raise SEIU's profile in legislative and community efforts.[28]

Fight for $15 and the Chinese Progressive Association played an important role in promoting a union organizing campaign at Medical Resources Home Health Corp in 2015. (Because they were not Medicaid-reimbursed, these workers labored outside the state bargaining unit.) The campaign illustrated some of the power as well as some of the challenges of the community/union organizing process.

Medical Resources

That year, a small group of medical resources workers—resentful about low and unpredictable pay—sought the help of the CPA. Chen explains:

> And so we started this campaign with just a few workers saying they're very unhappy, and we start writing letters to the company, saying "I want to know what the pay is. How do you determine how to get a raise, I want to see your policy for travel pay, because some people get more, some people get less." We started with that. And then the worker core started growing from four to five people to about a dozen, and then eventually we had twenty or thirty workers.

It took a while for the protesters to decide to turn their campaign into a union organizing drive. Chen understood the workers' reluctance, but also wanted to challenge it: "Whenever there's a union campaign, the thing that people like to do the most is to say 'Oh, the union just wants your dues,' and they would criticize unions, saying then your voice is not going to be heard." Thus, she says, "We did not talk about unionizing at all, throughout. But we were working with [SEIU Local] 1199, they were doing some research, and we were feeding them information about what do we think, realistically, what the workers can fight for? And we were also learning more about the industry, the structure, where the money is coming from, who it goes to, who are the decision-makers, and things like that. And eventually," she concludes, "the workers are like, 'Well, you know what, let's have a union drive.'"

Many of the workers were also dubious about SEIU's efforts to mobilize them for the Massachusetts Fight for $15 campaign. Recounts Chen: "I start talking to the workers about it, and they're like, 'I don't know, this is Fight for $15, I don't know if we can get fifteen, we're just asking for Boston's living wage [that at the time was $13.67], and already we think that's probably impossible, right?' But after we send them a first petition, they gave everybody who signed the petition a 45 cent increase! And then I was like, 'Well, that happened, and that means that they can pay you more, right?' But they only gave it to the people who signed the petition." The company's concession emboldened workers further, as did the June 2015 state decision on wages for home health-care workers paid by the state.

Just a few days after SEIU's wage victory for state-employed home health workers, workers at Medical Resource won a hard-fought union election. In September 2016, workers ratified their first contract with the agency. They won significant pay raises—though not enough to bring them up to the level of the state's Medicaid-reimbursed workers—as well as paid leave days and compensation for travel time and waiting time between appointments.[29]

The CPA served as a crucial bridge between the union and the many Chinese health-care workers. While SEIU had organizational resources and state-level clout, the CPA, as an ethnic social justice organization, had the deep roots in the community. "One of our big constituencies that we organize is the elderly. And the elderly, we start telling them about the home-care campaign, we're trying to reach out more, to more home-care workers. And they start asking their home care workers to contact CPA." CPA's collaboration with SEIU brought some significant victories. Chen reflected on the different, but potentially complementary, nature of the two types of organizations. "Some of [people's criticisms of unions] may be true, but all in all, if you work in a blue-collar industry, that's the best you can get. And this is how actually you can have the most influence, right? And build the most power. Because of that, we did publicity in the community."

Not all analysts are sanguine about the home health sector victories. The very strengths of social movement unionism could be perceived as weaknesses from the perspective of the labor movement. Leon Fink and Brian Greenberg argued that "home care, the biggest growth area for organizing in recent years, accentuated a tension already manifest in other ways between union leadership and its rank and file. More than any other organizing battles, home-care campaigns have been waged and won through the mobilization of media, church, and political allies *more than through the self-organization of the workers themselves*. The tangible gains from such campaigns . . . tend to turn the union political staff (themselves mostly young, college-educated professionals) into a kind of stand-in or steward for the poorly paid immigrant and minority members for whom they serve as advocates." Moreover, to the extent that home health-care workers are paid through Medicare and Medicaid, these campaigns are vulnerable to the critiques leveled against public sector unions, insofar as taxpayers employed in the nonunion private sector see their gains as an affront rather than a way of raising the floor for all.[30] Yet the college-educated Chen herself, like other Boston worker center staff, exemplifies how in immigrant communities many of the more educated staff share with the workers they seek to organize not only ethnicity, language, and culture, but also experiences of undocumentedness and low-wage, precarious labor.

Undocumentedness and the Challenges of Organizing

In addition to issues of labor market structure, workers' immigrant identities and legal-status issues bring particular challenges to labor organizing. Historically, immigrant workers' home-country orientation and short-term goals sometimes made them less likely to protest working conditions and wages that the native-born would consider intolerable. Many of Boston's recent immigrants share this home-country orientation, while also facing new issues that emerged in the late twentieth century related to immigration status and undocumentedness. Laws, policies, and enforcement have increasingly made workers' status unstable and fragile.

Undocumentedness can divide workers, and it can pose very real and concrete obstacles to labor organizing, especially in the Trump era. But immigrant rights can also serve as a key organizing issue for immigrant workers, as evidenced by the huge mobilizations in 2006 and 2017 that linked labor and immigrant identities.[31]

For immigrant and especially undocumented workers in Boston, immigration status is utterly central to their identity and position as workers. But their status brings with it an array of obstacles to labor organizing. Gladys Vega of the Chelsea Collaborative described a 2012 case at Boston Hides and Furs, a Chelsea animal hides processing wholesaler that was paying immigrant workers well under minimum wage. "We called a meeting with them," she recalls, "and it took us a little bit hard to get them organized, because they were so fearful about immigration. And they were so fearful about our organization, although some of them know Chelsea Collaborative. But when it comes to talking about their work conditions, they were like, no, they're gonna call immigration, like they were in a panic about seeking help." In this case, with support from Greater Boston Legal Services, the US Department of Labor ultimately sued the company and obtained $825,000 in back wages for fourteen employees—with no immigration status retaliation.

While worker centers emphasize that they support workers regardless of their immigration status, the immigrant community itself is far from united with respect to the rights of the undocumented. Says the CPA's Chen:

> Our community is quite divided on whether or not you support the undocumented. Because the people who came here what they call "the right way," say, "Well, I had to wait for fifteen years for my family to be reunited, and the people who come in undocumented are cutting the line! Why should we give them the right to do that? Doesn't it encourage more people to come in?" That's kind of like the general entire undocumented narrative within the community. And for us, in the workers center, we always have this discussion around "Why would it be important to not have a second-class citizen? Because they will be like second-class workers. And that actually jeopardizes the rights of all workers."[32]

Lídia Ferreira of the Brazilian Women's Group adds that legal status intersects with other aspects of immigrant vulnerability. If they work for employers from their home country, the employer may use this connection to threaten their families back home even as they also threaten to involve immigration authorities. After Trump's election, she explains,

> We had a meeting here with three workers who are suffering from wage theft, misclassification, and unpaid overtime. And also, they are suffering by threats by their employers. Because one of them had an accident at work, and when he decided to claim the workers' compensation to Brazilian Women's Group, the employers started to threaten him and his family in Brazil. And that is something unfortunately very common in our community. Because the employer knows their situation, their English, they start to say, for example, "I will report you to immigration if you decide to start a claim."

These fears seemed to be realized as the Trump administration's Immigration and Customs Enforcement, or ICE, began to cast its net more widely in detaining undocumented immigrants, which has had a sobering impact on the ability of workers to fight for their rights. In several cases nationally, including one in Boston, ICE apparently responded to tips from employers or to the very fact that workers filed a claim against an employer, in order to target undocumented workers.[33]

On May 1, 2017, the Massachusetts Attorney General's office reaffirmed its commitment to protecting the labor rights of all workers regardless of immigration status and protecting workers from status-related retaliation. "In Massachusetts, our labor and employment laws protect every worker, regardless of their immigration status," the Attorney General promised. "When dishonest employers hire undocumented workers under the table and then threaten them with deportation, it cheats the workers and makes it harder for honest businesses to compete. Today, my office is sending a message: if you're being threatened by your employer, our laws protect you."[34] But reality did not always live up to her words. In May 2017, a Honduran immigrant agreed to meet with his employer, a Boston-based construction company, after he filed a worker compensation claim. When the worker appeared at the appointed spot, ICE agents were waiting to arrest him.[35] Several other similar cases elsewhere in the country suggest that this was not a unique development. As government deportation priorities have been vastly expanded under the Obama and Trump administrations, employers' ability to threaten and control workers has also. These kinds of actions have chilling effects on immigrant workers' ability to fight for their rights and for worker centers to strengthen their organizing.

Even beyond the issue of their legal status, immigrant workers may have other reasons for being wary of attempts to organize. The issue of wage theft illustrates some of the challenges. Wage theft can happen when employers simply refuse to pay workers, or when they write bad checks, force workers to work off the clock, or misclassify workers as independent contractors to deny benefits. Community Labor United estimates that wage theft costs Massachusetts workers $700 million a year. Despite aggressive action by the state Attorney General's office, only a small portion is ever recovered. Wage theft has been a key issue in which Boston's worker centers have collaborated with the state's union federation to fight for a common goal: state-level legislation to hold parent industries responsible for violations like wage theft committed by subcontractors. The labor-supported bill passed the State Senate in 2016, but stalled in the House; it was reintroduced and remained under consideration as of early 2021.[36]

Many workers who have experienced wage theft approach a worker center hoping for help recovering their own lost wages. Centers generally want to engage workers in the larger legislative and public campaign, but for the workers, the end goal may be simply receiving their back wages. The contradiction illustrates the tensions in worker centers' dual mission as service providers, and as organizers for larger social change. In this respect, the questions and challenges facing worker centers mirror those facing unions: how to articulate and navigate connections between the narrower fight to protect workers' rights on the job and the larger goal of structural change in an economy increasingly inauspicious to these rights. Low-wage and immigrant workers may be among the most exploited by the system, but their status can also contribute to a worldview as individualistic and conservative as a stereotypically anti-immigrant white worker's. Immigrant workers are afraid of losing their jobs, but also of being reported to immigration enforcement and of repercussions to their families in their home countries.

Ferreira explained of her clients at the Brazilian Women's Group: "First we have to show them or educate them about the issues. We start to try to help them to think beyond the situation. It's difficult for them to see the light at the end of the tunnel, when you are talking about a long process, a campaign. Like last week we spoke with the two workers who came to the meeting, [but] they are [only] interested to receive their own payments, they are still waiting for so long. As a worker center, we need the workers to make the difference. We need their ability to go forward, to fight, to organize, to bring other workers to the solution."

Despite the unfavorable political climate and the many structural challenges her center faces, Chen tried to offer a hopeful perspective on labor-community relations after the 2016 election. Perhaps organized labor's weakened position could push it into greater focus on labor-community relations. "Labor is actually looking to partner with communities and worker centers to build a stronger movement," she says. "And I think that's very smart, because I think we're a very important strategic partner to the labor movement. And then labor needs to take stronger stands around immigrant rights, and housing issues, and other things."

Boston offers a complex landscape in which liberal, pro-worker, pro-union, and pro-immigrant ideologies infuse the city's self-image, while obscuring the marginalization and exploitation that many immigrant workers confront. The city's unions and worker centers play a crucial role in fighting for both legislative and grassroots solutions to its deep inequalities.

CHAPTER 10

Policy Group on Tradeswomen's Issues

A Collaborative Learning Community Crushing the Barriers to Women's Careers in the Construction Trades

Susan Moir and Elizabeth Skidmore

The authors of this story are two women: one is an academic researcher, and the other a carpenter who has moved into union leadership. Since 2008, we have collaborated on what one of us describes as a participatory action research (PAR) project and the other views as an organizing campaign. We share the goal of getting more women into the union construction trades. The results of this collaboration, and the industry partnerships that have been built, have changed the understanding and perception of gender in the construction industry in Massachusetts and have dramatically increased the number of women in the trades. We will tell you how this collaboration came about, where we see it going, and what ongoing challenges we continue to face.

In 2008, the research department at the Labor Resource Center at the UMass Boston was approached by a representative of the New England Regional Council of Carpenters. The carpenters' representative had been working to increase outreach and recruitment of women to apprenticeship in carpentry and union membership for twenty years. She and the labor center research director had previously worked together on issues of health and safety for tradeswomen and had co-authored a report on gender equity in pre-apprenticeship. This time, the carpenters' representative said to the researcher, "We have been trying and failing to get more women into the trades for decades. We need a think tank. Can we pull together the smartest people we know who care about this?"[1]

The story of how "Rosie the Riveter" was forced out of the factories at the end of World War II is well known. The contemporary history of the efforts, and failures, to open up male-dominated jobs in the construction trades to women, however, is less familiar.[2] As we began pulling together those "smartest people" we knew, we reviewed the story that tradeswomen had been living and creating since the 1970s. In April 1978, President Jimmy Carter signed Executive Order 11246 requiring that 6.9 percent of hours worked on federally funded construction projects be worked by women, a provision later made permanent. At that time, less than 3 percent of construction workers in the US were women.[3] The policy change was driven by the women's movement's demands for wage equality and access to better paying jobs in male-dominated fields. Following EO 11246, a wave of young women, many of them college-educated feminists, entered the trades. These women and their allies formed Tradeswomen's Organizations around the country and started pre-apprenticeship programs to train women in basic construction skills and provide them with the information and support they needed to apply to construction apprenticeship programs.[4] Women lobbied state and federal government agencies to provide funding for training. Hundreds of thousands of women went through these programs. Some undetermined number of those women pursued working in the trades by applying to apprentice programs or directly to contractors for employment. Occasionally, in some places the number of women working in construction increased to 5 and even 6 percent. However, most women never got through the application process; those who did were usually the first to be laid off when work slowed; the women who made it through the gauntlet that was the three- to five-year process from apprentice to journeywoman spent their working days in a hostile environment and spent their careers never seeing another woman at work.[5]

During this same era, participation by people of color (administratively termed "minorities") in the construction trades improved substantially, from a rate of 13 percent in the late 1960s to 20 percent in 2010 and 40 percent in 2020. Many factors have contributed to this change, including increased enforcement of equal opportunity and anti-discrimination laws, shifts in the racial demographics of the country, and other social changes following the Civil Rights and other social justice movements. The labor market also changed. The sons, nephews, and male family friends of white construction workers had a near-monopoly on apprenticeship and jobs in the industry for generations. As that traditional labor pool benefited from the well-paid middle-class jobs of their fathers, more of them went to college and into white-collar work. The resulting labor shortage was filled in part by "minorities"—but that meant minority men. Thirty years after the 6.9 percent goal for women in federal construction projects was set, when the carpenter came to see the academic in 2008, the workforce was just over 2 percent women.

Creating a Learning Community for Social Change

After the federal target was established, tradeswomen formed organizations across the country. Massachusetts, and especially Boston, was one of the centers of tradeswomen's organizing. By the mid-1980s, an initial wave of women who had entered several trades, a group that included electricians, carpenters, and plumbers, had successfully completed their apprenticeships and gone on to become journey-level workers. Women in the Building Trades (WIBT) was founded in 1986 and offered women pre-apprenticeship classes for almost twenty years.[6] The Boston Tradeswomen's Network (BTN) formed in 1990 to help women stay in the trades through mentoring and other forms of support. Although both organizations had dissolved by 2008, many of the people who had founded WIBT and BTN, or benefited from their efforts, were still around. At the recommendation of the researcher, those people— all of them women—were invited to attend a series of three to four meetings to review and evaluate their past efforts to increase the number of tradeswomen, and to explore the possibilities of a renewed initiative. This would not be the traditional think tank of a handful of professional experts; it would be a participatory process of community evaluation and knowledge building.

Outreach for the meetings was conducted by word-of-mouth, and twenty to thirty women showed up. In addition to current and former tradeswomen, several municipal, state, and federal government representatives who were involved in affirmative action policy and enforcement programs attended the meetings. These women had been working in isolation to enforce goals and support women entering the trades for years. The active participation of government representatives at this particular moment was not coincidental. The renewed interest in diversity issues nationally under the Obama administration and in

Massachusetts under Governor Deval Patrick's administration gave permission for lower-level officials to engage in this initiative. Patrick made his support for affirmative action explicit when he set up an Office of Access and Opportunity that was charged with pursuing racial and gender diversity issues across all state agencies.

The early meetings did not go smoothly. Old antagonisms and feuding factions who held each other responsible for the dissolution of various organizations came together in the room; tradeswomen who worked all day resented professional women who had the privilege and technology to make decisions; professional women, whose day jobs were to implement and enforce, contended with others' resentments over failed policies. Over several meetings, women aired their grievances and those who did not want to work with the group stopped coming. A decision on the name of the group solidified the commitment of those who remained. The name should not imply that this was an organization of tradeswomen or that the group would offer training. The name, they felt, should instead reflect the commitment to new ideas and strategies for reviving old efforts to increase women's access to good jobs in the construction trades. Before the end of 2008, the Policy Group on Tradeswomen's Issues (PGTI) was formed. Today, PGTI—a participatory research project and an organizing committee—is a learning community that shares knowledge, creates and evaluates practical strategies, and documents outcomes. It describes itself as a "multi-stakeholder collaboration of over seventy-five labor, community, government, and business partners that has been meeting every other month since 2008 with the singular purpose of crushing the barriers to women's entry into the construction trades. The PGTI goal is 20 percent tradeswomen by 2020."[7]

The Question Is "How?"

Early on, PGTI participants shared an understanding that knowledge of what had been done to increase the number of women in the trades was "siloed." Women in different trades and different unions had different experiences. Participants who worked in various government enforcement agencies had a great deal of information and experience, but these were subjective perspectives based on where they sat in the spectrum of government, labor, or community interest (or lack thereof) in affirmative action. The impulse for participants to generalize their own knowledge and experience dissolved quickly as it became clear that the initiatives, and their successes and failures, were disparate and often unconnected. The first three years of PGTI was a phase of explicitly building relationships in order to break down the silos of knowledge and experience and mapping who was doing what, and where. The first policy decision that PGTI participants made was to reject the longstanding controversy over "double counting" demographic data. In the tradeswomen's movement and other places where affirmative action goals for women and people of color existed simultaneously, there had been decades of discussions and disagreement over how to count a woman of color—as a woman, as a person of color, or both? This was further complicated when there were residency targets. How would a woman of color who was a resident in a covered jurisdiction be counted? PGTI said this woman should be counted three times. The following position was adopted its first year: "We do not oppose—in fact, we support— double and triple counting of women as 'female, minority and/or resident' for the purposes of collecting diversity data. Insofar as women of color are double counted, it incentivizes their access to these jobs and that is a good thing."[8] In addition to gathering and sorting the knowledge of those who had worked to increase women's access to the trades, PGTI's researchers conducted an extensive review of the literature on women and the construction trades, including case studies of "Bright Spots," or instances where women's participation had increased on single projects under intensive monitoring, only to fall back again to under 3 percent when the project was complete.

The 2011 PGTI report, *Unfinished Business: Building Equality for Women in the Construction Trades*, showed that the fundamental question of *why* women were not in the construction trades had been researched for decades, and the answers were consistent: women were not in the trades because they had been systematically excluded from apprenticeship and employment in male-controlled institutions, barring them from necessary education and exposure to relevant skills. These institutions have included all levels of construction industry stakeholders, from owners and developers who purchase and oversee construction, to the contractors and subcontractors who are the workers' employers, as well as the unions and apprenticeship programs that control the labor supply and train the workers. At every level, there has been historic discrimination and hostility toward women entering the construction trades and succeeding in them. *Unfinished Business* concludes that the "why" question has been answered many times and deserves no more study. Women have not been in the construction trades because men have kept them out.

The question for the future—the one that can change the past failures—is *how* can women's participation in the construction trades be increased up to and beyond the legally mandated 6.9 percent?[9] *Unfinished Business* documented that the industry's resistance to women entering the trades was in contradiction to the labor shortage that contractors and the industry's trade press had been lamenting since the mid-1990s.[10] The average age of construction workers in 2010 was forty; in 2017, it was forty-six. There is a critical need for younger workers and the traditional pool of young male family members of construction workers is not filling the need. Despite their fathers' good wages and upward mobility, the sons have gone to college. While they may work on a construction site during summer breaks from college, after graduation they are working in an office. The relevant *why* questions, therefore, might instead be: why keep out a willing workforce when faced with a growing shortage of workers?[11]

Unfinished Business also documented that the only viable career path for large numbers of women to enter the trades is through union apprenticeship. Numerous studies completed between 1998 and 2011 (see appendix) have found that while joint union apprenticeship programs have historically enrolled too few women, they still enroll twice as many women as nonunion programs. Contrary to commonly held but incorrect assumptions, joint union programs accept and graduate both women and people of color at much higher rates than nonunion programs.

PGTI participants spent three years building relationships, constructing baseline knowledge, and completing a foundational document. During those three years, the Massachusetts construction industry—like the industry nationally—was in the depths of the Great Recession. Fifty percent or more of building-trades workers were unemployed. Many had lost their health insurance and were running out of unemployment benefits. In a boom-and-bust industry, this was the deepest bust in decades. When PGTI participants began to raise questions of reviving efforts to increase the number of women in the trades, the response from many industry members was that it was not the right time. There were too many workers "on the bench" to think about bringing in new people. Within PGTI, discussions were focused on developing the alliances and strategies to push the issue as soon as doors began to open after the recession. When the door opened in 2011,

PGTI was well positioned to revive the movement and push for women to enter the trades.[12]

A Laboratory for How to Do It:
The UMass Boston Project Labor Agreement

In 2010, Governor Patrick and the Metro Boston Building Trades Council (MetroBTC), the umbrella organization for Greater Boston's construction unions, negotiated a Project Labor Agreement (PLA) for the reconstruction of the UMass Boston campus. In a city with almost forty institutions of higher education, UMass Boston is the only public university. It was built in the 1970s on a landfill with notoriously shoddy construction amid a corruption scandal. Reconstruction of the campus was projected to take ten years and cost $800 million.

Project Labor Agreements are pre-hire, union collective-bargaining agreements. Dating back to the 1930s, PLAs have ensured that major public works projects, such as the Hoover Dam and Cape Canaveral, were built safely and on time by skilled, qualified workers who were in turn guaranteed a good wage, job security, and health and pension benefits. The right of public entities to negotiate PLAs has been challenged and contested by the nonunion construction sector. In the case of UMass Boston—in no small part because the campus was so poorly built the first time—there was broad public and private agreement that construction needed to be closely monitored and that the workers who reconstructed the campus should have the benefits and protections of unionization. The UMass Boston PLA was standard in most respects: the work would be all union in exchange for a commitment for a negotiated process of labor disputes ("labor peace"), but it was unique in that it included very high workforce diversity requirements and the explicit commitment of the MetroBTC and its affiliated unions to provide the women, people of color, and Boston-resident workers who would meet those requirements. The diversity requirements modeled the City of Boston's Boston Resident Jobs Policy (BRJP), the highest diversity targets legally available at the time: 50 percent of construction workforce hours would be done by Boston residents, 25 percent by racial "minorities," and 10 percent by women.[13] As a state project, the diversity goals could have been set at the federal requirement of 15.3 percent minorities and 6.9 percent women. However, the unions and the Patrick administration chose to voluntarily include the BRJP's higher goals in the PLA, a groundbreaking development.

By contrast, in the 1980s and 1990s, the MetroBTC had opposed the creation and enforcement of the BRJP and all affirmative action efforts in construction. The UMass Boston PLA made a clean break with the exclusionary past of the building trades sector of the labor movement in Massachusetts and with the trades' historic resistance to any outside pressure to open up jobs to minorities and women.[14]

Meeting the goal for minorities would be a challenge, but it was attainable with the workforce available at the time. Since the mid-1990s, men of color had been entering the building trades in Massachusetts in larger numbers, and union projects in the city usually met the 25 percent "racial minority" benchmark. However, no progress had been made for women, and the local workforce rate was consistent with the national rate of 3 percent women. The unions would need tradeswomen to meet the goal they had agreed to. The newly elected head of the MetroBTC, Marty Walsh, initiated several recruitment efforts. He reached out to PGTI for advice; he met with the women of the Massachusetts Tradeswomen's Association (MTWA) to offer them his support and the support of the MetroBTC; he formed a partnership with the Boston Housing Authority, whose public housing residents were primarily women; and he established the MetroBTC's Building Pathways Pre-Apprenticeship Program to prepare people of color and women for entry into union apprenticeship programs. Since its founding, 40 percent of Building Pathways participants have been women and 80 percent of graduates have entered union apprenticeship.

In addition to setting high targets, the PLA included another innovation that would change the context for increasing women's participation in Massachusetts' construction workforce. It required the establishment of an Access and Opportunity Committee (AOC) that would monitor progress on the PLA diversity targets through an open and transparent process. The AOC would "serve as a central forum for representatives of all interested and affected individuals to exchange information and ideas and to advise the parties concerning the operation and results" of the new requirements. The AOC would also "assess the obstacles to success of achieving inclusion of minority and women workers in the construction opportunities and shall make recommendations for additional programmatic efforts to overcome some of those obstacles." PGTI participants, who had personally observed decades of similar initiatives that had failed to launch, lobbied for immediate commencement of the AOC and the inclusion of PGTI participants and other community representatives on the committee.

As it was with the earliest meetings of PGTI, the UMass Boston AOC got off to a slow and rocky start. An industry that for decades had been legally required to include women, but had never done so, had developed creative and customary processes to affirm the rightness and inevitability of excluding women. In early AOC meetings, a government or contractor representative responsible for enforcement would explain that no matter how hard contractors tried, it was impossible to find tradeswomen. They would blame the union. When the union came in the room and said they had the women, blame shifted down the hierarchy to the subcontractor. When various evasions and deceits were exposed, the women themselves were blamed. "They just don't want to do this kind of work," an enforcement official would say. When that excuse was challenged with evidence that women do want these jobs, the representatives of the old way of doing things threw up their hands and just claimed it would never happen.

But it did. Over months and years and through persistence and the continual evolution of a participatory model of exploration, learning, and documenting, AOC participants developed a collective analysis of what would work and would not work to increase the number of women at work building UMass Boston. Individuals, most but not all women, took the ideas that were generated collectively in PGTI and in the AOC meetings and tried them out in the field. Intensive monitoring and regular communication generated a growing set of best practices that increased women's numbers on site and kept the women working. The result was that the first project under the UMass Boston PLA, the Integrated Sciences Complex (ISC), attained what no other project in Boston ever had. Women worked 10 percent of the work hours on the ISC every month of the 24 months it took to build it. Out of that success, PGTI collected the proven best practices in a manual of checklists that were customized for all "stakeholders" of the industry: construction owners, developers, managers, contractors, subcontractors, building trade unions, training and apprenticeship programs, and community-based organizations. *Finishing the Job: Best Practices for a Diverse Workforce in the Construction Industry* provides guidance to each level of the industry in how to change the way they have been doing things—the way that keeps women out. It shows them, instead, the practices that bring women in and train them for successful careers as tradespeople.[15]

We have identified many of the key lessons of the ISC. Here are two key examples, which we regard as "game changers": Firstly, we have found that the truth is best learned when everyone is in the room. Contractors and union representatives have longstanding relationships. One may have worked for the other, or for his father. The union's business agent, meanwhile, is dependent on the contractor to get his members to work; the contractor is dependent on the agent for his workforce. They have been doing it this way for a long time. It is time-consuming to have multiple meetings with people who know or tell only half the story. It is much more effective to get everyone in the same room for corrective action meetings. In a business where the demands of the workforce are very fluid, wasting time can seriously impede changes if the job for the tradeswoman was completed last week. Secondly, if a woman is able to get on a contractor's core crew, the crew that goes to the job first and usually stays the longest, she may get more steady training and employment. Placing women on the core crew also reduces the problems that arise when contractors try to catch up with the required targets after the work has begun. "Catching up" causes both mathematical and human-resource problems. Mathematically, a contractor who has 0 percent women's hours for weeks at the beginning of a job may never be able to reach the 10 percent target before the crew is finished. The only means of catching up may be to replace male workers with tradeswomen, and that causes the human resource problem. PGTI has taken a strong public position against laying off tradesmen to add a tradeswoman to a crew. Not only will any woman who is added to the crew be blamed for the action, the support of union tradesmen is critical to the long-term goals of substantially increasing the number of women in the trades. That support is undermined by taking jobs from allies.

Finishing the Job and these game changers became tools for monitoring micro and short-term changes in women's participation on work sites. PGTI participants were also able to identify data for establishing baselines and assessing longer-term progress. The state Division of Apprentice Standards began reporting quarterly on the demographics of all registered apprentice programs. The City of Boston put years of data on women's (and "minority" and resident) work hours under the BRJP online. Initially, these data supported the local assumption that the rates of women working in the trades in Boston and enrolled in apprenticeship were slightly higher than the national rate at ±4 percent (perhaps due to the visibility of tradeswomen's organizing in the 1980s and 1990s), but they were also flat. Data in later years have supported anecdotal speculation that approximately half of the women who are entering the trades in Massachusetts are women of color. This in turn supports PGTI's advocacy of double counting and its practice encouraging unions and employers to privilege tradeswomen of color to meet their contractual obligation to secure a diverse workforce.

The PGTI Model: Integrating Supply and Demand

Along with the tools and best practices identified on the UMass Boston PLA, a larger theoretical framework emerged from a critique of the failed strategies of the past.[16] This framework had three key pillars:

- There was a fatal gap in past efforts between the *goal* of increasing women working in the trades and the *strategy* of training women to enter apprenticeship.

- The bridge across that gap was jobs. The historical practice of recruiting and training women for these jobs was a failed strategy. Supply needed the other half: demand. And demand would only come in the form of jobs that had effective commitments to hiring women.

- The UMass Boston ISC would devolve into just another "Bright Spot"—that is, a single case of success followed by the expected cyclical decline—if the lessons learned were not applied widely across the regional industry and the demand for women working in construction was not expanded.

The theoretical framework that developed to guide PGTI is a regional strategy of integration of both supply and demand. The supply is shaped by training women for the industry, and the demand comes from enforcing the hiring goals that get women working in the trades on construction sites.

For nearly thirty years, as thousands of women went through pre-apprenticeship, there was a constant and plentiful supply of women wanting and waiting to enter the trades. That supply had no impact on the baseline rate of women's participation in the construction trades or on increasing the number of women in the trades. Training women had created a surplus labor pool, because there had been no demand for women to work in construction. Presumably, demand should have been driven by the 6.9 percent target for women's hours in all federally funded construction, but the demand was hypothetical because there was no enforcement. Why there was no enforcement, however, is a contested question. The federal agency responsible for enforcement, the Office of Federal Contract Compliance (OFCCP), has had such a light presence in the industry that it is unknown to many stakeholders. Fear of litigation that potentially could have resulted in the 6.9 percent target being declared illegal may have contributed to OFCCP's cautious approach to its mandated responsibility.[17] However, an unenforced policy had no more impact on change than a policy overturned in the courts would have. PGTI's attempts to partner with OFCCP for greater government enforcement on regional construction projects that were covered by the federal target for women were exhaustive but ultimately ineffective.

But on the ISC and other projects that applied the best practices laid out in *Finishing the Job* and established AOC monitoring committees, women's participation on job sites was increasing. It was increasing because women were being hired by the contractors; there was demand for more women workers to meet the target of 10 percent imposed by the PLA. However, many of these contractors had been contractually obligated to hire women on other projects in the past. If they had worked on any project in Boston since 1980, they had signed a contract to hire 10 percent women. If they had ever worked on a federally funded project, they had committed to hire 6.9 percent women. What was different on the UMass Boston PLA? There was enforcement. Not government enforcement, which had proved to be non-existent and had contributed to a culture of flouting targets, but an open, public, and transparent process of continuous monitoring that developed through the community/labor partnerships and the collaborative efforts of those who participated in the AOC. It was critical that those reviewing the monthly progress on meeting workforce goals included more than just the owner and the general contractor or construction manager, which is how compliance meetings, if they were done at all, had been done in the past. By having the public in the room—in the form of PGTI, individual tradeswomen, the Building Trades Unions, community organizations, and community leaders—the construction industry "insiders" could no longer agree to not comply.

Given the success of the UMass Boston PLA in increasing women's access to work in the trades, the proven best practices of *Finishing the Job* and the model of continuous monitoring by the Access and Opportunity Committee were adopted by other projects. The largest and most visible is the Mass Gaming Commission's construction of two casinos. The $800 million casino project in Springfield provided a platform for expanding the work of the PGTI into western Massachusetts. With its 8 percent female workforce, the project exceeded the state and federal goals despite being in a rural area without Boston's history of organizing tradeswomen. At a second casino project in Greater Boston, 7 percent of the workers were women, and with over five hundred women working in total, it was likely the largest concentration of tradeswomen on any single construction work site anywhere in the country. The PGTI model is now being used in full or in part on about $6.7 billion worth of construction in Massachusetts. But the most reliable benchmark for progress is the data on women in registered apprenticeship. A study of Massachusetts apprenticeship data between 1997 and 2007 found that 928 women were enrolled in registered programs over that ten-year period, or an average of 93 per year, and that the rate of participation for women was 3.4 percent of all apprentices. A second baseline was taken in 2012, when there were 180 union and non-union women apprentices, or 4.2 percent of all apprentices in the trades. Halfway through 2020, the union sector of construction apprenticeship reached 9.5 percent women, with 676 active women apprentices. Ninety-five percent of all female construction apprentices in Massachusetts are in union programs. Progress in the nonunion sector has been flat since 2014 and continues to reflect the national trend of 3 to 4 percent women apprentices. See Figure 1 for trends in the union and nonunion sectors over the past eight years.

The Future and Its Challenges

There is no doubt that current economic and political conditions in Boston have created a robust context for the success of the PGTI's supply and demand model. The city has been in the middle of a historic building boom, and Boston's construction workforce increased by 50 percent between 2010 and 2017.[18] As of the end of 2019, the $15 billion in new construction permits that have been approved by the city's planning agency guarantee that the demand for new tradespeople will continue to accelerate. PLAs with major developers ensure that most of the construction within the city is done by union workers. Political support for increasing both gender and racial diversity in the workforce is very strong. Martin J. Walsh, the Building Trades Council leader who first championed a more diverse workforce and supported the first PGTI project at UMass Boston, became the mayor of Boston and continued to support the advancement of women in the trades. His successor as leader of the Metro BTC, Brian Doherty, has become a national voice for gender and racial justice and for opening the trades to historically excluded groups. Fourteen of the twenty-eight union apprenticeship programs in Massachusetts have increased their female participation by 20 percent or more in the past two years. Women are beginning to move into leadership positions as stewards and executive board members. The first woman of color business agent was brought on by the IBEW in the past year.[19]

The explicit goal of PGTI, "20 percent tradeswomen by 2020," is not just a slogan. Research on past efforts to increase women in the trades has made very clear that incremental progress on women's participation has not prevented cyclical setbacks. There is a historical pattern of "increase to 6 percent, drop back to 3 percent." In each case where women's numbers increased in response to activism around specific projects, the numbers have returned to the ~3 percent baseline when the project is complete. PGTI's regional approach and integration of supply and demand will not thwart the boom-and-bust cycles of the construction industry. When the Massachusetts construction economy inevitably depresses in some unknown number of years, tradeswomen will be laid off and the most vulnerable will leave the industry. The goal is to break the "6 percent, 3 percent" pattern by bringing a much larger number of women into the industry during this boom end of the cycle.

A consequence of PGTI's short-term successes is that, at the moment, there is a shortage of available qualified tradeswomen in the region. On AOC–monitored projects, the rate of tradeswomen on work sites is 7.5 percent—still too low, but twice the national average and above the federal 6.9 percent target. The demand for more tradeswomen comes both from reluctant contractors, who are pressured by AOC monitoring committees and from committed contractors who have bought into the goals and are increasing women's participation on additional projects. To meet the increased demand, PGTI and Building Pathways have formed a nonprofit, the Northeast Center for Tradeswomen's Equity (NCTE), to improve outreach and expand the pipeline to careers in the construction trades for women who might have no experience or knowledge of the opportunity. NCTE holds "Tradeswomen Tuesday" information sessions around the state at community colleges, career centers, high schools, and other locations, where women come to hear about how to enter the trades, and where working tradeswomen from the NCTE-sponsored "Tradeswomen's Speakers Bureau" tell their stories about how to get and stay in the trades. The Mass Gaming Commission has produced a public-service advertising campaign called "Build a Life That Works" on public transportation in Boston and Springfield. Over 18 percent of students in Massachusetts' vocational technical high school construction preparatory programs are girls, and their teachers and guidance counselors have formed Mass Girls in Trades (MAGIT) to connect their female students with careers in the trades. The first two years of targeted outreach to women has resulted in a database of over fifteen hundred women, 80 percent of whom are women of color, interested and actively pursuing careers in the union trades. These women receive information on open apprenticeships every month in addition to other opportunities, such as workshops offered by the unions to increase the diversity of apprenticeship applicants.

Even as the pool of available and qualified women grows, we continue to identify gaps in the pipeline. Opportunities for women are very uneven across the trades, with the laborers exceeding 16 percent women apprentices, but some mechanical trades still lagging at under 4 percent. Recently, gaps in the pipeline between the union hall and the apprentice training centers have become clearer. Apprenticeship programs are not entirely responsive to the market's labor demands. Program trustees control entry, and those in small programs continue to be reluctant to diversify their student bodies when it means not accepting as many of their traditional white male applicants. Unions, apprenticeship programs, and contractors make the greatest and fastest progress when they implement a practice of "Women First," taking the best women candidates first and filling in their member, trainee, and labor needs with men second. It's a radical idea, but one consistent with, and getting a boost from, larger social changes around gender.

"Women First" is both a theoretical paradigm and a radical organizing strategy. It is supported by PGTI's first documented research finding, that women have been systematically excluded from construction work because of their gender, and by conclusive evidence from twelve years of confronting and crushing intractable sexist barriers in the industry through collaborative organizing and participatory research. It is irrefutable that throwing women at the closed doors of an entrenched sexist institution has not changed the nature of the industry or the position of women within it. As organizers, we have analyzed the sexist barriers and taken them on, one by one; as researchers, at every stage, we have asked previously unasked questions, like how can we move the construction unions faster than their industry, the economy, and culture within which they live? Insofar as PGTI is a movement for the feminist transformation of an entire industry, partnership with the unions is indispensable, but not always reliable. Where the construction unions have led, groundbreaking changes in the region have happened; when progress has lagged, the unions have been tepid or absent partners.

The mashup of organizing and research that is PGTI provides a rich context for dialogue on this and other long-term questions and problems. We are guided by the mantra we recite together at the beginning of every PGTI meeting: *There is no silver bullet. We are in this together. We will never, never give up.*

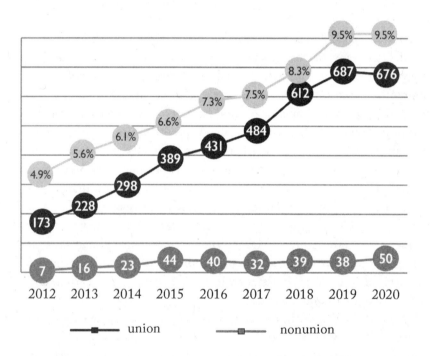

Figure 10.1: Trends in union and nonunion female construction apprentices in Massachusetts

CHAPTER 11

Organizing under Criminalization

Policing and Sex Workers' Rights in Rhode Island

Bella Robinson and Elena Shih

COYOTE and the Indoor Prostitution
Legislative Battle in Rhode Island

In June 2014, COYOTE (Call Off Your Old, Tired Ethics), Rhode Island's only sex-worker rights group, was contacted to assist a twenty-two-year-old sex worker who was facing a violent and abusive client in a motel room in Connecticut. COYOTE was the only organization that provided services to sex workers without requiring their exit from the trade working within fifty miles of the motel. Bella Robinson, the organization's founder and executive director, received intake information from the harassment victim, "Anna." Over the phone, she learned that Anna began selling sex while she was dating an ex-boyfriend, but when she became irritated with the relationship, she left him and tried to work as a sex worker independently. In her first appointment, she recalled meeting a pimp who offered to help maintain her safety, but quickly began controlling her in the months that followed.

In the brief intake call to Robinson, Anna reported that since meeting him, instead of offering protection, the pimp was restricting her movement and taking all her earnings. After a client had fallen asleep during a hotel stay one afternoon, Anna sensed the opportunity to seek help. She called COYOTE's hotline seeking immediate assistance to leave her pimp. Bella recorded her location and asked Anna about her immediate needs and if she wanted to report the pimp. Anna responded that she hoped to keep escorting without the pimp, but was reluctant to report him. She asked for a hotel room for the night so she could gain her bearings with a bit of independence for the evening.

Robinson made the hour-long drive to Connecticut, offered Anna fifty dollars in cash, and drove her to her mother's home in the state. Robinson explained to Anna that she could not offer her a place to stay or open a hotel room for her because doing so could expose her to charges for aiding prostitution, and under new anti-trafficking laws, to further charges of sex trafficking. In her organizing and public presentations about her work, Robinson toes a dangerous line, working for sex workers' rights and safety in a society where the industry is criminalized. As a public disclaimer, she often says, "I teach people how to stay safe but I'm not a market facilitator or a pimp or a madam."

This paradox, of organizing sex workers amidst the conditions of heightened criminalization, is the focus of this chapter. Since most approaches to labor organizing focus on collective action, the case of sex-worker-rights activism under rapidly escalating anti-trafficking policies creates significant challenges. For sex workers, ongoing criminalization poses fundamental barriers not only to associational power, but to the recognition of sex work as a form of labor at all. The aggressive policing of prostitution in Rhode Island has had dire consequences for sex workers' ability to organize against both state-sponsored and individual acts of violence. Echoing a chorus of sex-worker activists, this chapter argues that moral panics that claim that sex work is inherently exploitative must be understood within the context, not only of the criminalization of sex work, but the organizing and activism of its workers.

The History of Sex Work Law in Rhode Island

In the United States, sex work was not explicitly outlawed in many areas for at least the first century of the country's existence. Most states only criminalized prostitution around the time of the First World War, largely as a result of the actions of the Woman's Christian Temperance Union, among other social reform groups. Reformers referred to sex work as a "social disease," which could be cured by a combination of criminalization and rehabilitation.[1]

The nature of social reform meant that the social policies inherently sought to carve out roles of heroes and saviors, instead of that of allies.

The Mann Act of 1910 was created in order to halt the perceived growing threat of the "white slave trade," though a 1908 investigation by the Bureau of Investigation (now known as the FBI) into prostitution in New York City showed that most of the so-called "white slaves" in the city were, in fact, voluntary sex workers.[2] In this way, the Mann Act created a national perception of sex workers as victims. In 1913, the Supreme Court case *Hoke v. United States* decided that the United States federal government did not have the right to regulate the legality of sex work on a national level and that the decision was up to individual states.[3] Across the US, sex work remains legal in some counties in Nevada, and indoor prostitution was decriminalized in Rhode Island between 1980 and 2009.

COYOTE sued the state of Rhode Island in 1976, alleging that its anti-prostitution laws were far too broad and that many sexual acts between consenting adults could be seen as prostitution under the law. Although the case was eventually dismissed, in 1980 the Rhode Island General Assembly changed the prostitution laws in an attempt to make them more specific. In the process, they created a new legislative loophole that lasted almost thirty years, which outlawed street prostitution, but essentially made indoor prostitution legal. In 1998, the Rhode Island State Supreme Court ruled in *State v. DeMagistris* that the law criminalizing prostitution was "primarily to bar prostitutes from hawking their wares in public," and that someone who engages in sex work *privately* could not be prosecuted under this law. In 2003, charges against four women working at two Providence spas were dropped when their lawyer cited the 1998 state Supreme Court ruling, and a recriminalization campaign began soon after. After many unsuccessful attempts at new legislation beginning in 2005, recriminalization succeeded in 2009.[4]

Rhode Island's period of indoor-prostitution decriminalization is notably different than the legalization of prostitution in Nevada. Under legalization workers are required to register with the state, pay for licensing fees, submit weekly STD test results, and turn over earnings to brothel owners. Legalization thus creates a two-tier system of illegal workers and legal workers. In Nevada brothels, sex work takes place under a highly regulated system that requires workers to register so their names and personal information can be accessed by any public records request. This information can be used to discriminate against them in future employment, housing, and child custody cases, and puts them at risk from predators who might stalk them.

By contrast, in the years under decriminalization in Rhode Island there were no regulations—indoor commercial sex establishments had the same licensing regulations as all other businesses in the state. In Rhode Island, sex workers could work from home, at hotels, or for agencies like spas and massage parlors. Decriminalization has been shown to protect the health and safety of sex workers. For instance, in 2008, after the "Craigslist killer" robbed and murdered two women in Boston, he came to Rhode Island and tried to rob a local escort, but she dialed 911 and the police caught the man before he could harm anyone else. Reporting client violence and abuse to police is far riskier for sex workers under criminalization, who often report being jailed and arrested after seeking assistance to leave violent situations. These important distinctions between decriminalization and legalization frame the ongoing debate for sex worker rights.

Facing heightened advocacy from the national anti-trafficking movement, in November 2009, a new law recriminalized all commercial sex and solicitation in Rhode Island, regardless of whether it occurred on the streets or indoors. The law states that if found guilty of selling or soliciting sex, one can be fined up to $1,000 and incarcerated for up to six months. Further offenses could garner up to ten years of prison time in addition to fines of up to $10,000.[5] A number of sex workers, women's rights groups, anti-trafficking groups, and sex educators vehemently opposed the passage of this bill, arguing that arrests for prostitution-related offenses are more likely to hurt rather than help sex workers and victims of trafficking, and rarely lead to support of victims. In response, the Rhode Island branch of COYOTE was re-established in 2010 after several years of dormancy.

Continuing its fixation on ridding the state of sex trafficking, Rhode Island's government created an anti-trafficking task force in 2012 and the state's first anti-trafficking shelter in 2016. The anti-trafficking movement in Rhode Island has had direct consequences for sex-worker-rights organizations that refuse to demand sex workers exit prostitution as a mandatory requirement for assistance. Because sex-worker-rights organizations advocate for improved labor conditions, they face a considerable predicament in organizing as a criminalized group of workers.

The History of Anti-trafficking and Its Conflation with Sex Work

Anti-trafficking activism has risen since the year 2000 following the passage of the United Nations Palermo Protocol. It has been characterized by a number of "strange bedfellows"[6] made by its coalitions. It is comprised of radical feminists, such as the Coalition Against Trafficking of Women, and far-right, often evangelical Christians dedicated to ending trafficking, including organizations such as the International Justice Mission. These two groups, despite having vastly different stances on most social, economic, and political issues, have found common ground in their belief that all sex work is exploitative and thus a form of human trafficking, and that sex work should be made illegal. This "unholy alliance," as it is commonly known among sex workers, held significant power in the push for the 2000 Trafficking Victims and Protection Act, the first piece of US law to comprehensively deal with the issue of human trafficking.[7]

Sex-trafficking abolitionists correlate sex work with trafficking due to its intimate and erotic nature. Because women's sexuality has historically been regulated by state and religious institutions, radical feminists theorize that all sex work perpetuates the subjugation of women's bodies. Abolitionists argue that commercial sex still fundamentally caters to a male gaze that sees women as objects for sexual domination only. Due to this, sex work is regarded as a harmful act against women, similar to pornography.[8] Furthermore, class dynamics play into the radical feminist conversation: often those who oppose sex work have never experienced the socioeconomic position where economic survival is one's primary objective. Viewing prostitution as oppressive and anti-feminist, the humanitarian response of sex-work abolitionists is rooted in prosecution and punishment. The radical feminist enthusiasm to rely on policing requires a level of white, privileged comfortability with law enforcement that women of color, trans women, and immigrant women have not been afforded in the United States.[9] Rather than centering the expertise of sex workers by asking what they need to live safe and healthy lives, anti-trafficking organizations and radical feminists often reinforce puritanical values of punishment that rely on policing and prisons as solutions to the perceived dire issue of human trafficking.[10]

These debates have become particularly fraught in Rhode Island. University of Rhode Island scholar Donna M. Hughes has been the leading academic pushing for the criminalization of sex work in Rhode Island. She has published numerous articles on the "trafficking problem" in Rhode Island. These articles consistently assert the existence of a large transnational criminal network that traffics women and children from various countries, conflate labor trafficking with sex work, and recommend a carceral approach through the strengthening of police repression. Contemporaneously, a community of concerned academics raised concerns against Rhode Island's decriminalization of indoor prostitution. In 2008 and 2009, many letters were sent by academics from around the country to the Rhode Island State House in support of the state's indoor prostitution law. Academics, including the sociologist and criminologist Ronald Weitzer, noted that compared to street work, indoor sex work is generally much safer: There are lower rates of sexually transmitted infections, better working conditions, and lower rates of getting assaulted or robbed. In addition, the majority of indoor sex workers have not been trafficked against their will; instead, they have made the conscious decision to enter the trade. This academic opposition to criminalization, along with the methodological problems that come with trying to determine sex-trafficking victims, was not substantively discussed or mentioned in the public campaign for sex-work criminalization in Rhode Island. This opposition to criminalization was not substantively discussed or mentioned in the public campaign for the 2009 restrictions on sex work in the state.

COYOTE and other sex-worker rights organizations around the world assert that sex work and sex trafficking cannot be viewed as equivalent. However, the criminalization of sex work in Rhode Island is now synonymous with efforts to combat sex trafficking. Funds that arrive in the state under the mandate of combating trafficking, for instance, often do collateral harm by bolstering the policing and surveillance of sex workers. Furthermore, sex workers' voices are systematically excluded from policy discussions about human trafficking. In fact, the participation of sex workers in the efforts could be the best tool to combat sex trafficking—which legally refers to sex work done under conditions of force, fraud, or coercion, or involving a minor under the age of eighteen.

Sex Work as Work, Sex-Work Activism as Labor Activism

Following her first stint in prison after completing eight months of a three-year sentence for drug possession, like many ex-offenders, Bella

Robinson (Executive Director of COYOTE RI, and co-author of this chapter) was told to find a job as part of conditions for probation and parole. She was court-ordered to attend vocational training and completed a six-month-long data entry course, where she learned MS-DOS and WordPerfect. Six months later, Microsoft Windows had swept the country, and her training had become defunct. She chose to take a job working the graveyard shift at a group home for mentally disabled and autistic adults, where she was responsible for six to eight men and women. She checked on them through the night, woke them in the morning, and prepared them for their day. She earned a minimum wage but didn't qualify for food stamps, even though her earnings weren't enough to cover her living expenses, let alone provide the opportunity for savings. Following years of criminalization, Robinson saw that relative to work in retail, hospitality, and health care, sex work provided greater independence and work options. Now, as a sex-worker-rights activist, Robinson argues that efforts to criminalize or rescue prostitutes do more harm than good when there are few economic alternatives and solutions to poverty.

As the founder and director of COYOTE RI, Robinson advocates for sex work to be recognized as a legitimate type of labor, and through her work hopes that organized sex workers can access safe working conditions—conditions that once existed under decriminalization in Rhode Island. Beginning in 2014, she was encouraged to attend several labor training conferences, including the Regina V. Polk Women's Labor Leadership Conference and United Association for Labor Education Northeast Summer School for Union Women. She found that she was one of the only sex workers present, but learned that through understanding sex work *as* work, sex workers may understand themselves as people tied to a larger labor organizing and class struggle.

The rallying cry to understand sex work as work has existed since at least the late 1970s, when sex-worker-rights activist Carol Leigh first introduced the term "sex worker" to emphasize the labor dimensions of commercial sex. Still, the mainstream US labor movements and sex-worker-rights movements have seen limited cross-fertilization. At labor training conferences, Bella and other sex workers often felt confused and estranged from sessions that discussed union management, expressing that they felt that the union model of organizing did not fit sex workers who often work independently. At the same time, thinking through the discussions about organizing domestic workers—who similarly work in isolated, private locations—pointed to similarities that sex work shares with other types of women's work. Bella's participation in these labor conferences illuminated other commonalities as well. For instance, a role-playing exercise on collective bargaining, which drew on the experiences of unionized hotel workers in Chicago, illustrated a common struggle for safe and fair treatment on the job, despite the different legal statuses of hotel and sex work. Furthermore, the increasing entrenchment of the carceral state in monitoring undocumented workers has introduced an equally criminalized group of workers who, despite the various industries in which they work, are working under conditions of criminalization. Identifying these commonalities has been a vital part of learning to organize under criminalization.

Sex Workers' Participation in Research and Policy

Responding to the need for sex-workers' voices in policy discussions, COYOTE RI and Brown University's Center for the Study of Slavery and Justice recently conducted a 2014–2016 study of sixty-two sex workers in Rhode Island. The goal of the study was to measure the effects of the 2009 return to criminalized prostitution codes in Rhode Island. The study showed that sex workers working in Rhode Island are not simply desperate "victims" of evil traffickers. They come from various walks of life; in fact, 15 percent reported that they have been to graduate school. They are, however, much more vulnerable than other workers who do not work in a criminalized trade: 65 percent of sex workers surveyed said they would not report violence or crimes to the police for fear of arrest. For many, sex work is a form of labor that gives them the autonomy to create flexible schedules for schooling or parenting, avoid background checks, and sidestep questions about gaps in work experience. The responses point to numerous structural factors, including criminal records, or single-parenting young children, that create a mismatch between real people's employment needs and the jobs that are available to them. Significantly, these are the same decision-making processes that plague workers employed in a myriad of low-wage industries—not just sex work.

What's more, "rescue" attempts tend to make already precarious socioeconomic conditions for sex workers even worse. On October 26, 2016, an awards ceremony was held at the Providence Career and Technical Academy to honor police officers in Rhode Island for their "kindness and community policing."[11] Among the major achievements highlighted by this ceremony was the crackdown on fifteen massage parlors across the state, which police say were fronts for million-dollar sex-trafficking operations. What these accounts of "kindness" fail to mention is that these massage parlors were run by small groups of immigrant sex workers, who worked together and shared this space in order to ensure their safety. The recent crackdown on Asian massage parlors has made it more difficult for COYOTE RI to do outreach to Asian sex workers and to document the needs of that population, as they are being increasingly run underground. Shutting down massage parlors did not result in more safety for the women who work in them, but in their greater isolation, marginalization, and ultimately even deportation.

In the wake of a March 2016 human trafficking sting operation in Cranston that led to the arrest of thirty-one people—fourteen of whom were sex workers' clients—the Rhode Island ACLU published a statement to condemn the operation for "having little to do with trafficking, but a lot to do with embarrassing and penalizing consenting adults engaged in sexual conduct for a fee."[12] The ACLU's statement contends that operations in the name of "saving" or "helping" victims of sex trafficking have the major effect of stigmatizing sex workers and making their lives more precarious. It's a critique that echoes the concerns that sex workers have been vocal about for decades.

In the United States, the criminalization of both immigration and prostitution has deep historical roots. As Torrie Hester has pointed out, early-twentieth-century anti-prostitution laws made sex workers the second-largest deportable category of non-citizens in the United States. Motivated by a moral panic about the decency, respectability, and norms about appropriate women's work, deportation served to ensure that deviant women could be returned to their countries of origin "where friends, family, women's organizations, and religious officials could care for and reform them."[13] These various locations of underpaid, illegal, and undocumented work have continued to be the contemporary sites in which to police women workers.

The widespread attempts to prevent sexual exploitation through arrests are at the core of efforts to prevent human trafficking in the United States—and Rhode Island is certainly not an exception. These efforts heavily rely on the "pimp narrative," which assumes that sex work is inherently exploitative and that no individual would enter the sex industry without being coerced or deceived by a pimp or a trafficker. However, if we recall

Anna's story, told at the outset of this chapter, we see that she sought to escape from her pimp because he took all of her earnings, without offering the safety and a violent-free work environment. What Anna and others systematically protest, thus, are the labor conditions of sex work, not the work itself. These concerns additionally echo the coercive and exploitative nature of much low-wage labor alternatives to sex work.

Recommendations for Future Policy

The paradoxical nature of the efforts to reduce sex trafficking through criminalization show how sex workers' voices are ignored rather than uplifted, not only by the state and law enforcement but also by the very organizations that claim to advocate for them and protect them. Below are four policy and best-practice recommendations to both include and protect sex workers under the law, and to break the trend of stigmatization that has come to characterize anti-sex-trafficking work.

1. Actively engage with and include the voices of sex workers in community and health organizations

In order to have an agenda that seeks the protection and the well-being of sex workers, it is crucial to actively include them and center their ideas and expertise in these discussions. Current anti-trafficking and community health organizations in Rhode Island heavily rely on a universal victim rhetoric. While there is sex work that is happening under conditions of extreme exploitation—as is true with all kinds of labor—this narrative has excluded the voices and participation of the people involved. In order to remove these barriers and create a pathway through which sex workers can access services that they need, it is imperative that sex workers be included in these decision-making processes about their protection.

2. Interventions should seek to protect sex workers instead of criminalizing and stigmatizing them

While police officers are hailed as heroes by anti-trafficking organizations for allegedly rescuing victims of sex trafficking, the reality is that they have not only failed at their mandate of protecting sex workers, but they have directly contributed to the violence faced by sex workers. Relationships between the police and sex workers need to be improved drastically: the first step toward building these relationships is respect.

The police and media must cease publishing the names, addresses, and photographs of people arrested in prostitution stings.

Publishing the names of sex workers can damage their relationships with family members and others, and it jeopardizes their possibility of obtaining a legal job in the future. Media reports of police stings should also be careful not to sensationalize and celebrate sex-trafficking raids without providing a sober and honest account of the aftermath of such operations. Specifically, a raid-and-rescue operation often leaves sex workers without a place to work safely, without a way to feed their children or pay their rent, and often causes family separation through deportation. Criminalization has also made it easier for police officers to take advantage of sex workers and coerce sexual favors from sex workers. Police officers should not be allowed to engage in sexual contact with sex workers or victims of trafficking during prostitution stings or investigations.

3. Sex workers and third-party support agents should not be charged with pandering, promoting, or sex trafficking

Current legislation in Rhode Island makes it illegal for landlords to knowingly lease their properties to sex workers.[14] This provision exists because third-party agents are typically labeled as pimps or traffickers and housing is one area in which traffickers are believed to exert control over their victims. This blanket label obscures the diverse third-party relationships sex workers can have, many of which are meant to ensure their safety.[15] Trustworthy third-party support agents are often hired by sex workers to answer their phones and screen their clients, among other forms of support. These agents should be treated with respect, as their work is essential to ensuring the safety of sex workers. Due to the pervasive moral panic around sex trafficking, even sex-worker rights organizations are under threat of being labeled and criminalized as traffickers when they assist sex workers. These penalties for association pose unnecessary barriers to effective community organizing. Ultimately, such labels and policing measures lead to more stigma against sex workers, forcing sex workers to work in less safe conditions. Removing them from indoor spaces where there are other workers increases their vulnerability to violence and may force them to work on the street.

4. Consider decriminalization as a pathway to ensuring the health and safety of sex workers a priority

The decriminalization of consensual adult sex work has led to lower rates of STDs and rape for sex workers.[16] This clearly disproves the widespread and commonly accepted rationalization that criminalizing sex work enhances the safety of sex workers. On the contrary, decriminalization is the best model to ensure the human rights of sex workers. In order to truly help sex workers and victims of trafficking, community organizations need to put the health and safety of sex workers at the top of their agendas. In COYOTE's 2015 survey of sixty-two Rhode Island cis women sex workers, 24 percent of Rhode Island sex workers reported having been robbed or assaulted. Many also mentioned that if they went to a shelter or a medical facility and disclosed that they were a sex worker, staff demonstrated some bias and treated them unfairly. Any organization that promotes the stigmatization and criminalization of sex workers' is accepting the idea that the lives of sex workers are not valuable. Thus, laws that criminalize sex workers and traffickers—as well as their derivative practices, like "condom as evidence" laws—only serve to render the lives of sex workers and sex-trafficking victims more unsafe and have resulted in an increase of the rates of STDs without contributing to a decrease of exploitation, sexual or otherwise.[17]

It is important to recognize that the demands outlined above are not new, and that sex workers in the United States and globally have been fighting for their labor rights for decades. Community organizations and anti-trafficking organizations often refuse to prioritize the ideas, expertise, and rights of sex workers and victims of sex trafficking first. Anti-trafficking interventions thus create barriers for sex workers to access non-judgmental and compassionate services, and to organize within their communities.[18] For decades, sex workers have argued that sex work is work, and that sex workers' rights are workers' rights. However, until sex work is decriminalized and regarded as a legal kind of work, the labor organizing movement will be unable to reach its full potential—it will not be intersectional enough to win the demands of all working people.

Conclusion

Erik Loomis

The essays in this collection demonstrate the tremendous complexity and variety of labor problems, issues, and forms of resistance in the greater Boston area. Each chapter, whether I have the opportunity to mention it or not in this conclusion, significantly adds to our understanding of the contemporary labor movement in Boston. The region's labor struggle is a microcosm of the national movement within a political context that has somewhat insulated it from the worst of the anti-union attacks decimating organized labor elsewhere. Fifty years of deindustrialization, an ascendant conservative movement passing right-to-work legislation in the states and appointing extremist judges at the federal level, indifference from too many Democratic politicians, and a lack of new organizing from unions themselves have left the labor movement a shell of what it was in the 1950s. Southern New England reflects those trends, but the spirit of resistance among the region's workers, the ability to create and enact power on the local and state level, and the long history of labor struggle will keep the region in the forefront of the labor movement for a long time to come.

It's not all doom and gloom. The election of former Building Trades Council president Marty Walsh as Boston's mayor gives at least some unions almost unparalleled access to City Hall in one of the nation's largest cities. Rhode Island public sector unions won a continuing contract bill in 2019 which will stop cities from busting their public unions every time a contract expires, or unilaterally imposing wage and benefit deductions when the economy slips. Unions maintain real political power in Massachusetts and Rhode Island, and it shows—at least sometimes.

Still, unions have often struggled to elect state-level politicians who are responsive to the needs of the region's working class. Rhode Island governor Gina Raimondo, a long-time favorite of the *Wall Street Journal* editorial page—never a good sign for workers—rose to power by dramatically cutting union pensions for state workers during her term as state treasurer from 2011 to 2015. And while unfunded pensions were a legitimate problem for Rhode Island, the ease with which she rode roughshod over the state's public sector unions to enact these "reforms" says much about the limited political pull they have, especially when many private sector unions used little political capital to help their union sisters and brothers. Raimondo may be a Democrat, but when it comes to the hard-earned gains of workers, she aligns herself with capital consistently. The situation is hardly better in Massachusetts, where despite the state's liberal reputation, the Republican Charlie Baker is in his second term as governor, hardly making the Bay State a union paradise.

We also have to ask just what union strength has really gotten the region's working class as a whole, versus union members themselves. As Aviva Chomsky and Steve Striffler point out in this book's introduction, Walsh's victory was a coup for the building trades, but nothing about his election victory or his administration has led to a militant labor movement ready to take on the challenges of the immediate present. The sobering situation is that much about the contemporary labor movement actively prevents it from growing into a large-scale social movement. Unions have frequently prioritized the short-term interests of their own members over the working class as a whole. They have often fought with each other as much as they have battled the bosses. But we have to look at these issues in the context of what unions do. A labor union represents its dues-paying members first and foremost, ensuring that their members have work, that they have a fair contract, and that they have representation on the job. This is not a bad thing, even if these day-to-day realities get short shrift in leftist writings. The trades do very well with the massive boom in central city construction. Building trades exist to build, and it's highly unlikely those unions would ever pass up jobs that will put their members to work in the short term in exchange for vague long-term promises of a Boston that is livable and affordable for the working class. It's also unfair to blame them for that.

But none of this can make us forget the fact that the Boston working class is really struggling to survive in our new Gilded Age and that unions have largely been caught flat-footed in their response. As many essays in this book demonstrate, the lived economy of Boston's workers is very different than the one portrayed on CNBC and in the pages of the *Wall Street Journal*. Massachusetts might be the world's fourth-wealthiest nation per capita if it were an independent country, but Boston and the region as a whole has some of the nation's worst income inequality with an urban center that's increasingly a playground for the wealthy, and decaying, deindustrialized towns that make up the outer core of the modern suburbs centers of poverty. An elite set of high-paid workers in the financial, medical, and knowledge sectors drive up the cost of living and also rely on a bevy of low-paid service workers who live in the city's poorer neighborhoods or in the distant deindustrialized towns; these service workers, in turn, struggle with underfunded social services, from schools to health care to transportation. Neighborhoods dominated by people of color are prime targets for new developments, radically driving up housing costs and gentrifying the last affordable areas. The conditions aren't quite so grim yet in Rhode Island, but Providence is rapidly gentrifying as well, with the city's West End changing by the month. Like the rest of the nation's urban centers, income inequality defines working people's lives in southern New England.

The labor movement, as presently constructed, is rather ill-suited to address the broader needs of the working class on a mass scale. The building trades simply are not equipped for mass organizing, going back to their original structure in the nineteenth century. They remain an internally powerful force in the region's labor movement but do not organize on an industrial basis and cannot organize the existing New England workforce. The collapse of manufacturing work in New England—in 2018 Massachusetts lost half the jobs it had in 1990, and many more since 1920—means that the large industrial sector unions that formed the backbone of the CIO are either no more or are mere shells of themselves. The growth of low-wage worker unions such as the Service Employees International Union has certainly helped fill the big policy vacuum that the industrial unions left, and while this is true to some extent of the public sector unions as well, many of them, such as the teachers' unions, are inherently middle-class organizations and understandably have different priorities.

This has made the labor movement a rather tenuous ally of other progressive organizations at a time when both American democracy and a century of union-won gains face nearly unprecedented threats. The longstanding position within the labor movement—that the only unions that should comment on a given social issue are those whose jobs are directly affected by it—remains strongly felt. This is, frankly, parochial at a time when the house of labor is crumbling. And yet, on the biggest issues of the day, ones that have enormous implications for the working class, this rule holds. Nowhere is this more damaging in terms of organizing and recruiting a new generation of activists than climate change. The northeast is already seeing significant effects of climate change, including more humid summers, stronger storms, and increased erosion that will make many coastal neighborhoods unlivable. Moreover, we know that higher temperatures and humidity levels will have disproportionate effects on the poor, including a higher risk of death from heat stroke in housing without air conditioning and growing asthma rates resulting from increased numbers of cockroaches. Climate change will arguably be the greatest crisis the history of humanity has faced, and it requires a comprehensive response that must include unions. But both nationally and in New England, the old parochial stance of the labor movement has taken precedence. Laborers International Union of North America (LIUNA) President Terry O'Sullivan has attacked climate activists and the Green New Deal for supposedly destroying jobs, while attempting to intimidate other union leaders from speaking out in favor of programs to fight climate change based on the old standard that it doesn't affect their members' jobs. The Rhode Island LIUNA local has followed the union's national leadership in waging a bitter and contentious battle to create a liquefied natural gas plant in the state, leading many of the state's environmental activists to conclude that unions will never be an ally in the climate fight. While environmentalists absolutely need to do more to make sure that clean energy jobs are also union jobs, the overall situation suggests that labor lacks the ability to ally with other groups for the struggles ahead; more importantly, this is what many progressive groups now think. Labor is simply not strong enough to operate without allies. Fighting for a green energy future in New England that is also a union energy future should be a top priority of every union in the region.

Whether on climate or poverty, social movement unionism has a critical role to play in rebuilding the labor movement. With over half of Massachusetts union members in the public sector, these unions have to lead the way. As Enid Eckstein's essay demonstrates, the public sector's embrace of public goods in a time of radical privatization and its willingness to ally with progressive groups outside of organized labor points a strong way forward. These alliances have often focused on the struggles of people of color to live with dignity, starting to undo the "tangle of exclusion," as Chomsky describes the region's fraught history of race and labor. The region's strong teachers' unions show robust power in state legislatures and with voters, which it demonstrated when Massachusetts voters overwhelmingly rejected Question 2 in 2016. The measure, strongly supported by Governor Baker, would have lifted the cap on charter schools in the state. Its defeat helped to save the public good of a universal K-12 education from privatization.

Moreover, low-wage-worker unions like SEIU are spending resources to build the necessary community alliances for broad-based social unionism. Harris Gruman's essay on Raise Up Massachusetts notes the importance of economic justice coalitions of unions, community activists, and politicians that slowly build up economic power for the working class. As slow as these movements are—and we are a long ways from something like sectoral bargaining in Massachusetts that would really transform the lives of workers—they are absolutely critical for the future of the labor movement. The advantage of Raise Up is how it replicates union movements, seeking big contracts that cover huge numbers of workers— up to a million, in the dreams of those behind Raise Up. The problem, as Gruman puts it, is that "unions are almost the only vehicle expressing the financial power of working people." The same goes for their politics. This is why Republicans are taking direct aim on their existence.

New England is one of the only places where unions still have significant state-level power, making Baker more reticent than other Republicans to destroy them. But New England's labor movement is as impacted by national-level decisions as any other part of the nation. With a US Supreme Court seeking to eviscerate union rights, not to mention an anti-union Department of Labor and National Labor Relations Board under the Trump administration, unions are less able to fund organizations such as Raise Up Massachusetts or the worker centers that Chomsky describes that empower immigrant workers at the bottom of the economic ladder. Worker centers have the potential to provide a path toward organizing marginalized workers. But their future is far from assured; they are threatened by political attacks on the unions who fund them and corporate attempts to get them legally classified as labor unions so they can fall under the nation's restrictive labor laws. SEIU has provided a lot of funding for these innovative alternative models of worker organizing, but it has lost significant financial resources after 2018's *Janus v. AFSCME* Supreme Court decision. Among other things, it has had to reduce its funding for the Fight for $15, which was one of the most creative methods to empower long-forgotten workers and put income inequality on the political table once again. Fight for $15 inspired people across the country to vote for minimum wage increases, but it brought no new members into SEIU while costing the union millions of dollars. This is a difficult dilemma with major implications for the future of organizing.

Eric Larson's honest and realistic portrayal of the promises and challenges of grassroots anti-racist organizing through the Rhode Island Solidarity School demonstrates the difficulty of mass organizing. The need for anti-racist organizing within unions and among the working class generally is unquestionable, but the question no one has answered is how to muster the time and resources to do it while fighting all the other battles required of the labor movement. The Solidarity School has done brave work on this issue, but progress is slow and difficult. Moreover, while working with coalitional organizations such as Jobs with Justice can provide necessary infrastructure, it is not without its own problems. The decline of Rhode Island's Jobs with Justice chapter after its director suddenly disappeared in 2017, which Larson does not discuss, shows how dependent such organizations and thus coalitional efforts generally can be on a single person. In fact, the entire history of the left demonstrates the constantly tenuous nature of this sort of work, where one or two people often keep an idea alive.

The future of the labor movement also requires a focus on underground economies, as Bella Robinson and Elena Shih's essay shows us. These underground economies include sex work, sweatshop labor, drug cultivation and distribution, undocumented workers no matter where they labor, or other under-the-table work. In order to provide safe and dignified working conditions for these laborers, we have to bring them into the light, which means legalizing their work and lives. Rhode Island's brief experiment between 1998 and 2009 with the semi-decriminalization of prostitution conducted indoors allowed the state's sex workers an unusual amount of safety. Unfortunately, those who whip up fears about sex trafficking led to the end of this experiment, and in the aftermath sex workers' lives became much more dangerous. Whether or not there is a real path toward unionization of underground-economy workers, the labor movement must extend its reach to the region's least-empowered workers as it struggles to rebuild itself. The aristocracy of labor is not the future in an era of growing contingency, desperation, and marginalization.

Like the rest of the labor movement, workers in southern New England must focus on four major principles moving forward. First, unions simply must devote more resources to organizing. Traditions of militant unionism can still lead the fight for justice, as the interview with IUE-CWA Local 201 leader Jeff Crosby demonstrates. Even in decimated industries, real leadership exists that can inspire, train new leaders, and set an agenda for a new generation.

Perhaps the most promising sector for this organizing has been in higher education. The region is unique in the nation in that nearly all of its institutions of higher education are privately owned, and many of them are the nation's most elite, expensive, and massively endowed. Harvard is the standard-bearer here. It has been in the spotlight many times in the last several years. Under the presidency of the historian Drew Gilpin Faust, Harvard garnered a union-busting reputation that should shame any historian who has written on the injustices of the past. Alas, Faust made her bargain with the capitalists who give huge donations to the institution. Amy Todd's essay about organizing contingent faculty at Brandeis demonstrates both the potentials and difficulties of mobilizing faculty labor. While universities remain popular institutions with the general public, few sectors of the economy engage in more consistent union busting. The private schools in the Boston area have consistently fought against higher education unionizing over the past few decades. Todd's discussion of her and her fellow adjunct faculty at Brandeis is a valuable window into the intransigence of wealthy institutions with multibillion dollar endowments, operating more as hedge funds than as employers, squeezing faculty at the bottom of the pay scale, even though granting them everything they wanted would cost a small fraction of the institution's overall budget. Too often, senior faculty, more obsessed with professional privilege than social justice, side with anti-union administrations to protect their own identities and the belief that they "deserve" what they have achieved. Recent unionization campaigns among graduate students at Harvard and Brown have seen a shift in administration's attitudes, but it remains to be seen what will happen when (perhaps even before this book's publication date) the National Labor Relations Board will once again return to the decision of the Bush years that graduate students are not employees and thus not eligible for collective bargaining rights. Institutions may be confident enough in that future that not actively fighting their graduate students seems the better bet.

The potential for organizing in higher education is also by no means limited to academia. Carlos Aramayo's essay on university cafeteria-worker organizing in Boston's elite colleges demonstrates the rank exploitation of a largely immigrant workforce laboring for subcontractors such as Chartwells, where they serve the newest generation of the global elite and face racism and sexual harassment. Carefully building alliances with both unions and student organizations, the cafeteria workers—now organized with UNITE HERE Local 26—have won major victories over the last decade. A twenty-two-day strike at Harvard in 2016 gave the nation a window into the region's rampant income inequality, with the nation's most prestigious and wealthy institution of higher education attempting to squeeze its poorest workers on health care. Overall then, at least some of Boston's unions have done a pretty good job of expanding into new sectors of the economy, but in order to roll back the losses of the last several decades, university worker organizing should only be the tip of the iceberg.

Second, New England's unions also need to use their political power in a more systematic way, working together to build power for all, instead of fighting amongst themselves or taking short-term measures to help themselves at the expense of other workers. In 2014, when Providence moved toward raising the municipal minimum wage for hotel workers after a long struggle led by UNITE HERE Local 217, the Rhode Island state legislature, overwhelmingly controlled by Democrats, passed a bill (borrowed from right-wing Oklahoma) forbidding it. The ban was enabled by more politically conservative unions who sold out UNITE HERE and the other low-wage worker unions fighting for it. That's unacceptable and a sign of the dismal infighting that undermines a strong political stance by unions.

As we move forward it's important to avoid romanticizing alternative forms of the labor movement that might reduce the emphasis on political influence and lobbying, instead promoting direct-action democracy within unions. There's certainly nothing wrong with democratic unionism, but I suggest two caveats. First, there is a broad assumption that democratic unionism would lead to more left-leaning results, but the history of rank-and-file activism against union leadership, often led by white workers angry over desegregating unions, demonstrates that this may not be true. Second, there's little historical evidence from the American labor movement that unions can be successful without a strong political game that breaks the alliance between employers and government.

It's true enough that the older labor framework built around the National Labor Relations Act is broken, perhaps irrevocably. At the very least, the NLRB's partisan nature, which has gotten much worse over the decades, provides no long-term path forward for New England's workers. But there is absolutely nothing in American history to suggest that workers can win gains in the face of a hostile government. Rather, it is critical to influence government, as workers did during the early years of the New Deal, with the militant 1934 strikes that helped precipitate the National Labor Relations Act. Whatever the labor movement looks like in the future, it has to have the centralized force to influence politics if it will consolidate any victories it gains on the picket line. It's nice to think about an extremely democratic and decentralized movement based on the principles of the Industrial Workers of the World, but the historical record simply does not support such an approach.

Third, and perhaps most importantly given the national media depiction of the working class—which the Trump election has reduced the most diverse part of the nation into white men from the Midwest—unions absolutely must focus their organizing efforts on women and people of color. This is true for several reasons. First, white men in the United States are simply hard to organize into unions, more so than women or people of color, especially in the last several decades. Second, any union movement that focuses on the needs of white men in order to fulfill facile political expediencies or romantic visions of the movement's past will shoot itself in the foot by failing to organize for the future. Third, for those who often ask why the American left never developed the way it did in Europe, the clearest answer is that white workers have usually, albeit not always, chosen their identity as whites over their identity as workers. The first major national law to come out of the labor movement was the Chinese Exclusion Act in 1882, and the movement supported immigration exclusion for over a century beyond that. There simply is no there there in focusing on white men as the future of organized labor. It makes little sense demographically or strategically. That's different than giving up on white men, but the movement's future leaders are necessarily going to be mostly women and people of color.

Fourth, New England workers need to use their ultimate power: to withhold their labor from the bosses. As the labor movement declined after 1980, strikes became incredibly rare. New England saw more strikes during this fallow period than most parts of the nation, but still, people could go years without laying eyes on a striking worker. The return of the strike as labor's major weapon over the last few years has heartened many of us. 2018 saw the largest number of strikes in the United States since 1986; 2019 saw nearly as many, and there is little reason to believe that these numbers will decline over the next several years. Workers are again realizing the real power they have as growing income inequality, community support for unions, and a renewed sense of class-based militancy have changed the nation's politics. The return of the strike is critical for the future of the labor movement in Boston and around the country because the more people strike, the more other workers will see them, take courage, and believe they can win their own demands through walking off the job. Let's not romanticize striking: it's a scary action, especially if you, like most of your coworkers, have some combination of student loan payments, rent or house payments, child-care bills, elder-care expenses, and health-care debt. People worry about losing their jobs. But when you see how the strike can lead to real victories, and you live in a culture where striking is a norm instead of an outlier, much of that fear goes away. Solidarity from other unions lifts your spirits and your own victory gives courage to others. That is part of the recent story in New England. It was a critical part of the origins of the nation's labor movement. And a revived labor movement must center the power of the strike.

While I suppose this conclusion has not been a cheery and optimistic look at the contemporary labor movement, Boston-area unions should be proud of their recent moves to make their movement look more like the city. Historically, the Boston labor movement was hostile to Black workers, and that hostility bled into other parts of the city's life, most notoriously in the anti-busing protests of the 1970s and the resistance to court orders to hire Black teachers. Boston labor has made a lot of progress, but also still has far to go. Even today, Boston teachers and police officers are overwhelmingly white. And it is true that there is a significant disconnect between what union membership and union leadership often looks like. The greater Boston area is tremendously diverse, yet the leadership of many locals remains white and male.

Nonetheless, a lot of the region's unions, reflecting a national trend, are making significant improvements, both in terms of hiring and promoting women and people of color and in finding new ways to organize the most marginalized workers, as I've already discussed. There is reason for optimism in southern New England. As Susan Moir and Elizabeth Skidmore demonstrate in their essay on women in the construction trades, it can be done with strong political and union leadership backed by pressure from below to change their ways. Marty Walsh's Building Pathways Pre-Apprenticeship Program has funneled women into the building trades at a rate that is slowly changing that male bastion of work. Moreover, as with all labor regulations, enforcement is critical, which is why so many women have worked on the reconstruction of UMass Boston. Boston's building trades have taken significant steps to diversify their hiring practices, breaking with a long history of racial exclusion. That break might have come awfully late, but it is still laudable now that it is here. It is absolutely critical for the entirety of the labor movement to continue along this path in order to build its capacity to fight for the working class today and in the future.

One of the most important recent moments in the region's labor history was the Stop and Shop strike in the spring of 2019. Thirty thousand workers affiliated with the United Food and Commercial Workers walked off the job as Stop and Shop's parent company, the multibillion-dollar Belgian conglomerate Ahold Delhaize, attempted to decimate employee health care. This became New England's entry into the strike wave of the late 2010s. It demonstrated the robust nature of the Boston-area labor movement and the culture of solidarity it has retained after a century of strong unionism. Stop and Shop lost millions of dollars. The Teamsters refused to deliver goods to the stores, undermining the company's ability to keep shelves full and stores open. Members of other unions and sympathetic community members came out to walk the picket lines or deliver food and water to the strikers. Many shoppers chose other stores to find what they needed, often at the suggestion of the strikers themselves when they talked to the customers they knew from their years on the job.

The Boston area has not, however, been struck by the recent wave of teachers' strikes that have inspired workers across the nation. That's largely because the region has strong teachers' unions with political muscle and reasonably funded schools. They haven't needed to engage in big strikes. Instead, they've helped teachers in other parts of the nation make it through their own struggles. All these strikes reflect a growing impatience with the inequality of the new Gilded Age. The Stop and Shop strikers and the entire Boston-area labor movement have the potential to lead us into a new era of labor militancy. Whatever the future brings in terms of government repression of unions, the labor movement is continuing to evolve to meet new challenges, and New England workers will play a key role in the struggle for justice.

NOTES

Introduction

1   City of Boston, Mayor's Office of Workforce Development, "Boston's Workforce: An Assessment of Labor Market Outcomes and Opportunities," March 2016, 41, https://owd.boston.gov/wp-content/uploads/2016/03/2015-Office-of-Workforce-Development-Workforce-Report-Booklet_v1_r8_spreads.pdf.

2   Jamie Ducharme, "Why Are Boston's Nurses So Damn Angry," *Boston Magazine*, October 1, 2017; Jane McAlevey, "The Massachusetts Nurses Union Is Reviving the Strike," *The Nation*, July 19, 2017; Jessica Bartlett, "Tufts Medical Center Reaches Tentative Deal with Nurses Union," *Boston Business Journal*, December 18, 2017.

3   Ducharme, "Why Are Boston's Nurses So Damn Angry"; McAlevey, "The Massachusetts Nurses Union."

4   Bartlett, "Tufts Medical Center."

5   Richard Yeselson has discussed the notion of the union fortress in his "Fortress Unionism," *Democracy: A Journal of Ideas* 29 (2013).

6   James R. Green and Hugh Carter Donahue, *Boston's Workers: A Labor History* (Boston: Boston Public Library, 1979), 115–20.

7   US Department of Commerce, Bureau of Economic Analysis, "News Release," May 17, 2018, https://www.bea.gov/news/2018/real-personal-income-states-and-metropolitan-areas-2016.

8   City of Boston, Mayor's Office of Workforce Development, "Boston's Workforce."

9   Janelle Jones, "State Unemployment Rates by Race and Ethnicity at the End of 2016 Show Progress, but Not Yet Full Recovery," Economic Policy Institute, February 8, 2017, https://www.epi.org/publication/state-unemployment-rates-by-race-and-ethnicity-at-the-end-of-2016-show-progress-but-not-yet-full-recovery/; Boston Redevelopment Authority, "Poverty in Boston," March 2014, http://www.bostonplans.org/getattachment/f1ecaf8a-d529-40b6-a9bc-8b4419587b86, 4–5.

10   Boston, Mayor's Office of Resilience and Racial Equity, "Resilient Boston: An Equitable and Connected City," July 13, 2017, 18, http://www.adaptationclearinghouse.org/resources/resilient-boston-an-equitable-and-connected-city.html; https://www.boston.gov/sites/default/files/document-file-07-2017/resilient_boston_digital.pdf.

11   Barry T. Hirsch and David A. Macpherson, "The Union Membership and
     Coverage Database, 2017," *www.unionstats.com*; Heiwon Kwon and Benjamin
     Day, "The Politics of Labor in Boston," in Lowell Turner and Daniel B. Cornfield,
     eds., *Labor in the New Urban Battlegrounds: Local Solidarity in a Global Economy*
     (Ithaca, NY: Cornell University Press), 100.

12   See Ruth Milkman and Ed Ott, eds., *New Labor in New York: Precarious Workers
     and the Future of the Labor Movement* (Ithaca, NY: Cornell University Press,
     2014); Ruth Milkman, *L.A. Story: Immigrant Workers and the Future of the U.S.
     Labor Movement* (New York: Russell Sage Foundation, 2006); Ruth Milkman,
     Joshua Bloom, and Victor Narro, *Working for Justice: The L.A. Model of Organizing
     and Advocacy* (Ithaca, NY: Cornell University Press, 2010); see also Lowell
     Turner and Daniel B. Cornfield, eds., *Labor in the New Urban Battlegrounds: Local
     Solidarity in a Global Economy* (Ithaca, NY: ILR Press, 2007).

13   Green and Donahue, *Boston's Workers*, 106, 118.

14   See Clete Daniel, *Culture of Misfortune: An Interpretive History of Textile Unionism
     in the United States* (Ithaca, NY: Cornell/ILR Press, 2001); William F. Hartford,
     *Where is Our Responsibility? Unions and Economic Change in the New England
     Textile Industry, 1870–1960* (Amherst: University of Massachusetts Press, 1996).

15   Green and Donahue, *Boston's Workers*, 106.

16   Kwon and Day, "The Politics of Labor in Boston," 97–98.

17   Michael Joseph Piore, "The Role of Immigration in Industrial Growth: A Case
     Study of the Origins and Character of Puerto Rican Migration to Boston," MIT
     Department of Economics Working Paper 112A (May 1973), 23. See Mel King,
     Chain of Change: Struggles for Black Community Development (Boston: South End
     Press, 1981), 95–100 on the United Community Construction Workers. More
     recently, Donna Jean Murch, *Living for the City: Migration, Education, and the
     Rise of the Black Panther Party in Oakland, California* (Chapel Hill: University of
     North Carolina Press, 2010) has explored radicalization of second-generation and
     new Black migrants from the South to Oakland, California, during that city's
     post-WWII industrial decline. See Elizabeth Hafkin Pleck, *Black Migration
     and Poverty: Boston 1865–1900.* (New York: Academic Press, 1979), 117, on the
     northern-born origin of 1960s urban rioters.

18   See Judith Stein, *The Pivotal Decade: How the United States Traded Factories for
     Finance in the 1970s* (New Haven: Yale University Press, 2011); Jefferson Cowie,
     Staying Alive: The 1970s and the Last Days of the Working Class (New York: The
     New Press, 2012); Lane Windham, *Knocking on Labor's Door: Union Organizing
     in the 1970s and the Roots of a New Economic Divide* (Chapel Hill: The University
     of North Carolina Press, 2017).

19   See Windham, *Knocking on Labor's Door,* 65; Bill Fletcher Jr. and Fernando
     Gapasin, *Solidarity Divided: The Crisis in Organized Labor and a New Path
     toward Social Justice* (Berkeley: University of California Press, 2008) 43; Nelson
     Lichtenstein, *State of the Union: A Century of American Labor* (Princeton, NJ:
     Princeton University Press, 2003).

20   James E. Blackwell, "Jobs, Income, and Poverty: The Black Share of the New
     Boston," in Phillip L. Clay, ed., *The Emerging Black Community in Boston:
     A Report of the Institute for the Study of Black Culture* (Boston: University of
     Massachusetts at Boston, 1985), 6–79, 43.

21   Barry Bluestone and Mary Huff Stevenson, *The Boston Renaissance: Race, Space, and Economic Change in an American Metropolis* (New York: Russell Sage Foundation, 2000), 15, 94–95; Colin Gordon, "Declining Cities, Declining Unions: Urban Sprawl and U.S. Inequality," *Dissent Magazine*, December 10, 2014.

22   City of Boston, Boston's People and Economy, 2012, 207, https://www.boston. gov/sites/default/files/fy12-volume1-bostons-people-and-economy.pdf.

23   Bluestone and Stevenson, *Boston Renaissance*, 42–45; Ronald P. Formisano, *Boston against Busing: Race, Class, and Ethnicity in the 1960s and 1970s* (Chapel Hill: University of North Carolina Press, 2004), 225.

24   Green and Donahue, *Boston's Workers*, 113.

25   Green and Donahue, *Boston's Workers*, 119.

26   Windham, *Knocking on Labor's Door*, 153.

27   Piore, "Role of Immigration in Industrial Growth," 6. These numbers include a much smaller population of Cuban migrants.

28   Piore, "Role of Immigration in Industrial Growth," 11–12.

29   Piore, "Role of Immigration in Industrial Growth," 14.

30   Mayor's Office of Workforce Development, "Boston's Workforce," 31; Commonwealth of Massachusetts, Executive Office of Labor and Workforce Development (EOLWD), Employment and Wages (ES-202), http://lmi2.detma. org/lmi/lmi_es_a.asp#IND_LOCATION; EOLWD Employment and Wages Report, http://lmi2.detma.org/lmi/lmi_es_b.asp?AT=05&A=000051&Y=2016& P=00&O=50&I=1013~1&Iopt=1&Dopt=TEXT. Although 1979 was the peak in numbers, the percent of workers in unions had started to decline much earlier. See Gerald Meyer, "Union Membership Trends in the United States" (Washington DC: Congressional Research Service, 2004).

31   Katie Johnson, "Office Dogs, Yoga Classes, Good Pay—Welcome to the Modern Mass. Factory," *Boston Globe*, June 5, 2018.

32   Commonwealth Corporation and Massachusetts Department of Higher Education, Massachusetts Healthcare Chartbook, 2013, http://www.mass.edu/ nahi/documents/Mass_Healthcare_Chartbook.pdf.

33   Commonwealth Corporation and Center for Labor Markets and Policy, Drexel University, "Health Care Employment, Structure, and Trends in Massachusetts, Chapter 224, Workforce Impact Study," December 2016, http://commcorp.org/ wp-content/uploads/2017/07/Resources Health-Care-Workforce_Employment-Structure-and-Trends-in-Massachusetts.pdf, 3.

34   Randy Albelda and Marlene Kim, "A Tale of Two Decades: Changes in Work and Earnings in Massachusetts, 1979–1999," MassBenchmarks vol. 5, no. 2. (2002): 12–17.

35   Bluestone and Stevenson, *The Boston Renaissance*, 8, 5.

36   City of Boston, *Boston's People and Economy*, 208.

37   Bluestone and Stevenson, *Boston Renaissance*, 15.

38   Albelda and Kim, "A Tale of Two Decades," 14. According to Albelda and Kim, in the late 1970s Hispanics were 1.4 percent of the workforce, Blacks 3.1 percent, and Asians and Native Americans 1.1 percent. Two decades later, Hispanics were 5.3 percent, Blacks 5.1 percent, and Asian and Native Americans 3.3 percent.

39 Edwin Meléndez, "Latino Poverty and Economic Development in Massachusetts," in Edwin Meléndez and Miren Uriarte-Gastón, eds. *Latino Poverty and Economic Development in Massachusetts* (Mauricio Gastón Institute, 1993), 15. For an in-depth study of urban decline and Latino immigration in Lawrence see Llana Barbar, *Latino City: Immigration and Urban Crisis in Lawrence, Massachusetts, 1945–2000* (Chapel Hill: University of North Carolina Press, 2017).

40 Albelda and Kim, "A Tale of Two Decades," 16.

41 Meléndez, "Introduction," in Meléndez and Uriarte-Gastón, *Latino Poverty*, 4.

42 Blackwell, "Jobs, Income, and Poverty," 48.

43 Centro (Center for Puerto Rican Studies, Hunter College, City University of New York), "Puerto Ricans in Massachusetts, the United States, and Puerto Rico, 2014," Centro DS2016US-07, April 2016, https://centropr.hunter.cuny.edu/sites/default/files/PDF/STATE%20REPORTS/2.%20MA-PR-2016-CentroReport.pdf.

44 James Jennings, Barbara Lewis, and Richard O'Bryant, "Blacks in Massachusetts: Comparative Demographic, Social and Economic Experiences with Whites, Latinos, and Asians," William Monroe Trotter Institute, University of Massachusetts Boston, *William Monroe Trotter Institute Publications* 29 (2015), 23.

45 Harris Gruman, personal communication, September 22, 2017.

46 David Pihl, Jasmine Kerrissey, Tom Juravich, "The State of Labor and Employment in Massachusetts," *Working Paper Series* (Labor Center, University of Massachusetts, Amherst, September 4, 2017) 5, 17.

47 Andrew M. Sum, Ishwar Khatiwada, Joseph McLauglin, Mykhaylo Trubskyy, and Sheila Palma, "Recapturing the American Dream: Meeting the Challenges of the Bay State's Lost Decade," MassInc, December 2011, https://massinc.org/research/recapturing-the-american-dream-meeting-the-challenges-of-the-bay-states-lost-decade/, 5, 11.

48 In 1959, the top 10 percent of households took home 40.9 percent of income; in 2010, they took 51.4 percent. Sum et al., "Recapturing the American Dream," 11; Estelle Sommeiller, Mark Price, and Ellis Wazeter, "Income Inequality in the U.S. by State, Metropolitan Area, and County," Economic Policy Institute, June 16, 2016, http://www.epi.org/publication/income-inequality-in-the-us/#epi-toc-3.

49 Katie Johnston, "Most Jobs Added in Boston since Recession Called Low-Paying," *Boston Globe*, September 22, 2015.

50 See Evan Horowitz, "Is the Mass. Economy Slanted Against Blacks, Hispanics?" *Boston Globe*, August 18, 2015.

51 Kwon and Day, in *Labor in the New Urban Battlegrounds*, 106.

52 Pihl et. al., "The State of Labor and Employment in Massachusetts," 8.

53 Ruth Milkman noted that the legacy of pre-New Deal, AFL-style unionism in Los Angeles proved a strength as deindustrialization, corporate anti-union attacks, and the weakening of federal labor supports and the NLRB undermined the CIO model of unionism. See her *L. A. Story: Immigrant Workers and the Future of the Labor Movement* (New York: Russell Sage Foundation, 2006).

54 Yeselson, "Fortress Unionism."

55   Kwon and Day, *Labor in the New Urban Battlegrounds*, 97–98.

56   Katie Johnston, "Millennials, White-Collar Workers and Bringing New Life to Unions," *Boston Globe*, March 12, 2018.

57   Katie Johnston, "MIT Pay Raise Shows Janitors' Union Clout," *Boston Globe*, July 1, 2016.

58   Pihl et. al., "The State of Labor in Massachusetts," 18.

59   Janice Fine, "Worker Centers," *Race, Poverty & the Environment* 14, no. 1 (2007): 57.

60   Victor Narro, "Worker Centers and the AFL-CIO National Convention," *Law at the Margins*, August 31, 2018, www.lawatthemargins.com/perspectives-worker-centers-and-the-afl-cio-national-convention/.

61   See the AFL-CIO's website: https://aflcio.org/what-unions-do/social-economic-justice/worker-centers.

Chapter 1

1   James R. Green and Hugh Carter Donahue, *Boston's Workers: A Labor History* (Boston: Boston Public Library, 1977), 118.

2   Saskia Sassen, *The Global City: New York, London, Tokyo* (Princeton: Princeton University Press, 1991).

3   This definition is used frequently by researchers to indicate class, in part because it is hard to find data that gets at the better definitions of class which include measures of workers' relation to production or the degree of control they may have over their work time or over other workers. Education level, then, is a very rough indication of the working class.

4   As a benchmark, the average unemployment rate in Massachusetts from 2005 to 2007 was 4.8 percent, and for 2013 to 2015 it was 5.7 percent (US Bureau of Labor Statistics, Unemployment Rate in Massachusetts [MAUR], https://fred.stlouisfed.org/series/MAUR).

5   Each year of data is a 1 percent sample of all households in the state. As is customary with a sample survey, we use the ACS-assigned person weights to get estimates of total population.

6   Zero earnings indicate someone who was not employed, so we exclude them. Self-employed workers can report negative earnings. However, less than 0.1 percent of all earners report negative earnings in the 2013–15 period.

7   Sassen, *Global City*.

8   The ACS only asks about workers' primary jobs. It is possible, therefore, that workers with second jobs are engaged in the gig economy.

9   US Department of Commerce, Bureau of Economic Analysis, 2017, Regional Economic Accounts, Data: Interactive Tables for Gross Domestic Product by State and by Metropolitan Area, https://www.bea.gov/regional/index.htm.

10   Using a standard OLS regression, workers in Boston earn 1.7 percent more than workers in its suburbs (statistically significant at the 90 percent level) while they earn 13.6 percent more than workers in the non-metro region (statistically significant at the 99 percent level).

11　Earnings at the median are at the exact midpoint of all workers' earnings (i.e., 50 percent earn more while 50 percent earn less). Similarly, the earnings at the 20th decile represents the earnings of the worker in which 80 percent of all workers earn more while 20 percent earn less.

12　To do this we sum the total amount of earnings earned by workers in each quintile and divide this amount by the sum of all earnings. The percentages of earnings shares held by each quintile add up to 100 percent.

13　This is calculated by subtracting the share of total earnings held in each quintile in 2005–2007 from those in 2013–2015 (depicted in Figure 1.3). Because we are looking at a change in the total shares and the shares add up to 100 percent of all income, one quintile's earnings gain is due to another one's loss (that is, the sum of the changes must equal zero).

14　This is a common definition used in the literature. See Jérôme Gautié, Niels Westergaard-Nielsen, and John Schmitt with Ken Mayhew, "The Impact of Institutions on the Supply-Side of the Low-Wage Labor Market," in *Low-Wage Work in the Wealthy World*, ed. Jerome Gautié and John Schmitt (New York: Russell Sage Foundation, 2010), 147–82.

15　We only look at workers that earn positive earnings of $1.00 or more an hour.

16　The differences are statistically significant at the 99 percent level of confidence.

17　One example of a low-wage professional worker with high levels of education is pre-school teachers. They work long hours but receive relatively low pay.

Chapter 2

1　James R. Green and Hugh Carter Donahue, *Boston's Workers: A Labor History* (Boston: Boston Public Library, 1979), n.p.

2　Meagan Day, "UC Workers on Strike," *Jacobin*, May, 2018.

3　Tom Juravich, William F. Hartford, and James R. Green, *Commonwealth of Toil: Chapters in the History of Massachusetts Workers and Their Unions* (Amherst, MA: University of Massachusetts Press, 1996).

4　Priscilla Murolo, "Five Lessons from Public Sector Unions," *Labor Notes*, June 11, 2018.

5　Heidi Shierholz, "The Numbers of Workers Represented by a Union Held Steady in 2019 While Union Membership Declined," Economic Policy Institute, January 22, 2020, www.epi.org/publication/2019-union-membership-data/.

6　US Department of Commerce, Bureau of the Census, "State Distribution of Public Employment in 1960," March 31, 1961, 8; Barry T. Hirsch and David A. Macpherson, *Union Membership and Coverage Database*, "Union Membership, Coverage, Density, and Employment by State and Sector, 1983–2019," www.unionstats.com.

7　Juravich et al., *Commonwealth of Toil*, 142.

8　Commonwealth of Massachusetts, Department of Labor Relations, *A Guide to the Massachusetts Collective Bargaining Law*, 11th ed., 2016, http://www.mass.gov/lwd/labor-relations/a-guide-to-the-ma-collective-bargaining-law-11-8-16.pdf; John Kifner, "Public Workers Strike in Massachusetts," *New York Times*, June 22, 1976.

9   Hirsch and MacPherson. "The Union Membership and Coverage Database, 2017," www.unionstats.com; Heiwon Kwon and Benjamin Day, "The Politics of Labor in Boston," in Lowell Turner and Daniel B. Cornfield, eds., *Labor in the New Urban Battlegrounds: Local Solidarity in a Global Economy* (Ithaca, NY: Cornell University Press), 100; David Pihl, Jasmine Kerrissey, and Tom Juravich, "The State of Labor and Employment in Massachusetts," *Working Paper Series*, Labor Center, University of Massachusetts, Amherst, September 4, 2017, https://www.umass.edu/lrrc/sites/default/files/UMass_Labor_Day_Report_8-25-17.pdf.

10 Jake Rosenfeld, "Government Is Not the Answer: Why Public Sector Unions Won't Rescue Labor," *Talking Points Memo*, March 17, 2014.

11 Brentin Mock, "Boston City Government Has a Racial Pay Disparity Problem," *CityLab*, July 21, 2017.

12 Edgar B. Herwick III, "How Urban Flight Led to Boston's Residency Requirement," *WGBH News*, June 12, 2014; City of Boston, "Residency Requirements for City Workers," https://www.boston.gov/departments/human-resources/residency-requirements-city-workers; and Andrew Ryan, "Boston's Residency Rule Routinely Flouted," *Boston Globe*, July 6, 2014.

13 John Goodman and Gary Loveman, "Does Privatization Serve the Public Interest?" *Harvard Business Review*, August–September 1991.

14 Richard Hogarty, "Downsizing the Massachusetts Mental Health System," *New England Journal of Public Policy* 12, no. 1 (1996).

15 Massachusetts Teachers Association, *The Threat from the Right Intensifies*, May 2018, www.massteacher.org/-/media/massteacher/files/initiatives/privatization/threat-from-the-right-2018.pdf

16 Meizhu Lui, "Fighting Racism as the First Order of Business: Lessons from a Marxist-Inspired Union Organizing Experience," *Class, Race and Corporate Power* 5, no. 3 (2017), 7.

17 Michael Greenstone and Adam Looney, "A Record Decline in Government Jobs: Implications for the Economy and America's Workforce," *Brookings*, August 3, 2013, www.brookings.edu/blog/jobs/2012/08/03/a-record-decline-in-government-jobs-implications-for-the-economy-and-americas-workforce/.

18 *Frontline*, "Interview: Grover Norquist," September 2, 2004, https://www.pbs.org/wgbh/pages/frontline/shows/choice2004/interviews/norquist.html.

19 Ed Pilkington, "Right Wing Alliance Plots Assault to Defund and Defang America's Unions," *The Guardian*, August 30, 2017.

20 US Bureau of Labor Statistics, "Union Members in Wisconsin—2019," February 19, 2020, https://www.bls.gov/regions/midwest/news-release/2020/pdf/unionmembership_wisconsin_20200219.pdf

21 Josh Bivens, Lora Engdahl, Elise Gould, et al., "How Today's Unions Help Working People," Economic Policy Institute, August 24, 2017, http://www.epi.org/publication/how-todays-unions-help-working-people-giving-workers-the-power-to-improve-their-jobs-and-unrig-the-economy/.

22 Elise Gould and Will Kimball, "Right to Work States Still Have Lower Wages," *Economic Policy Institute*, Briefing Paper #395, April 22, 2015, http://www.epi.org/publication/right-to-work-states-have-lower-wages/.

23   Kellie Lunney, "Romney Again Targets Government Employees," *Government Executive*, August 15, 2012.

24   Katherine Cramer Walsh, "Political Understanding of Economic Crises: The Shape of Resentment toward Public Employees," in *The Costs of Crisis: Popular Responses to the Great Recession*, eds. Nancy Bermo and Larry Bartels (Russell Sage Foundation, forthcoming).

25   Cynthia Estlund and William E. Forbath, "The War on Workers: The Supreme Court Ruling on Harris v. Quinn Is a Blow for Unions," *New York Times*, July 2, 2014.

26   "Massachusetts Home Health Workers Build Strength Despite Obstacles," *1199 Magazine*, April 16, 2019.

27   "Resolution: An Injury to One Is an Injury to All," MA AFL-CIO Constitutional Convention, October 17–18, https://www.massaflcio.org/system/files/ma_afl-cio_2017_convention_resolutions_0.pdf.

28   A major funder of "Yes on 2" was later fined almost half a million dollars for failing to disclose its donors. See Kathleen McNerney and Meghna Chakrabarti, "Unmasking Dark Money behind Charter School Ballot Question," WBUR, September 15, 2017.

29   Matt Murphy, "Group Insurance Commission Relents," *Taunton Daily Gazette*, January 25, 2018.

30   Rebecca Rainey and Ian Kullgren, "1 Year After Janus, Unions Are Flush," *Politico*, June 17, 2019.

31   Robin Urevich, "Mark Janus Wants His Union Dues Back," *American Prospect*, July 11, 2019; Ann C. Hodges, "The Aftermath of *Janus v. AFSCME*: An Ongoing Assault on Public Sector Unions," American Constitutional Society, March 2020, www.acslaw.org/wp-content/uploads/2020/02/Janus-v.-AFSCME-An-Ongoing-Assault-on-Public-Sector-Unions.pdf.

32   Hirsch and Macpherson, *Union Membership and Coverage Database*.

Chapter 3

1   Chuck Turner, "People's Platform: Economic Development," video, November 9, 2017, Boston Neighborhood Network, https://bnntv.org/vod/peoples-platform/peoples-platform-chuck-turner-economic-development-part-1.

2   Barry Bluestone and Mary Huff Stevenson, *Boston Renaissance* (New York: Russell Sage Foundation, 2000), 386; Lane Windham, *Knocking on Labor's Door* (Chapel Hill: University of North Carolina Press, 2017).

3   Jim Vrabel, *A People's History of the New Boston* (Amherst, MA: University of Massachusetts Press, 2014), 230; Vijay Prashad, "This Ends Badly: Race and Capitalism," in Jordan T. Camp and Christina Heatherton, eds., *Policing the Planet* (New York: Verso, 2016), 291.

4   Bluestone and Stevenson, *Boston Renaissance*, 206ff.; Boston Area Research Initiative (Northeastern University), "An Evaluation of Equity in the Boston Public Schools' Home-Based Assignment Policy," July 2018, https://www.northeastern.edu/csshresearch/bostonarearesearchinitiative/wp-content/uploads/sites/2/2018/07/Final-Evaluation-of-Equity-in-BPS-HBAP.pdf; WBUR Learning Lab, "Massachusetts' School-to-Prison Pipeline, Explained," April

21, 2015, learninglab.legacy.wbur.org/topics/massachusetts-school-to-prison-
pipeline-explained/.

5   See Marilyn Halter, *Between Race and Ethnicity: Cape Verdean American
        Immigrants, 1860–1965* (Champaign: University of Illinois Press, 1993); Waters,
        Black Identities: West Indian Immigrant Dreams and American Realities (New
        York: Russell Sage, 1999), 34–36. Of course, these categories could overlap:
        West Indian migrants to the southern United States could then join southerners
        moving north. See also Jie Zong and Jeanne Batalova, "Caribbean Immigration
        in the United States," Migration Policy Institute, September 14, 2016, www.
        migrationpolicy.org/article/caribbean-immigrants-united-states.

6   Waters, *Black Identities*, 91; Johnson describes local support for the 1938 Labor
        Rebellions, including events with Claude McKay in 1938 and Eric Williams
        in 1943 and campaigns for participation in the native Black labor movement
        in Violet Showers Johnson, *The Other Black Bostonians: West Indians in Boston,
        1900–1950* (Bloomington: Indiana University Press, 2006), 90, 93. Lara Putnam
        describes the spread of radical ideas in West Indian migrant circuits in *Radical
        Moves: Caribbean Migrants and the Politics of Race in the Jazz Age* (Chapel Hill:
        University of North Carolina Press, 2013).

7   *Autobiography of Malcolm X* (New York: Ballantine Publishing Group, 1964)
        46–47.

8   *Autobiography of Malcolm X*, 340.

9   Johnson, *The Other Black Bostonians*, 84; Daniels, *In Freedom's Birthplace*, 373–74;
        Schneider, *Boston Confronts Jim Crow*, 175.

10   Mel King, *Chain of Change: Struggles for Black Community Development* (Boston:
        South End Press, 1981), 9; Jeanne Theoharis, "'They Told Us Our Kids Were
        Stupid': Ruth Batson and the Educational Movement in Boston," in *Groundwork:
        Local Black Freedom Movements in America*, ed. Jeanne Theoharis and Komozi
        Woodard (New York University Press, 2005), 20; Johnson, *The Other Black
        Bostonians*, 118. Nelson's father worked as a tailor at the Charleston Navy Yard,
        30.

11   King, *Chain of Change*, 10–11.

12   See below and especially, King's conversation with Omar Cannon, Leo Fletcher,
        Elma Lewis, Marion McElhaney, and Byron Rushing in King, *Chain of Change*,
        291–95.

13   King, *Chain of Change*, 49–50; 51–52.

14   King, *Chain of Change*, 59, 61, 63; 95–96; 98; 105.

15   Massachusetts Association of Minority Law Enforcement Officers, Inc., "History
        of Mamleo," www.mamleo.org/history.html.

16   Boston Society of Vulcans, "Founding and History," www.bostonvulcans.org/
        founding-history/.

17   Llana Barber, *Latino City: Immigration and Urban Crisis in Lawrence,
        Massachusetts, 1945–2000* (Chapel Hill: University of North Carolina Press,
        2017), 196–97, shows how suburban state legislators in Massachusetts promoted
        the state's welfare reform of 1995 that "served as a model" for the 1996 national
        welfare reform; Richard Rothstein, *The Color of Law* (New York: W.W. Norton,
        2017).

18   Lance Carden, *Witness: An Oral History of Black Politics in Boston* (Boston College, 1989), 66.

19   Ronald P. Formisano, *Boston Against Busing: Race, Class, and Ethnicity in the 1960s and 1970s* (Chapel Hill: University of North Carolina Press, 1991), 13.

20   Ana Patricia Muñoz, Marlene Kim, Mariko Chang, et al., "The Color of Wealth in Boston," Federal Reserve Bank of Boston, March 25, 2015, www.bostonfed. org/publications/one-time-pubs/color-of-wealth.aspx.

21   Carden, *Witness*, 42.

22   King, *Chain of Change*, 157, 41, 129, 159.

23   Ruth Batson, *The Black Educational Movement in Boston: A Sequence of Historical Events* (Northeastern University School of Education, 2001), 376, 378.

24   See King, *Chain of Change*, especially chaps. 3, 7, 13, 14; Yawu Miller, "Black Educators Celebrate 50 Years of Advocacy," *Bay State Banner*, December 16, 2015; Jeanne Theoharis, "They Told Us Our Kids Were Stupid"; Robert A. Jordan, "Blacks Fear the Worst from 2 ½," *Boston Globe*, March 23, 1981.

25   See, for example, "US Court Pares Judge's Control on Boston Schools in Rights Case," *New York Times*, September 30, 1987.

26   Irene Sege, "A Calm Hand at the Helm of the Teachers Union," *Boston Globe*, October 1, 1983.

27   Ann Bradley, "Teachers Lambaste Order in Boston's Desegregation Case," *Education Week*, May 30, 1990.

28   Ann Bradley, "Teachers Lambaste Order"; Bruce Gellerman, "Boston Public School System Seeks to Increase Diversity Among its Teachers," WBUR, September 14, 2015; Jeremy C. Fox, "Boston Struggles to Diversify Teaching Ranks," *Boston Globe*, August 24, 2015.

29   The Campaign for Education of the Whole Child," The Alliance for the Education of the Whole Child, January 2006, www.citizensforpublicschools.org/ wp-content/uploads/2009/08/whole_child_report.pdf.

30   "Black and Hispanic Teachers Bear Disproportionate Impact of New 'Objective' Evaluation System," *Boston Union Teacher*, April 2013.

31   Lawyers Committee for Civil Rights and Economic Justice, "Broken Promises: Teacher Diversity in Boston Public Schools," March 2018, www.lawyerscom. org/wp-content/uploads/2018/03/Broken-Promises-Teacher-Diversity-Position-Paper.pdf.

32   BTU for All, "Progressive Principles," www.btuforall.com/jessicas-platform/.

33   For Colonial, see James Green, *Taking History to Heart* (Amherst: University of Massachusetts Press, 2000), 110–12; Thomas Juravich, William F. Hartford, and James Green, *Commonwealth of Toil* (Amherst: University of Massachusetts Press, 1996), 130–36. For Boston City Hospital, see Meizhu Lui, "Fighting Racism as the First Order of Business: Lessons from a Marxist-Inspired Union Organizing Experience," *Class, Race and Corporate Power* 5, no. 3 (2017), www. digitalcommons.fiu.edu/classracecorporatepower/vol5/iss3/2: 7. For General Electric, see Jeff Crosby, this volume.

34   See Mark Erlick and Jeff Grabelsky, "Standing at a Crossroads: The Building Trades in the Twenty-First Century," *Labor History* 46, no. 4 (November 2005):

421–45. For further detail on Black workers' struggles and white union resistance in the construction industry, see James E. Blackwell, "Jobs, Income, and Poverty: The Black Share of the New Boston," in Phillip L. Clay, ed., *The Emerging Black Community in Boston: A Report of the Institute for the Study of Black Culture* (Amherst: University of Massachusetts at Boston, 1985): 6–79; David Goldberg and Trevor Griffey, eds., *Black Power at Work: Community Control, Affirmative Action, and the Construction Industry* (Ithaca, NY: ILR Press, 2010); Chuck Turner, "Sharing the Pie: The Boston Jobs Coalition," *Labor Research Review*, 1. no. 12 (1988); Donovan Slack, "Fewer Residents Get Building Jobs," *Boston Globe*, September 10, 2009; Fred Barbash, "Court Upholds Cities' Rules on Jobs Residency," *Washington Post*, March 1, 1983; Initiative for a Competitive Inner City (ICIC), "Case Study: What Works: Building Pathways Creates Pathway to Boston's Well-Paying Construction Jobs," icic.org/construction/works-building-pathways-creates-pathway-bostons-well-paying-construction-jobs/; Matt Rocheleau, "Construction Hiring Goals Not Met in Boston," *Boston Globe*, May 18, 2015; Matt Rocheleau, "Mayor Calls on Construction Firms to Hire More Minorities, Women, Residents," *Boston Globe*, November 29, 2016.

35 Fred Barbash, "Boston's 'Reverse Discrimination' Case May Be Declared Moot," *Washington Post*, April 19, 1983.

36 Andrea Estes, "Court Halts Racial Decree for Fire Department," *Boston Globe*, March 28, 2003.

37 Danielle Ossher, Courtney Brooks, and Walter V. Robinson, "City Firehouses Still Stuck in a Racial Divide," *Boston Globe*, August 1, 2010.

38 Ossher, Brooks, and Robinson, "City Firehouses Still Stuck in a Racial Divide"; Lawrence Harmon, "Boston's Police Test," *Boston Globe*, March 9, 2013; Yasmin Amer and Ally Jarmanning, "Groups Want a Change in How Boston Fire and Police Hire Military Veterans," WBUR, February 14, 2018; Delores Handy, "As More Officers Reach Retirement, Boston's Police Force Is Becoming Less Diverse," WBUR, June 21, 2017.

39 Amer and Jarmanning, "Groups Want a Change"; Harmon, "Boston's Police Test"; Yawu Miller, "Police Seek More Diverse Recruit Pool as Minority Numbers Drop," *Bay State Banner*, July 9, 2014.

40 Barber, *Latino City*.

41 Andrew Ryan, "A Brand New Boston, Even Whiter than the Old," *Boston Globe*, December 11, 2017.

42 Windham, *Knocking on Labor's Door*; Debbie Gruenstein Bocian, Keith S. Ernst, and Wei Li, "Unfair Lending: The Effect of Race and Ethnicity on the Price of Sub-Prime Mortgages," Center for Responsible Lending, May 31, 2006.

43 Dudley Street Neighborhood Initiative, "Declaration of Community Rights," www.dsni.org/about-us.

44 Dom Apollon, "Got a Record? You Can Still Get a Job in Massachusetts," *Colorlines*, September 3, 2010; Martin Desmarais, "City Updates CORI Reform Ordinance," *Bay State Banner*, April 16, 2014; Boston Workers Alliance: Fighting for Jobs and CORI Reform, web.archive.org/web/20110725101525/http://bostonworkersalliance.org/?page_id=2.

45 See Black Economic Justice Institute, www.bejii.org and Boston Ujima Project, www.ujimaboston.com.

46 "Boston Jobs Coalition Supports Boston Resident Jobs Policy Ordinance," *Sampan*, January 26, 2017.

47 Highlighted in print (Peter Medoff and Holly Sklar, *Streets of Hope: The Fall and Rise of an Urban Neighborhood* [1994]) and film (*Holding Ground: The Rebirth of Dudley Street*, directed by Mark Lipman and Leah Mahan [1996] and their follow-up effort, *Gaining Ground: Building Community on Dudley Street*, [2013]).

48 Penn Loh, "Land, Co-ops, Compost: A Local Food Economy Emerges in Boston's Poorest Neighborhoods," *YES Magazine*, November 7, 2014. See also Steve Dubb, interview with Aaron Tanaka, *Community-Wealth.org*, November 2015, www.community-wealth.org/content/aaron-tanaka.

Chapter 4

1 The United Electrical Workers (UE) was an early leftist CIO union committed to radical democratic and anti-racist structures. It was expelled from the CIO in the organization's anti-communist purge of 1949 to 1950.

Chapter 5

1 Brandon J. Dixon and Caroline S. Engelmayer, "Citing Harvard, Northeastern Dining Workers Brace for Strike," *Harvard Crimson*, September 21, 2017.

2 See Lisa Prevost, "For Boston Seaport, G.E. Was Just a Start," *New York Times*, June 14, 2016.

3 See for example, Tim Logan, "Akamai Gets $700L Tax Subsidy for Kendall Expansion," *Boston Globe*, September 21, 2016; John Chesto, "IBM granted $2.5M in tax breaks for locating digital health venture," *Boston Globe*, September 23, 2015; and David L. Chandler, "A new era set to begin in Kendall Square," *MIT News*, May 17, 2016, http://news.mit.edu/2016/new-era-kendall-square-initiative-cambridge-planning-board-0518.

4 The City of Boston's 2017 city master plan, *Imagine Boston 2030*, highlights the growth of new economy industries alongside the service sector. See City of Boston, *Imagine Boston 2030*, imagine.boston.gov, 74–75.

5 I am the elected President of UNITE HERE Local 26 and have previously worked as its Financial Secretary Treasurer and Organizing Director.

6 *Boston Magazine*, "Single Family Home Prices in Greater Boston 2017," www.bostonmagazine.com/best-places-to-live-2017-single-family-homes/.

7 Jim Hammerand, "Here's the Salary You Need to Afford a Home in Boston and 49 Other Metros," *Boston Business Journal*, December 18, 2017.

8 City of Boston, *Imagine Boston 2030*, 92. This report also points out that while Boston's median income is comparable to the national average, the median home value in Boston is more than two and a half times the national average.

9 *Boston Magazine*, "Single Family Home Prices."

10 City of Boston, *Imagine Boston*, 86, 296.

11 City of Boston, *Imagine Boston*, 86–87. See also the Spotlight Team, "Boston. Racism. Image. Reality. The Spotlight Team Takes on Our Hardest Question," *Boston Globe*, December 10, 2017, , see,.

12 Tim Logan, "Average Boston-Area Rent Falls for the First Time in Almost 7 Years," *Boston Globe*, January 5, 2017.

13 Massachusetts Health Policy Commission, *Annual Health Care Costs Trend Report, CTR 2016* (February, 2017), www.mass.gov/anf/budget-taxes-and-procurement/oversight-agencies/health-policy-commission/publications/2016-cost-trends-report.pdf, 27.

14 Massachusetts Health Policy Commission, *Annual Health Care Costs*, 20, 11, 6.

15 Katie Johnston, "Supporters of Higher Minimum Wage Urge Lawmakers to Enact Hike," *Boston Globe*, September 19, 2017.

16 David Scharfenberg, "Mass. Poised to Be Pacesetter for Minimum Wage," *Boston Globe*, June 14, 2014.

17 Sarah Toy, "Mass. Wage Theft Bill Seeks to Tackle Growing Problem," *Lowell Sun*, May 29, 2017.

18 See Paul Solomon, "A Lawyer and Her Client Weigh in on the Overtime Scam," *PBS NewsHour*, June 18, 2015, www.pbs.org/newshour/economy/making-sense/working-overtime-doesnt-always-equate-overtime-pay; Gloria Dawson, "Meet the Lawyer Challenging the Food-Delivery Industry," *Eater*, December 29, 2015.

19 See the *Boston Globe*'s editorial endorsement, "Yes on Question 4: Earned Sick Time for All," October 25, 2014.

20 As the organizing director and later financial secretary treasurer of Local 26 during this period, I have a unique, albeit biased, view of the work of UNITE HERE Local 26. While I will rely on some published sources for this discussion, I have also drawn on my memory and personal experience of these events.

21 Victor Silverman, "Victory at Pomona College: Union Strategy and Immigrant Labor," *Labor Studies Journal* 40 no. 1 (2015): 8–31.

22 Jessica Teich, "Chartwells," *Woof Magazine*, April 6, 2012, www.woof-mag.com/2012/06/04/chartwells/. This article is the best journalistic account of the campaign to unionize Northeastern cafeteria workers. Chartwells is the food service provider that runs the cafeterias at Northeastern University.

23 Teich, "Chartwells."

24 Local 26, "Northeastern University Food Service Workers Vote to Unionize," April 13, 2012, http://www.local26.org/2012/04/northeastern-university-food-service-workers-vote-to-unionize/.

25 Local 26, "Cafeteria Workers at Lesley and Simmons Join UNITE HERE Local 26," October 4, 2013, http://www.local26.org/2013/10/cafeteria-workers-at-lesley-and-simmons-join-unite-here-local-26/.

26 United Students Against Sweatshops, "'The Numbers Said It All': Northeastern Chartwells Workers Win Union," http://usas.org/the-numbers-said-it-all-northeastern-chartwells-workers-win-union/.

27 The Northeastern contract was the first new contract negotiated during the wave of campus organization. It included a five-year job guarantee for immigrants if their protected status is revoked. The economics of the contracts that followed it are basically the same.

28 Mike Kramer, personal communication, February 6, 2018.

29 I have written in detail about this campaign elsewhere, see Carlos Aramayo, "Lessons from the 2016 Harvard Strike," *International Labor and Working-Class History* 91 (Spring, 2017): 175-177.

30 "The demand[s]," wrote Mike Kramer, the organizing director who oversaw the Harvard strike, "gave workers a common language to address a varied set of problems and one which was easily understood by a diverse set of potential allies" (Kramer, personal communication, February 6, 2018).

31 See, for example, Danielle Doug, "Harvard University dining hall workers strike over wages and health-care costs," *Washington Post*, October 5, 2016; Katie Rogers, "No End in Sight to Strike by Harvard's Cafeteria Workers Over Wages," *New York Times*, October 11, 2016; and Michelle Chen, "The First Campus Strike in Over 30 Years Is Happening at Harvard," *The Nation,* October 11, 2016.

32 Hamilton Nolan, "Idiots Who Run Harvard Let Their Low-Wage Workers Go on Strike," *Deadspin*, October 5, 2016.

33 Local 26, "Dining Hall Workers at Northeastern University Announce Strike Vote, Prepare for Potential Strike," September 20, 2017.

34 Local 26, "Dining Hall Workers."

35 See Danny McDonald, "Northeastern Dining Hall Workers Vote to Authorize Strike," *Boston Globe*, October 5, 2017.

36 Northeastern News, "Northeastern University to Host Clinton Global Initiative," *News@Northeastern*, https://news.northeastern.edu/2017/02/northeastern-university-to-host-clinton-global-initiative-university/.

37 I suspect that the readiness of many millennial students to come to the aid of organizing and striking cafeteria workers comes in part from a combination of their racial and ethnic diversity and the contingent nature of jobs in the innovation economy. Many of these students are first-generation college attendees and the children of immigrant parents. As such, they have personal and experiential affinity with Black and brown cafeteria workers struggling to make ends meet. In addition, as has been widely reported, the innovation economy is notoriously contingent. Students looking toward first jobs find the new economy insecure and uninviting; economic insecurity is not the privilege of workers in the service industry.

38 See Julia Carrie Wong, "Facebook Worker Living in Garage to Zuckerberg: Challenges Are Right Outside Your Door," *Guardian*, July 7, 2017; Nitasha Tiku, "The Second Class Citizens of the Google Cafeteria," *ValleyWag*, December 19, 2013; and UNITE HERE, "Cafeteria Workers at Yahoo Unionize, Join Workers' Movement for Equality in the Tech Industry, December 15, 2017, http://unitehere.org/cafeteria-workers-at-yahoo-unionize/.

Chapter 6

1 The author wishes to thank Dorothy Nelson, retired Lecturer in English at UMass Boston and NTT faculty activist, for reading and commenting on a draft of this article. Richard Vedder, "There Are Really Almost No Truly Private Universities" *Forbes*, April 8, 2018.

2 Barbara Gottfried and Gary Zabel, "Social Movement Unionism and Adjunct Faculty Organizing in Boston," in *Steal This University: The Rise of the Corporate*

University and the Academic Labor Movement, ed. Benjamin Johnson, Patrick Kavanaghm, and Kevin Mattson (London: Routledge, 2003).

3   Tenure-stream faculty at private universities are a different case. Until 2015, they were barred from unionization as a result of a 1980 Supreme Court ruling, *National Labor Relations Board v. Yeshiva University.* This ruling upheld a lower-court decision that tenure-stream faculty at private universities constitute management, not labor, and thus had no *need* to unionize, as they are already well-treated and have a substantial role in institutional governance. A 2015 NLRB ruling, however, reversed that decision (Scott Jaschik, "Big Union Win," *Inside Higher Education,* January 2, 2015; Kim Tolley, Marianne Delaporte, and Lorenzo Giachetti, "Unionizing Adjunct and Tenure Track Faculty at Notre Dame de Namur University," in *Professors in the Gig Economy: Unionizing Adjunct Faculty in America,* ed. Kim Tolley [Baltimore: Johns Hopkins University Press, 2018], 104–22).

4   "Tuition and Fees," www.brandeis.edu/student-financial-services/tuition-calculator/tuition.html.

5   James R. Green and Hugh Garter Donahue, "Epilogue: Boston Workers Since World War II" in Green and Donahue, *Boston's Workers: A Labor History* (Boston Public Library, 1977), 115–20.

6   Cathy Sandeen, "MOOCs Moving On, Moving Up," *Inside Higher Education,* June 22, 2017.

7   Bureau of Labor Statistics, US Department of Labor, 2017, *Occupational Outlook Handbook,* Postsecondary Teachers, www.bls.gov/ooh/education-training-and-library/postsecondary-teachers.htm.

8   A. J. Angulo, "From Golden Era to Gig Economy: Changing Contexts for Academic Labor in America" in *Professors in the Gig Economy,* ed. Kim Tolley (Baltimore: Johns Hopkins University Press, 2018), 3–26.

9   Bureau of Labor Statistics, US Department of Labor, New England Information Office, Boston Area Employment: October 2018, www.bls.gov/regions/new-england/news-release/areaemployment_boston.htm.

10   Deirdre Fernandes, "Adjuncts Help Colleges Expand Their Online Programs," *Boston Globe,* October 23, 2017; Fernandes, "Adjuncts Seek Better Pay, Benefits through Legislation." *Boston Globe,* June 29, 2017.

11   Nell Gluckman, "Want to Be a 'Volunteer Adjunct'? Southern Illinois U. Is Hiring," *Chronicle of Higher Education,* April 24, 2018.

12   Blaine Greteman, "Don't Blame Tenured Academics for the Adjunct Crisis," *Chronicle of Higher Education,* February 22, 2017.

13   Claire Potter, "Angry about Adjuncting?" *Inside Higher Education,* October 16, 2017.

14   Gary Zabel, "Critical Revolutionary Praxis in the Neoliberal University," *Works and Days* 33–34, nos. 65/66, 67/68 (2016–17): 200.

15   For an analysis of gig work in the sciences see Roberta Kwok, "Flexible Working: Science in the Gig Economy," *Nature* 550 (2017): 419–21; Johanna Mayer, "Uber, but for Scientists," *Science,* January 19, 2018.

16   See, for example, Max Moran, "Faculty to Grow Union Effort," *Justice,* September 8, 2015; Rachel Riley, "Brandeis Faculty Petition to Join Higher

Education Union," *Boston Globe*, November 4, 2015; Abigail Gardener, "Brandeis Faculty Forward Continues Collective Bargaining," *Brandeis Hoot*, March 24, 2017; Daniel Souleles, "Leaving Brandeis," *Brandeis Hoot*, March 31, 2017,

17 Souleles, "Leaving Brandeis."

18 Waltham City Council, "Resolution," 2015, brandeisfacultyforward.org/wp-content/uploads/2015/02/Waltham-City-Council-Resolution.pdf.

19 Gottfried and Zabel, "Social Movement Unionism," 210.

20 Modern Languages Association, "Report of the MLA Task Force on Doctoral Study in Modern Language and Literature," May 2014, apps.mla.org/pdf/taskforcedocstudy2014.pdf.

21 Zabel, "Critical Revolutionary Practice," 196.

22 Joe Berry, *Reclaiming the Ivory Tower: Organizing Adjuncts to Change Higher Education* (New York: Monthly Review Press, 2005).

23 Berry, *Reclaiming the Ivory Tower*, XI.

24 Amy Todd, "Challenges to Organizing Academic Labor," *Anthropology News* 53, no. 4 (April 2012).

25 Marya R. Levinson, "Univ.'s Unique Contract Structure Makes Adjunct Union Unnecessary," *Brandeis Hoot*, October 30, 2015; Harry Mairson, October 30, 2015, comment on Levison, "Univ.'s Unique Contract Structure."

26 Peter Schmidt, "Union Efforts on Behalf of Adjuncts Meet Resistance Within Faculties' Ranks," *Chronicle of Higher Education*, April 9, 2014.

27 William Herbert, "The Winds of Change Shift: An Analysis of Recent Growth in Bargaining Units and Representation Efforts in Higher Education," *Journal of Collective Bargaining in the Academy* 8, no. 1 (2016).

28 Gottfried and Zabel, "Social Movement Unionism," 210.

Chapter 7

1 See Thomas Frank, *Listen, Liberal* (New York: Henry Holt and Company, 2016).

2 Evan Horowitz, "If Mass. Was a Country, It Would Be among World's Richest." *Boston Globe*, June 10, 2015.

3 Massachusetts Budget and Policy Center, "2017 State of Working Massachusetts," https://www.massbudget.org/reports/swma/wages-income.php.

4 Greg Ryan, "Ballot Boxing: How Businesses Are Gearing up for 2018 Ballot Clashes," *Boston Business Journal*, September 21, 2017.

5 Moishe Postone, *Time, Labor, and Social Domination* (Cambridge University Press, 1996).

Chapter 8

1 Tyler Pager, "Donald Trump Claims to Remake GOP as Party of 'the American Worker,'" *Boston Globe*, February 24, 2017; Sean Higgins, "Teachers Union Head Met Privately with Steve Bannon," *Washington Examiner*, November 1, 2017; Philip Bump, "Donald Trump Got Reagan-like Support from Union Households," *Washington Post*, November 10, 2016.

2   Eduardo Bonilla-Silva, *Racism without Racists: Color-Blind Racism and the Persistence of Racial Inequality in America* (Lanham: Rowman & Littlefield Publishers, 2014).

3   Shiva Maniam, "Most Americans See Labor Unions, Corporations Favorably," *Pew Research Center*, January 30, 2017, www.pewresearch.org/fact-tank/2017/01/30/most-americans-see-labor-unions-corporations-favorably/; Eric Larson, "Black Lives Matter and Bridge Building: Labor Education for a 'New Jim Crow' Era," *Labor Studies Journal* 41, no. 1 (2016): 36–66.

4   Ian Haney-Lopez, *Dog Whistle Politics: How Coded Racial Appeals Have Wrecked the Middle Class* (Oxford University Press, 2014).

5   Michelle Alexander, *The New Jim Crow: Mass Incarceration in the Age of Colorblindness* (New York: New Press, 2012), 164, 141.

6   Jane McAlevey, *No Shortcuts: Organizing for Power in the New Gilded Age* (Oxford University Press, 2016).

7   Bill Fletcher and Fernando Gapasin, *Solidarity Divided: The Crisis in Organized Labor and a New Path toward Social Justice* (Berkeley: University of California Press, 2008); Paul Johnston, *Success While Others Fail: Social Movement Unionism and the Public Workplace* (Ithaca, NY: ILR Press, 1994); Ray M. Tillman and Michael S. Cummings, eds., *The Transformation of U.S. Unions: Voices, Visions, and Strategies from the Grassroots* (Boulder, CO: Lynne Rienner Publishers, 1999).

8   Janice Fine, *Worker Centers: Organizing Communities at the Edge of the Dream* (Ithaca, NY: ILR Press, 2006); Barbara Ransby, *Ella Baker and the Black Freedom Movement: A Radical Democratic Vision* (Chapel Hill: University of North Carolina Press, 2003); Linda Briskin, "Union Renewal, Postheroic Leadership, and Women's Organizing," *Labor Studies Journal* 36, no. 4 (December 2011): 508–37.

9   Bruce Nissen, 2004, "The Effectiveness and Limits of Labor-Community Coalitions: Evidence from South Florida," *Labor Studies Journal* 29, no. 1 (2004): 67–89.

10 Amanda Tattersall, *Power in Coalition: Strategies for Strong Unions and Social Change* (Ithaca: ILR Press, 2010); Amanda Tatersall, "The Power of Union-Community Coalitions," *Renewal: A Journal of Social Democracy* 19, no. 1 (2011); Amy B. Dean and David B. Reynolds, *A New New Deal: How Regional Activism Will Reshape the American Labor Movement* (Ithaca: ILR Press, 2009).

11 Larry Cohen, "Introduction: Stand Up! Fight Back!" in *Jobs with Justice: 25 Years, 25 Voices*, ed. Eric Larson (San Francisco: PM Press, 2013), 1–10.

12 Robin D. G. Kelley, *Race Rebels: Culture, Politics, and the Black Working Class* (New York: Free Press, 1994); Ransby, *Ella Baker*; E.P. Thompson, *The Making of the English Working Class* (New York: Vintage Books, 1966).

13 Eric D. Larson, "Ode to the American Century: Ambivalent Americanism and the Founding of the Jobs with Justice Coalition," *Labor* 12, no. 3 (2015): 53–74.

14 Bill Fletcher Jr., and Fernando Gapasin, "The Politics of Labour and Race in the USA," *Socialist Register* 39: 261.

15 Kwame Ture and Charles V. Hamilton. *Black Power: The Politics of Liberation in America* (New York: Vintage Books, 1992); Alethia Jones, Virginia Eubanks,

and Barbara Smith, eds., *Ain't Gonna Let Nobody Turn Me Around: Forty Years of Movement Building with Barbara Smith* (Albany: SUNY Press, 2014).

16 Audre Lorde, *Sister Outsider* (Freedom, CA: Crossing Press, 1984), 114–23; Ransby, *Ella Baker*, 188. Ransby discusses the "group leadership" of Black working-class women in the Black Freedom and Civil Rights movements.

17 Laura Flanders, "Building Movements without Shedding Differences: Alicia Garza of #BlackLivesMatter," *Truth-Out.Org*, March 24, 2015; Barbara Ransby, "Ella Taught Me: Shattering the Myth of the Leaderless Movement," *Colorlines*, June 12, 2015; Angela Y. Davis, *Women, Race & Class* (New York: Vintage Books, 1983); Jeremy Brecher and Tim Costello, *Building Bridges: The Emerging Grassroots Coalition of Labor and Community* (New York: Monthly Review Press, 1990).

18 Sean Thomas-Breitfeld, Linda Burnham, Steven Pitts, Marc Bayard, and Algernon Austin, "#BlackWorkersMatter (Excerpt)," Discount Foundation: Neighborhood Funders Group, 2015, www.nfg.org/sites/default/files/resources/Black%20Workers%20Matter%20Report%202015.pdf; Alicia Garza Tometi, Patrisse Cullors, and Opal, "An Interview with the Founders of Black Lives Matter," 2016, www.ted.com/talks/alicia_garza_patrisse_cullors_and_opal_tometi_an_interview_with_the_founders_of_black_lives_matter.

19 Lorde, *Sister Outsider*, 114–15.

20 Cherríe Moraga, "Preface," *This Bridge Called My Back: Writings by Radical Women of Color*, ed. Cherríe Moraga and Gloria Anzaldúa (Watertown, Mass: Persephone Press, 1981), xlvi.

21 Nancy MacLean, *Democracy in Chains: The Deep History of the Radical Right's Stealth Plan for America* (New York: Viking, 2017); Corey Robin, "The First Neoliberals," *Jacobin.com*, April 28, 2016.

22 "Rhode Island Solidarity School Mission Statement, 2013," document in author's collection.

23 Jerry Tucker and other reform-minded UAW members also created Solidarity Schools in the 1990s.

24 Myles Horton, Brenda Bell, John Gaventa, and John Marshall Peters, *We Make the Road by Walking: Conversations on Education and Social Change* (Philadelphia: Temple University Press, 1990), 219.

25 These organizations include Rhode Island Council 94 AFSCME, SEIU Healthcare New England, Carpenters Local Union 94, General Teamsters Local 251, United Auto Workers Local 571, Providence Street Youth Movement, Providence Student Union, English for Action, the Olneyville Neighborhood Association, and Direct Action for Rights and Equality.

26 INCITE!, ed., *The Revolution Will Not Be Funded: Beyond the Non-Profit Industrial Complex* (Boston: South End Press, 2007); Dean Spade, *Normal Life: Administrative Violence, Critical Trans Politics, and the Limits of Law* (Durham: Duke University Press, 2015).

27 Jo Freeman, "The Tyranny of Structurelessness," *Berkeley Journal of Sociology* 17 (1972): 151–65.

28 The school has also been mindful to not replicate or compete with the labor education efforts of other local working-class organizations. Both the local racial

justice organization and the local immigrants' workers' centers offer intensive political education programs to their members. The local labor studies institute offered a "training" course for organizers that focused on technical skills for campaign work; the Solidarity School opted to be a discussion-oriented "school."

29 Jorrell Kaykay, telephone interview with the author, September 16, 2017. Jeffrey Santos, a founding member of the advisory committee, echoed these sentiments in our September 21, 2017 interview, as well.

30 Jesse Strecker, telephone interview with the author, September 14, 2017.

Chapter 9

1 Centro: Center for Puerto Rican Studies (Hunter College, City University of New York), "Puerto Ricans in Massachusetts, the United States, and Puerto Rico, 2014," April 2016; centropr.hunter.cuny.edu, 5. Many Puerto Ricans settled elsewhere in the state: there were 199,207 Puerto Ricans in Massachusetts in 2000, 266,125 in 2010, and 308,028 in 2014. The Hispanic or Latino population of the state also jumped, from 428,729 in 2000 to 627,654 in 2010 and 730,094 in 2014 (2).

2 Boston Redevelopment Authority, "Imagine All the People," rev. ed., June 2009, www.bostonplans.org/getattachment/c84782e4-01fd-4930-9939-f28b35ee9a84.

3 Boston Redevelopment Authority, "Boston by the Numbers, 2015," www.bostonredevelopmentauthority.org/getattachment/1fd5864a-e7d2-4ebc-8d4a-a4b8411bf759, 8.

4 Boston Redevelopment Authority–Research Division, "New Bostonians 2013–2014," March 2014, www.bostonplans.org/getattachment/08c87f4c-a651-45f9-bb42-04a55bae8b3b.

5 The census separates the "Hispanic" question from the "race" question, and those choosing "Hispanic" can identify as any race. Some publications, however, treat "Hispanic" as a race and don't break down the race of those identifying as Hispanic. "Boston by the Numbers," 8–10.

6 Andrés Torres, "Latinos and Labor: Challenges and Opportunities," *New England Journal of Public Policy* 11, no. 1 (1995): 147–60, 150; 149; 151.

7 Torres, "Latinos and Labor," 154.

8 Janice Fine, "A Marriage Made in Heaven? Mismatches and Misunderstandings between Worker Centres and Unions," *British Journal of Industrial Relations* 45, no. 2 (2007): 335–60, 341.

9 Fine, "A Marriage Made in Heaven?" 344. See Jane McAlevey with Bob Ostertag, *Raising Expectations (and Raising Hell): My Decade of Fighting for the Labor Movement* (New York: Verso, 2012), for an inside look at the pitfalls of this SEIU approach.

10 Corey Kurtz, "Worker Centers: Vehicles for Building Low-Wage Worker Power," (MA Thesis, Tufts University, May 2008), 82–83.

11 Kurtz, "Worker Centers," 82–83.

12 Kurtz, "Worker Centers," 82–83.

13 Fine, "A Marriage Made in Heaven?" 335.

14 Kurtz, "Worker Centers," 8.

15 See Aviva Chomsky, *Linked Labor Histories: New England, Colombia, and the Making of a Global Working Class* (Durham: Duke University Press, 2008), and Ardis Cameron, *Radicals of the Worst Sort: Laboring Women in Lawrence, Massachusetts, 1860–1912* (Champaign: University of Illinois Press, 1993).

16 See Chomsky, *Linked Labor Histories*, 142–78 for a discussion of how faltering New England textile manufacturers relied on immigrant workers as they prepared to shut down or relocate in the 1980s and 90s.

17 For some of the CPA's history, see Peter Kwong, *The New Chinatown* (New York: Hill and Wang, 1996), 160–73. Quotes come from Karen Chen, interview with author, January 25, 2017.

18 A lawyer and paralegal from Greater Boston Legal Services, which collaborated with the CPA on the campaign, give more detail on the process. See Cynthia Mark and Evonne Yang, "The Power-One Campaign: Immigrant Worker Empowerment through Law and Organizing," *Clearance Review: Journal of Poverty Law and Policy* 36, no. 3–4 (2002): 264–74.

19 Mark and Yang, "The Power-One Campaign," 265.

20 Katie Johnston, "MIT Study: Immigrants Vital to Boston's Economy," *Boston Globe*, May 18, 2017; Eduardo Porter, "Home Health Care: Shouldn't It Be Work Worth Doing?" *New York Times*, August 29, 2017.

21 Paraprofessional Healthcare Institute (PHI), *U.S. Homecare Workers: Key Facts*, phinational.org/sites/phinational.org/files/phi-home-care-workers-key-facts.pdf; Commonwealth Corporation and Center for Labor Markets and Policy, Drexel University, "Healthcare Employment, Structure, and Trends in Massachusetts, Chapter 224 Workforce Impact Study," December 2016, www.commcorp.org/wp-content/uploads/2017/07/Resources_Health-Care-Workforce_Employment-Structure-and-Trends-in-Massachusetts.pdf; Amy Baxter, "One in Four Direct Care Workers Are Immigrants," *Home Health Care News*, June 21, 2017; Robert Espinoza, "Immigrants and the Direct Care Workforce," PHI Research Brief, June 2017, phinational.org/sites/phinational.org/files/research-report/immigrants_and_the_direct_care_workforce_-_phi_-_june_2017.pdf.

22 Leigh Anne Schriever, "The Home Health Care Industry's Organizing Nightmare," August 18, 2015, https://tcf.org/content/commentary/the-home-health-care-industrys-organizing-nightmare/.

23 Eileen Boris and Jennifer Klein, *Caring for America: Home Health Care Workers in the Shadow of the Welfare State* (New York: Oxford University Press, 2015), 164; Eileen Boris and Jennifer Klein, "'We Were the Invisible Workforce': Unionizing Home Care," in Dorothy Sue Cobble, ed., *The Sex of Class: Women Transforming American Labor* (Ithaca: ILR Press, 2007), 188–89. On the background of ACORN, the ULU, and the Boston campaign see also Vanessa Tate, *Poor Workers' Unions: Rebuilding Labor from Below* (Chicago: Haymarket Books, 2000), 111–19, and Keith Kelleher, "ACORN Organizing and Chicago Healthcare Workers," *Labor Research Review* 1, no. 8 (1986).

24 See Steve Early, *The Civil Wars in U.S. Labor: Birth of a New Workers' Movement or Death Throes of the Old?* (Chicago: Haymarket Books, 2011), 167–71 for a discussion of these issues and their impact on Boston organizing. See also Leon Fink and Brian Greenberg, *Upheaval in the Quiet Zone: 1199/SEIU and the Politics of Health Care Unionism* (Champaign: University of Illinois Press, 2009), 209–43.

Boris quote in Kris Maher, "Unions Target Home Workers," *Wall Street Journal*, June 19, 2013.

25 Alana Semuels, "Home Healthcare Ruling May Inhibit Growth of Powerful Union," *Los Angeles Times*, June 30, 2014.

26 Jeffrey Krassner, "A Prescription for Growth," *Boston Globe*, November 8, 2007; Alejandra Cancino, "SEIU Stops Collecting Fees from Non-Member Home Health Workers," *Chicago Tribune*, August 12, 2014; Semuels, "Home Healthcare Ruling."

27 Mary Moore, "Unions Gained Ground in Bay State Last Year," *Boston Business Journal*, February 1, 2013; Katie Johnston, "Mass. Home Health Workers Win Wage Hike to $15 an Hour," *Boston Globe*, June 26, 2015.

28 "Fight for 15 Home Care," www.fightfor15homecare.org.

29 Katie Johnston, "Mass Home Healthcare Workers Win Wage Hike to $15 an Hour," *Boston Globe*, June 26, 2015; SEIU Press Release, "Home Care Workers at Medical Resources Vote to Unionize Despite Illegal Management Tactics, June 30, 2015," www.1199seiu.org/breaking_home_care_workers_at_medical_resources_vote_to_unionize_despite_illegal_management_tactics; Jessica Bartlett, "Newly Unionized Workers at Newton-Based Home Health Agency Secure Raises," *Boston Business Journal*, Jul 27, 2016; 1199SEIU Press Release, "Medical Resources Caregivers Win First Contract," September 22, 2016, www.1199seiu.org/massachusetts/medical-resources-caregivers-win-first-contract.

30 Fink and Greenberg, *Upheaval in the Quiet Zone*, 285–86. Italics in original.

31 See Kim Voss and Irene Bloemraad, *Rallying for Immigrant Rights: The Fight for Inclusion in 21st Century America* (Berkeley: University of California Press, 2011).

32 For an in-depth study of these divisions, see David G. Gutiérrez, *Walls and Mirrors: Mexican Americans, Mexican Immigrants, and the Politics of Ethnicity* (Berkeley: University of California Press, 1995).

33 Michael Grabell, "They Got Hurt at Work—Then They Got Deported," NPR, August 16, 2017, www.npr.org/2017/08/16/543650270/they-got-hurt-at-work-then-they-got-deported; Michael Arria, "Why Defending Workers' Rights Means Fighting ICE's Deportation Machine," *In These Times*, August 21, 2017.

34 Attorney General Maura Healey, Press Release, "On International Workers Day, AG Healey Issues Advisory on Protections for Immigrant Workers," May 1, 2017, www.mass.gov/ago/news-and-updates/press-releases/2017/2017-05-01-protections-immigrant-workers.html.

35 Shannon Dooling, "An ICE Arrest After a Workers' Comp Meeting Has Lawyers Questioning if It Was Retaliation," WBUR, May 17, 2017, www.wbur.org/news/2017/05/17/ice-arrest-workers-comp.

36 Katie Lannan and Colin A. Young, "Wage Theft Demands Legislative Response, Advocates Say," *Hull Times*, June 21, 2017.

Chapter 10

1 Susan Moir and Elizabeth Skidmore, "Designing a Pre-Apprenticeship Model for Women Entering and Succeeding in the Construction Trades," Report from the Center for Women and Work (University of Massachusetts Lowell, 2007).

2   Brigid O'Farrell and Suzanne Moore, "Unions, Hard Hats, and Women Workers," in *Women and Unions: Forming a Partnership* (Ithaca, NY: ILR Press, 1993); Kate Braid "The Culture of Construction, or Etiquette for the Non-Traditional," in Marjorie Griffin Cohen, ed., *Training the Excluded for Work* (Vancouver: BC Press, 2003); C. Goldin, "Understanding the Gender Gap: An Economic History of American Women," in P. Burstein, ed., *Equal Employment Opportunity: Labor Market Discrimination and Public Policy* (New York: Aldine de Gruyter Inc., 1994), 17–26.

3   Susan Eisenberg, *We'll Call You if We Need You: Women's Experiences Working in Construction* (New York: Cornell University Press, 1998).

4   Barbara Byrd, "Great Work if You Can Get it: Women in the Skilled Trades," in M. C. King, ed., *Squaring Up: Policy Strategies to Raise Women's Incomes in the United States* (Ann Arbor: University of Michigan Press, 2001), 200–25; Fran Moccio, *Live Wire: Women and Brotherhood in the Electrical Industry* (Philadelphia: Temple University Press, 2009); Vivian Price, "Race, Affirmative Action, and Women's Employment in US Highway Construction," *Feminist Economics* 8, no. 2 (2002).

5   Louise Vetter, "The Vocational Education Option for Women," in Sharon Harlan and Ronnie J. Steinberg, eds., *Job Training for Women: The Promise and Limits of Public Policy* (Philadelphia: Temple University Press, 1990), 91–113; Susan Moir and L. S. Azaroff, "The Boston-Area Research Circle on Health and Safety for Women in Construction: An Innovative Participatory Method for Coloring in the Picture of a Special Work Environment," *New Solutions: A Journal of Environmental & Occupational Health Policy* 17, nos. 1–2 (2007).

6   Women in the Building Trades Archive at Sophia Smith Collection, Smith College, asteria.fivecolleges.edu/findaids/sophiasmith/mnsss500.html.

7   PGTI: The Policy Group on Tradeswomen's Issues, "About PGTI," www.policygroupontradeswomen.org.

8   It would be almost a decade before we had the data to demonstrate the power of this decision. Anecdotally, we could see that more women of color were interested in the trades and it appeared that more women of color were entering apprenticeship. By 2017, we had enough data to confirm this observation. Based on 2.5 million hours worked by women in the City of Boston in 2013 to 2019, we know that 54 percent of those hours were worked by women of color and that tradeswomen of color are in fact the majority in Boston.

9   The federal mandate of 6.9 percent women's hours covers federally funded construction. The state of Massachusetts has also mandated 6.9 percent women's hours on all public and publicly assisted construction in the state.

10   Susan Moir, Meryl Thomson, and Christa Kelleher, "Unfinished Business: Building Equality for Women in the Construction Trades," Labor Resource Center Publications 5, 2011.

11   C. Menches and D. Abraham, "Women in Construction: Tapping the Untapped Resource to Meet Future Demands," *Journal of Construction Engineering and Management* 133, no. 9 (2007): 701–7.

12   Erin Johansson and Benjamin Woods, "Building Career Opportunities for Women and People of Color: Breakthroughs in Contruction," Jobs with Justice Education Fund and North American Building Trades Unions Tradeswomen

Committee, November 2016, www.jwj.org/wp-content/uploads/2016/12/
JWJEDU_NABTU_Report_2016_OnlineVersion_small.pdf.

13 University of Massachusetts Building Authority, Project Labor Agreement
for the UMass Boston Campus Between Building and Construction Trades
Council of the Metropolitan District and the New England Regional Council of
Carpenters, October 20, 2010, www.umassba.net/wp-content/uploads/2014/05/
Project-Labor-Agreement-for-UCRR-project-at-UMass-Boston-Campus.pdf.

14 Ravi K. Perry, "Governor Deval Patrick and the Representation of Massachusetts'
Black Interests," *Trotter Review* 20, no. 1 (2012).

15 PGTI, "Finishing the Job: Best Practices for Diverse Workforce in the
Construction Industry," May 2016, www.pgtiblog.files.wordpress.com/2016/06/
the-pgti-model-integrating-supply-and-demand-for-women-in-the-construction-
industry.pdf.

16 PGTI, "The PGTI Model: Integrating Supply and Demand for Women in the
Construction Industry," 2016, www.policygrouppontradeswomen.org/wp-content/
uploads/2020/07/The-PGTI-Model-v2-7.20.pdf.

17 Fear of litigation has not been unfounded. The courts have repeatedly required
proof of a disparity between those working in construction and those who claim
exclusion and discrimination. PGTI is conducting Regional Workforce Disparity
Studies to support enforcement efforts by municipalities. These studies have
found substantial disparities between the number of women who are working
in the construction trades and women in the region who are willing and able
to enter the industry. See Sofya Aptekar, "Springfield Construction Industry
Disparity Study," 2018, www.policygrouppontradeswomen.org/wp-content/
uploads/2019/02/springfield-disparity-study-4.18.pdf.

18 The Boston Planning & Development Agency, Research Division, "Boston's
Economy 2019," www.bostonplans.org/getattachment/33993523-dce0-4cfd-
903c-5eb8744733e8.

19 As this book goes to publication, we are in the sixth month of the Covid 19
pandemic and an era of unprecedented challenges for all aspects of public health
and the economy. PGTI and its partners are focused on ensuring healthy work
sites and continuing the progress toward fair employment for tradeswomen and
tradespeople of color that has been made in Massachusetts over the past decade.
We are in dialogue with industry leaders about the need to reject traditional
ways of operating, such as lack of transparency in job placement and "last hired,
first fired," that reinforced historic gender and racial discrimination in the
construction workforce.

Chapter 11

1 Brian Donovan, *White Slave Crusades: Race, Gender, and Anti-Vice Activism,
1887–1917* (Champaign: University of Illinois Press, 2006); Kayla Blackman,
"Public Power, Private Matters: The American Social Hygiene Association and
the Policing of Sexual Health in the Progressive Era," MA Thesis (University of
Montana, 2014).

2 Jessica Rae Pliley, *Policing Sexuality* (Cambridge: Harvard University Press, 2014).

3 *Hoke v. United States*, 227 U.S. 308 (1913).

4   Lynn Arditi, "How R.I. Opened the Door to Prostitution," *Providence Journal*, November 14, 2014.

5   2009 Rhode Island Code, Title 11 - Criminal Offenses, Chapter 11-34.1 - Commercial Sexual Activity § 11-34.1-7, Pandering or permitting prostitution – Not allowed.

6   Elizabeth Bernstein, "The Sexual Politics of the 'New Abolitionism,'" *differences* 18, no. 3 (2007): 128–51.

7   International Committee on the Rights of Sex Workers in Europe, "Feminism Needs Sex Workers, Sex Workers Need Feminism: Towards a Sex-Worker Inclusive Women's Rights Movement," *ICRSE Briefing Paper*, 2016.

8   Catherine A. MacKinnon, *Toward a Feminist Theory of the State* (Cambridge: Harvard University Press, 1989), 113, 127.

9   Victoria Law, "Against Carceral Feminism," *Jacobin.com*, October 17, 2014.

10 Law, "Against Carceral Feminism"; International Committee, "Feminism Needs Sex Workers"; Robyn Maynard, "Carceral Feminism: The Failure of Sex Work Prohibition," www.robynmaynard.com/writing/carceral-feminism-the-failure-of-sex-work-prohibition.

11 "Providence Police Officers Honored for Bravery, Kindness," *Providence Journal*, October 26, 2016.

12 American Civil Liberties Union of Rhode Island, "ACLU Statement on Cranston Police Department Prostitution Sting Operation," March 14, 2016, www.riaclu.org/news/post/aclu-statement-on-cranston-police-department-prostitution-sting-operation.

13 Torrie Hester, *Deportation: The Origins of US Policy* (University of Pennsylvania Press, 2017), 84.

14 OpenDoors of Rhode Island, "Rethinking Arrest: Street Prostitution & Public Policy in Rhode Island," 2009, opendoorsri.org/sites/default/files/RethinkingArrest.pdf.

15 Global Network of Sex Work Projects, "Criminalisation of Third Parties and Its Impact on Sex Workers' Human Rights," June 13, 2017, www.nswp.org/resource/criminalisation-third-parties-and-its-impact-sex-workers-human-rights.

16 Elizabeth Nolan Brown, "Study: To Lower Rape and STD Rates, Decriminalize Prostitution," *Reason.com*, July 15, 2014.

17 L. Cameron, J. Muz, and M. Shah, "Crimes of Morality: Unintended Consequences of Criminalizing Sex Work," UCLA Working Paper, 2016. Condom-as-evidence laws permit law enforcement officers to stop, search, and arrest people for suspicion of prostitution if they are carrying condoms.

18 Noah D. Zatz, "Sex Work/Sex Act: Law, Labor, and Desire in Constructions of Prostitution," *Signs: Journal of Women in Culture and Society* 22, no. 2 (Winter 1997): 277–308; Svati P. Shah, "Sex Work in the Global Economy," *New Labor Forum* 12, no. 1 (2003): 74–81.

Index

About the Editors

Aviva Chomsky is professor of history and coordinator of Latin American Studies at Salem State University. The author of several books, Chomsky has been active in Latin American solidarity and immigrants' rights issues since the 1980s. She lives in Salem, Massachusetts.

Steve Striffler writes and teaches about labor, migration, and the left in relation to Latin America and the United States. He recently published *Solidarity: Latin America and the US Left in the Era of Human Rights*, which explores the history of US-Latin American solidarity from the Haitian Revolution to the 2000s.

About Haymarket Books

Haymarket Books is a radical, independent, nonprofit book publisher based in Chicago. Our mission is to publish books that contribute to struggles for social and economic justice. We strive to make our books a vibrant and organic part of social movements and the education and development of a critical, engaged, international left.

We take inspiration and courage from our namesakes, the Haymarket martyrs, who gave their lives fighting for a better world. Their 1886 struggle for the eight-hour day—which gave us May Day, the international workers' holiday—reminds workers around the world that ordinary people can organize and struggle for their own liberation. These struggles continue today across the globe—struggles against oppression, exploitation, poverty, and war.

Since our founding in 2001, Haymarket Books has published more than five hundred titles. Radically independent, we seek to drive a wedge into the risk-averse world of corporate book publishing. Our authors include Noam Chomsky, Arundhati Roy, Rebecca Solnit, Angela Y. Davis, Howard Zinn, Amy Goodman, Wallace Shawn, Mike Davis, Winona LaDuke, Ilan Pappé, Richard Wolff, Dave Zirin, Keeanga-Yamahtta Taylor, Nick Turse, Dahr Jamail, David Barsamian, Elizabeth Laird, Amira Hass, Mark Steel, Avi Lewis, Naomi Klein, and Neil Davidson. We are also the trade publishers of the acclaimed Historical Materialism Book Series and of Dispatch Books.